CW01346315

NEMVUS

© Copyright 2016 by Nemvus Productions.
Illustrated and edited by L. Renée Bayard.

First Edition
2nd Printing

ISBN: 978-0-9974321-2-1   *Paperback*
ISBN: 978-0-9974321-0-7   *eBook*

Nemvus Productions
   916 Goldenwood Glen
   Placerville, CA 95667

Any internet references contained in this work are current at publication time, but the author cannot guarantee that a specific location will continue to be maintained.

COGNITIVE TYPE

THE ALGORITHM OF HUMAN CONSCIOUSNESS AS REVEALED VIA FACIAL EXPRESSIONS

by

J. E. SANDOVAL

NEMVUS PRODUCTIONS

TABLE OF CONTENTS

Preface .... *xi*

PART I – INTRODUCTION .... *xiii*
  1. Epistemology of Psychology *1*
     1. The Problem In Quantifying Consciousness *1*
     2. The Psychology Of Facial Expressions *4*
  2. Of Consciousness *7*
     1. Continuity Of Consciousness *9*
     2. Perception & Judgment *10*
     3. The Necessity For Abstract & Concrete Perception *11*
     4. The Necessity For Logical & Ethical Judgment *12*
     5. The Necessity For Proactivity & Reactivity *14*
     6. The Oscillations *15*
         a. Proactive Perception & Reactive Perception ... *16*
         b. Proactive Judgment & Reactive Judgment *19*
     7. The Four Function Oscillation Pairings *20*
         a. The Ne-Si & Ni-Se Oscillations *22*
         b. The Fe-Ti & Fi-Te Oscillations *27*
     8. The Whole Of A Cognitive Type *33*
         a. Hierarchy *34*
  3. Judgment & Perception *38*
  4. The Energetic Quadrants *45*
     1. Compass as the Lead Process *45*

CONTENTS

2. Articulator as the Lead Process	*48*
3. Explorer as the Lead Process	*52*
4. Worldview as the Lead Process	*56*

PART II – FUNCTIONS — *63*

5. Fi | Reactive Ethical Judgment	*65*
6. Ti | Reactive Logical Judgment	*78*
7. Fe | Proactive Ethical Judgment	*86*
8. Te | Proactive Logical Judgment	*98*
9. Si | Reactive Concrete Perception	*106*
10. Ni | Reactive Abstract Perception	*114*
11. Ne | Proactive Abstract Perception	*121*
12. Se | Proactive Concrete Perception	*127*

PART III – TYPES — *133*

13. FiNe | Edamin	*139*
1. The Seelie Fairy	*141*
2. The Scientist	*142*
3. The Sensitivist	*144*
14. FiSe | Edavin	*147*
1. The Indie Artist	*149*
2. The "Vegetarian"	*151*
3. The Unseelie Haughty	*151*
4. The Harmonious Seelie	*152*
15. TeSi | Edamer	*155*
1. The Entrepreneur	*157*
2. The Eccentric Nerd	*159*
3. The Historian	*160*

CONTENTS

    4. The Logistical Ethicist   *161*
16. TeNi | Edaver   *165*
    1. The Fervent Eccentric   *167*
    2. The Physicist   *168*
    3. The Executive   *171*
17. SiFe | Malein   *175*
    1. The Traditionalist   *179*
    2. The Silly-Serious   *180*
    3. The Eternal Parent   *181*
18. NiFe | Valein   *185*
    1. The Guru   *187*
    2. The Contentious Visionary   *188*
    3. The Grandfather   *189*
    4. The Covert Addict   *190*
19. NeTi | Maleer   *195*
    1. The Comedian   *197*
    2. The Dabbling Theorist   *198*
    3. The Introverted Extrovert   *199*
20. SeTi | Valeer   *203*
    1. The Sensationalist   *205*
    2. The Analytical Sensationalist   *206*
    3. The Anti-Sage   *207*
21. TiNe | Alemin   *211*
    1. The Minimalist   *213*
    2. The Armchair Philosopher   *214*
    3. The Technical Scholar   *215*
    4. The Psychoanalyst   *217*
22. TiSe | Alevin   *221*

CONTENTS

    1. The Technical Specialist — *223*
    2. The Ace Athlete — *224*
    3. The Poised Actor — *224*
23. FeSi | Alemer — *229*
    1. The Matriarch — *231*
    2. The Charismatic Charmer — *232*
    3. The Martyr — *233*
    4. The Philosophical Moralist — *234*
24. FeNi | Alever — *237*
    1. The Alpha Visionary — *239*
    2. The Oracle — *240*
    3. The Persona-Sensitive Sensationalist — *241*
    4. The Academic Advocate — *241*
25. SiTe | Medain — *245*
    1. The Encyclopedia — *247*
    2. The Lawyer-Politician — *248*
    3. The Practical Dabbler — *249*
    4. The Witty Jester — *250*
26. NiTe | Vedain — *253*
    1. The Deadpan — *255*
    2. The Political Critic — *256*
    3. The Sarcastic Jester — *256*
    4. The Practical Mystic — *257*
27. NeFi | Medaer — *261*
    1. The Scattered Entrepreneur — *264*
    2. The Faux-Fe Seelie — *264*
    3. The Introverted Extrovert — *265*
28. SeFi | Vedaer — *269*

1. The Seelie Socialite	*271*
2. The Manager	*272*
3. The Feisty Unseelie	*273*
4. The Gypsy	*274*
29. Function Quadrants	*276*
30. On Vultology	*280*
31. On Demographics of Type	*296*
PART IV – TYPOLOGIES	*303*
32. On Myers-Briggs & Keirsey	*305*
33. On Socionics	*316*
34. On Experimentation	*321*
35. Origin & Credits	*325*
PART V – APPENDIX	*327*
36. Listing of People's Types	*329*
37. Lexicon of Visual Signals	*336*
38. Terminology	*339*
39. Bibliography	*348*

CONTENTS

1. The Socio-Socialist ... 272
2. The Manager ... 275
3. The Frisky Investor ... 277
4. The Gypsy ... 277
29. Problem Quadrants ... 279
30. On Voltology ... 280
31. On Some Supplies of Love ... 296

PART D — TYPOLOGIES

32. On Meta-Biology & Robotics ... 305
33. On Biofonics ... 316
34. On Experimentation ... 321
35. Origin & Credits ... 325

PART V — APPENDIX

36. Listing of People's Types ... 329
37. Lexicon of Verbal Signals ... 346
38. Terminology ... 450
39. Bibliography ... 474

x

PREFACE

In my personal study of human psychology I have found no greater teacher than the late psychologist Carl Gustav Jung in presenting an initial explanation of psychological interplays. I therefore owe much of my progress and the creation of this book to his former works. The psychology first described by C.G. Jung is an encompassing philosophy of the psyche, but one hitherto lacking in external quantification; a complication not atypical within the realm of psychoanalysis. Hence, as evident as the reality of psychological types may have appeared in the mind of the Swiss psychologist, and despite the immense efforts made to convey with precision the reality of these psychologies, the absence of an empirical quantifier gave rise to a plethora of misinterpretations of his writings, and skepticism which remained unresolved for the past one hundred years. However, the initial discovery he conceived is indispensable to the conclusions found herein, as this work is the physical realization of that very same essential psychology – it is the crystallization of that same phenomenon, which was first understood only via abstractions and intangible impressions, now understood through a concrete and quantifiable form.

This book deals primarily with the identification of the types, as it is a sufficiently challenging undertaking for a single book to make a concise empirical case for their existence. And when I consider the infinite volumes that may be written about each of these sixteen equations as they manifest in diverse forms and times, I'm drawn by necessity to specialize my focus toward one element of their reality – their physiological quantification – which is the most pertinent and lacking element to a comprehensive study of these types. It is my desire that through this book the existence of said types can be seen to be an empirical

PREFACE

reality, rather than a speculative psychology, and efforts may be directed to the full understanding of these sub-classes within our own species.

The insertion of a concrete quantifier for a formerly abstract theory naturally obliges us to revise the entire model in light of the new information. As such it is not necessary, although greatly recommended, to have a prior understanding of Jungian theory to comprehend the contents of this book. It now becomes possible to observe which initial hypotheses of Jung's work were incomplete, to identify in precisely what ways they were lacking, and to correct our perception to align with what is evident. Therefore although the psychological basis is in large part the same, *cognitive type* differs from Jung's *psychological type* in ways that will be explained as we delve deeper into these pages.

PART I

INTRODUCTION

EPISTEMOLOGY OF PSYCHOLOGY

1. THE PROBLEM IN QUANTIFYING CONSCIOUSNESS

The age-old dilemma of quantification, fundamentally married to psychoanalysis, arises from our attempt to make objective sense of the apparatus which births subjectivity – using that very same subjective apparatus. It is the endeavor to comprehend consciousness, which itself is intangible and unavailable for direct examination to an outside individual – and only marginally available to the awareness of the individual himself. It is no mystery, then, that the question of the human psyche's operation has remained unanswered for the whole of human history, though it has defined every aspect of its culture and deliberations.

A multitude of rationalizations and systems can be postulated to describe the operation of the psyche, but without also having an objective anchor point to double-check their fidelity, they remain incomplete classification systems generating some sense of order to the otherwise confusing array of information flowing from the psyche. But the question of the nature of consciousness is not a trivial one, and if we desire to gain any legitimate understanding of its operation we must first approach the topic by asking: what epistemic approach is most suited to understanding human consciousness? The unavailability of consciousness for direct examination, being by its very nature an abstraction – much like sight is the abstraction formulated by the information of the eye – has traditionally restricted the study to either the components that generate it, or the effects that it causes; neurology and behavior.

The neurological approach is certainly the most quantifiable, but brings with it a series of new dilemmas. The information the brain produces in the form of electromagnetic waves and synaptic firings is not a direct representation of the psychic experience of the individual – but a cryptic representation, which cannot be translated without a behavioral comparison point. We discover what this neural activity corresponds to when a physical/behavioral effect is observed occurring during the presence of said neural activity. In light of this, the challenge of deciphering the psyche is one which cannot bypass the requirement for keen psychological interpretation of behavior but which also requires cooperation with neuroscience and any other available empirical means of quantification. The psyche cannot be understood objectively while being divorced from subjectivity; it can only be understood by making sense of subjectivity in an objective manner – hence making the *human* element indispensable. The abstract and concrete elements of perception are both equally necessary for complete understanding – and it is also crucial that the subjective experience be revered as well as the objective one. An academic approach too far leaning toward the objective and concrete directions will fail to capture a truly intelligent understanding of reality, even though it may appear captivating to hold a sight which has an available quantification for each component in its tapestry. It attains this certainty at the compromise and loss of much more breadth of insight which isn't formatted in a structure quite as rigid and defined – but formatted nonetheless. The over-emphasis toward this form of empiricism is not what I desire to advocate, as it is an illusion to consider the concrete to be by default more empirical than the abstract, when often times abstract representation – perhaps seen clearest in the field of mathematics – can best represent the overlying dynamics of reality. It's in like form as mathematics that I refer to formulas and equations of psychic dynamics, which individual human subjects serve to represent, but which exist independent of any particular individual.

In a similar vein, I wish to also make note of the scarcity of psychological progress within the last century where the dominating approach to psychological investigation has been conducted through compartmentalized studies with an isolated focus. A hypothesis is formulated which addresses one specific

1. EPISTEMOLOGY OF PSYCHOLOGY

behavior, trait or exhibited symptom from the infinite effects that result from the human equation – and a study is conducted in which these behaviors and symptoms are quantified by means such as the patient's account of their experience, a polygraph, multiple-choice answering sheets, or some other measure. Aggregated results are taken from these studies and summarized in statements of statistical averages based on responses. The shortcoming of such an approach, specifically when directed toward comprehending an apparatus such as the human psyche, is that the fractal nature of the human equation re-generates new rationalizations, opinions and reactions to reality which themselves transition continually with each generation of humanity. Attempts to isolate and study a single aspect of the Collective's expressions are akin to photographing the contours of a lightning strike then using that photograph as the cornerstone for the shape of all lightning streams. The human psyche is a system of *adaptation* and its very triumph, as the most successful evolutionary instrument, lies in its capacity for the seamless mass-assimilation of memetics and cultures. Its adaptive capacity is enormous and a deep consideration of this reality quickly brings into light what sort of approach is needed for its quantification. It must be understood by the rules of its cognitive dynamics; by the formulas which give rise to this infinite feedback cycle – and less by the specific effects observed at any given time.

Perhaps the most striking example of this over-dependency on segmented behaviorism to inform on the nature of an individual is seen in the *Diagnostic and Statistical Manual of Mental Disorders* of the American Psychiatric Association. This manual is commonly used as a guide to understanding the nature of a patient – when it is instead at best a statistical record of the landscape and opinions of the present culture and its standards for, as well as deviations from, normalcy. Such a manual does not inform on psychological dynamics, as its purpose is in providing medical practitioners a tangible and consensual means of diagnosing diseases by the present lore. In the enthusiasm and philosophy born from the scientific revolution's success in the fields of medicine and physics, the same reductionist philosophy has been ill-applied to the study of the psyche. Although this form of empiricism carries explanatory power, their methodologies and executions provide a very crippling approach in psychology; constricting authentic insights by only accepting information in a format differing from the dynamic way it exists in the mind. The fallacy within this approach is well understood, yet hitherto widely accepted out of necessity and for lack of a more substantial solution. However, I postulate that the solution to a dynamic yet concrete approach to psychology lies in another, vastly overlooked, avenue of study which is intimately linked to, and indicative of, psychological experience – namely facial expressions.

2. THE PSYCHOLOGY OF FACIAL EXPRESSIONS

While there is little argument that facial expressions themselves convey psychological states, their relation to psychic experience has been primarily explored through the emotional dimension. The work by Dr. Paul Ekman during 1960-1970 served to establish that while there's indeed ample variance among cultures/races in deliberate gesturing, there are numerous expressions that are universal to humanity. That is to say, regardless of race or cultural exposure, our facial muscles contract in particular ways as an automatic response to certain emotional states. In his book *Telling Lies* (1975), Ekman conducts a study in which people of an aborigine culture with no prior exposure to the developed world were recorded making the expressions that correspond to their emotional states. The results perfectly aligned with what Ekman had observed in the developed world. Through this study Ekman demonstrated the Darwinian relation between the face and human emotions. It is because of this that we can rightly assume that the study of facial expressions (which we might better term **Vultology**, from the Latin *vultus* "face" and Greek *logos* "knowledge") carries within it at the very least one dimension of truth about the nature of the human experience of consciousness. The challenge then becomes the proper discrimination between elements and expressions that are fun-

1. EPISTEMOLOGY OF PSYCHOLOGY

damental and those expressions which are contrived by upbringing. This avenue of objective analysis presents a new dimension for exploring the psyche than the aforementioned neuroscience and behaviorism. This is possible only because there is a direct connection between our facial muscles and our central nervous system – the former operating essentially as an extension of neural activity. However, what is not highlighted in Ekman's work, and what is the apex of my research in this book is that microexpressions are not only emotional indicators, but cognitive indicators – and more specifically, they are able to tell us the rhythm of processing a person utilizes on a regular basis.

This can be demonstrated by focusing on individual patterns of body language. When a person is observed for a consistent period of time, it becomes evident that they utilize a particular set of facial signals. In other words, people have a unique "signature" to their expressions and the major locus of their facial expressions fall in this perimeter, with a small percentage of outliers. This initial observation lead me to deeper questioning in which I also saw that certain signals appeared clustered together in people. Part of one individual's "signature" was identically represented in another individual, while another half was not – but was seen in other individuals. It became evident then that the phenomenon I was observing could not be deciphered using isolated subjects but through understanding the connections between a multitude of people. I saw that what was needed was a relational approach to this challenge, in which data is related from a variety of angles for patterns and differences. Keeping in mind that the psyche operates in an algorithmic fashion, the idea was to identify the nature of this algorithm in generating the multiple cognitive signals that display on the faces of people.

The following chapter takes the form of an abstract, or thesis, of the overlying concepts contained in the remainder of this book, while the subsequent chapters work to establish the principles first outlined therein. It is not my intention to at once definitively assert a conclusion about the nature and operations of this phenomenon, but instead to lay a foundation from which a new field of study could be opened. Parallel avenues, such as

COGNITIVE TYPE

that of EEG & fMRI tracking, are also deeply important to the investigation of this material. The exploration of these avenues alongside cognitive type is a topic that I hope may be addressed further in another study.

2

OF CONSCIOUSNESS

The phenomenon of consciousness, from its very placement within human physiology, gives multiple implications about its own nature. If we begin by considering that sentience is one sub-system of human biology, then we understand that the entirety of its manifestation has its origin within our genome and is confined to certain biological realities.

In previous eras it was difficult for us as a species to comprehend how so many diverse perspectives, infinite ideas, concepts, abstractions, dreams and languages could be confined by such a finite container; the body. And indeed this has been one of the grounds from which the belief of an extra-body sentience, or the eternal soul, has predominated history. As Jung noted in his book *Archetypes and the Collective Unconscious* (1969), much of that mysticism comes from our own unconscious – which appears to us to bring forth knowledge from some unknown place seemingly outside of us[1]. But the mechanism which gives rise to consciousness as well as the unconscious can be explained without resorting to an outside source. All of our imaginings and thoughts stem from a finite genetic coding, and immediately this in itself presents the question: how could infinite thoughts be generated by a finite code?

From a mathematical perspective the answer is quite straightforward. The human psyche could not produce the infinite variations it does, using such a finite code, without it also being a *feedback equation*. The information generated by our body's collision with our environment – what becomes our *individuality* – is not part of our genome, yet within that finite code we have the instructions which give birth to all the billions of different perspectives in our species through exposure to life.

1: Archetypes and the Collective Unconscious, par.8 C.G. Jung – 1969

This brings the focus of this chapter directly into **cognitive science**, which attempts to understand the systemic workings of cognition as a computational mechanism. What I am attempting in this book is essentially a detailed explanation of the nature of this equation, according to the multiple patterns visible in our countenance and how they reveal to us the quality of our thoughts during these expressions.

I must first begin by stating one premise; that complex systems are a congealing of smaller linear systems (like vectors) which each have but one operation. A system, however complex, is at its roots comprehensible as a collection of pieces which each have an individual function. If we take the human body as an example, we see that it is comprised of individual but interactive systems such as the cardiovascular, digestive, endocrine, skeletal, muscular and epidermal. These systems themselves are comprised of sub-systems, such as the digestive system's stomach, liver, gallbladder, pancreas, intestines – which are divisible further into cells, each also being its own sub-system. Magnifying further we see additional sub-systems within those cells, such as ribosomes which help produce certain molecular structures. However, once we magnify to the molecular level we begin to see things differently. While each molecule can be magnified further and seen as yet another system at the subatomic level, molecules play a vector-like role in the body. A single protein molecule may have but a single designated task, such as binding with a receptor site or forming the lining of a membrane, but in combination with other proteins, more complex tasks are formed. Yet even though the same protein may be reused for other process in the body, the function of each molecule in the human body is linear. The task of the scientist is to understand complex systems to their most elemental level – to untangle their causality to a point that can't be reduced further – as well as see the placement of each miniature process in the grand scheme of things.

This approach to functional differentiation is also applicable to the psyche. Despite the psyche not being a literal object, the energetic causality it undertakes is itself a system and can be

2. OF CONSCIOUSNESS

understood by fundamental principles. In this way, a variation of reductionism is indeed applied but to *psychic energies* rather than behaviors. Through this careful deduction we too can see logical necessities manifest, mutual-exclusions expressed, and vector operations arise from cognitive dynamics. We learn that certain processes cannot handle more than one operation – such as how an introverted process cannot extrovert itself into the world whatsoever – and these necessities become evident as a result of isolating the components of a system.

If a certain apparatus is expressing a multitude of contradictory attributes and operations, then we know that this apparatus is a complex system in itself – existing at a higher level of complexity than the fundamental elements that define it. There is a cause to that duality that is due to at least two subordinate components of that system which need to be defined. The full clarity of the system is only seen when it has been reduced to its most basic components, so that each component that causes each effect is understood for its own quality. No doubt, the overall outcome of these psychic systems interplaying in an actual human – such as an *Introvert* – reveals various properties, due to the complex feedback loop that transpires between the elements involved. However, in isolation introversion *itself* or an introverted processes cannot be responsible for any extroverted expression by virtue of its definition (or vector). The same is applicable to all other true dichotomies of our cognitive apparatus, as I'll be touching on below.

1. CONTINUITY OF CONSCIOUSNESS

Not all components of the brain are concerned with the creation of consciousness, and a great part of them are preoccupied with the difficult task of regulating all other systems in the body. However, for the formation of consciousness, there are two predominant neural processes at work: the synthesis of data and the process of decision-making. What I will hereafter quantify as our *Cognitive Type* is the sequence in which one's brain processes information and makes decisions. It is a rhythm of brain activity responsible for the way in which we construct our

COGNITIVE TYPE

perception of reality and navigate within it. The specific rhythm of brain activity we possess remains constant from our very earliest days throughout our lifetime.

The most elemental component of this algorithm is a never ending oscillation between eternally conflicting processes in the psyche. Our awareness remains continuous, not static, because of this never-resolving tension among antagonistic processes. Were this tension to resolve, the algorithm of consciousness would cease – but by remaining unresolved, the psyche is in a continual challenge between data absorption and processing.

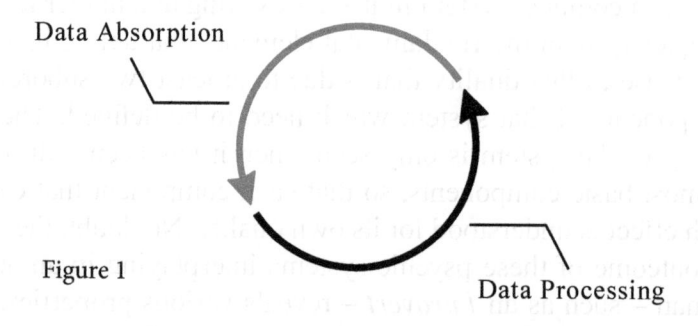

Data Absorption

Figure 1

Data Processing

The psyche aims to resolve all incoming information by categorizing each component, but it fails to achieve this due to the endless stream of data entering the psyche. However, it is equally dependent on this data's introduction in order to operate – as it would have no purpose without perceived information to discriminate between. The psyche can no more cease to perceive as it can cease to process – even if the operation is taking place outside of conscious awareness.

2. PERCEPTION & JUDGMENT

This oscillation wheel between data absorption and processing is what C.G. Jung termed Perception and Judgment; however the definition herein will contain a few peculiarities not mentioned in Jung's definition. The role of Perception in the psyche is the **synthesis** of information. Data synthesis is the automatic population and correlation of information into the

2. OF CONSCIOUSNESS

psyche absent of any conscious scrutiny of the data. There are two types of perceptive data; incoming and pre-existing, and synthesis is the process of associating the incoming data to the pre-existing – the specifics of this process will be explained further in the next chapter.

As rightly defined by C.G.Jung, Perception is an irrational process, though not necessarily because the connections it makes are linked improperly, but because the links are formed incidentally, not through rational deduction. Associations made by the perception processes are made on the basis of shared attributes – data is connected so long as it relates to other data, independent of any rational justification for the association within parameters of laws or axioms.

Thus anomalies/contradictions in logic as well as ethics will exist in perception and go unchecked for as long as the data is not critiqued with a judgment process. Perception processes draw associations, while the judgment processes break associations that cause contradictions according to the judgment process' criteria of measure. The process of discrimination, also known as Judgment, is the deliberate arrangement of incoming data into **harmony**; it is the recognition and elimination of contradiction – be it logically or ethically.

3. THE NECESSITY FOR ABSTRACT & CONCRETE PERCEPTION

Furthermore the psychic recognition of the data obtained by the perceptive organs requires the cooperation of more than one operation. The perception of the world is done both in the **literal** and in the **implied** sense. Literal perception is that which intakes reality in a realistic and tactile form as it appears before our senses. Implied perception intakes reality via proxy, extracting from the environment instead what it alludes to, rather than what is.

Both of these forms of data intake are necessary for the comprehension of reality. Were we without abstract perception, we would be incapable of seeing beyond the immediately observable – unable to foretell coming events or imagine alternatives to situations. Were we without concrete perception, our minds would never form a tactile and correct concept of reality and would be utterly lost in an abstract delusion where imagination is taken as literal reality.

4. THE NECESSITY FOR LOGICAL & ETHICAL JUDGMENT

The decision-making apparatus is equally divided into two components according to the themes it is responsible for administering; themes which have often been differentiated as the conflict between the **Heart** and **Mind**. While such terms are far too broad to be of use for our purposes, the general concept present in them is not unrelated to the phenomenon underlying this dichotomy. A more precise definition would be to say the Heart, so to speak, is that which manages decisions that deal with Humanity and living things: it is the principle of Ethic. The Mind, so to speak, is that which manages decisions that pertain to non-living things: it is the principle of Logic. Both processes operate on the principle of *reason* but in different topics and with different criteria. This separation is also essential as the criteria for Logical decision making left to itself may generate an erroneous choice that is entirely inhumane, but which appears most reasonable to it. Likewise the criteria for Ethical decision making by itself would cause an erroneous romanticizing of reality, applying the principle of Ethic to all realms, including the non-living, anthropomorphizing all of life and being incapable of understanding or managing situations objectively when needed.

As was clarified by James Hillman, an early student at the C.G. Jung Institute, the process of Ethic, or "Feeling", is not the same as emotions, though emotions are often present alongside it [2]. But I feel I must make a further clarification as to what relationship the Ethical process has to the emotional register of an individual, beginning by contrasting it against the operation of the Logical process.

The Logical process is one disassociated from the emotional register. It is a process that discerns between data, but it does so without any recognition of things outside of the of prin-

---

2: A Note on Multiple Analysis and Emotional Climate at Training Institutes, James Hillman – 1962

2. OF CONSCIOUSNESS

ciples of deduction. It is sequential reasoning; if this → then this. A process associated to the emotional center is likewise a process that discerns between data, but it does so within a different framework; different parameters. The sequence of "if → then" is processed within the context of bodily experience. The aim is not logical consistency but a consistency of the body/emotional-register with the principles of survival/life versus death. The aim of logical consistency is without consideration of the body as anything more than a data source. Logic has no bias for its own body. Consequently, "Ethics" can be defined as the proper alignment to, and management of decisions in the context of life & death, where life is the central bias and aim. Consistency versus inconsistency is to logic as life versus death is to ethics.

The Logical process differentiates itself from the personal self and thus does not perceive one's own importance as anything more than yet another variable within the information registered. It can only possess this lack of bias, and thus be a dispassionate process, through this lack of self-investment. If a creature existed who was purely logical and entirely lacking the ethical dimension, its absence of regard for its own life would not take long to terminate its own existence. Fortunately the human psyche is not so one-dimensional as to make us entirely motivated by logic or strictly by the impetus for survival. Both are present in each individual and the interplay between these two dynamics can indeed become very complex. One soon finds logical reasons to support ethical pursuits (and vice versa) as dispassionate analysis is used to inform the ethical process. Through this convergence, the ethical and logical processes can better execute their respective decisions. This collaborative dynamic I will hereafter refer to as harmonizing.

We also understand that the matters which motivate humanity toward self-preservation lie within the instinctual and "reptilian brain" [3]. The ethical discernment process is not itself those impulses, nor would I suggest it lies within the limbic system, but it draws from them pre-existing parameters from which to formulate judgment. The logical process generates its

3: The Third Vision, pg.25, Dr. Francis H. Vala MD – 2012

COGNITIVE TYPE

parameters naturally via exposure to the environment, using initially only the discernment between similarity and dissimilarity. It would, if it existed in isolation, attempt this process in whatever universe – with whatever laws – it woke up to, creating an organized catalog of parallels from the data presented to it by the perception processes. This would not be true of the ethical process, as it would – if awoken in a universe with alternate laws – conceive this universe using pre-existing "human" archetypes and measure the substances and perceptive impressions available through that human judgment. It would define more and less valuable substances depending on their capacity to cause or prevent death – however it came to understand it.

5. THE NECESSITY FOR PROACTIVITY & REACTIVITY

This following differentiation pertains more to the direction of energy flow within the psyche and less to a psychic function. I will be describing two terms in this section: **proactive** and **reactive**. These correspond directly with C.G. Jung's objective and subjective attitudes, also known as introversion and extroversion. Rightly so, Jung distinguished this axis from the others as a causal mechanism akin to the heart's systolic and diastolic relationship. The proactive process is one ever leaving the subject, while the reactive process is ever returning to the subject [4].

As mentioned previously the human psyche maintains continuity via a feedback system, and this motion must be maintained through a direction of energy flow; the psychological processes cycle within either a proactive or reactive direction. This dual process is by no means unique to our psyche as it imitates the same causality that exists in countless natural systems from electric currents to biological sex. Were there no proactive/reactive divide, there would be nothing initiating an interaction or dialogue between the two opposing aspects of the psyche: they would remain static. As a causal necessity of a feedback cycle, one must feed into the other, which in turn responds and that response is absorbed again by the first process – and this cycle

4: Psychological Types, par.6, C.G. Jung – 1921

continues ad infinitum.

It is due to the presence of this innately cyclical quality that I would add an amendment, or perhaps clarification, to Jung's definition of the introversion-extroversion duality and hence why I prefer to use the terms proactive and reactive. As I hope will be seen in the whole of this book, a fundamental property of cognitive elements is **oscillation**. The necessity for one to feed into the other was not explicitly highlighted by Jung, who viewed the two terms as more contrasted and capable of retaining their own nature at the suppression of the other. But the contrary is true, as they are much more dependent on each other than this and not just for a healthy operation. In any sort of processing, even within cases of strong suppression, both aspects of the cycle can very well be seen operating and transpiring continually within every passing second.

6. THE OSCILLATIONS

The perception & judgment duality, abstract & concrete duality, as well as the logical & ethical duality – each contain an oscillation relationship sustained via one process being proactive whilst the other remains reactive. If perception is proactive, then judgment is reactive, if logic is proactive then ethics are reactive, and vice versa. To further complicate things, within perception itself there exists a duality, as extroverted perception cycles into introverted perception – and the same applies to judgment; extroverted judgment cycles into introverted judgment.

The algorithm of consciousness is a complex net of interwoven oscillations. While there is no simple way to perfectly visualize all oscillations in one diagram, the diagram below is an approximation depicting these eight relationships. As you'll notice in the diagram there are two solid circles running horizontally, and two dashed circles running vertically. In the top dark circle we have proactive judgment cycling into reactive judgment, and at the bottom we have proactive perception cycling into reactive perception. While these two processes are happening separately, there is also a dialogue between these two cycles as the dotted circles indicate – likewise following a proactive/

COGNITIVE TYPE

reactive direction. This arrangement is necessary to ensure communication between all elements, interconnecting the insights of each process by allowing a mode of transference. These four oscillations are the foundation of our cognitive type, and the continual cycling of these four oscillations within us at each passing second is what generates our consciousness.

Proactive Ethics
Proactive Logic
Proactive Judgment

Reactive Ethics
Reactive Logic
Reactive Judgment

Reactive Perception
Reactive Abstract
Reactive Concrete

Proactive Perception
Proactive Abstract
Proactive Concrete

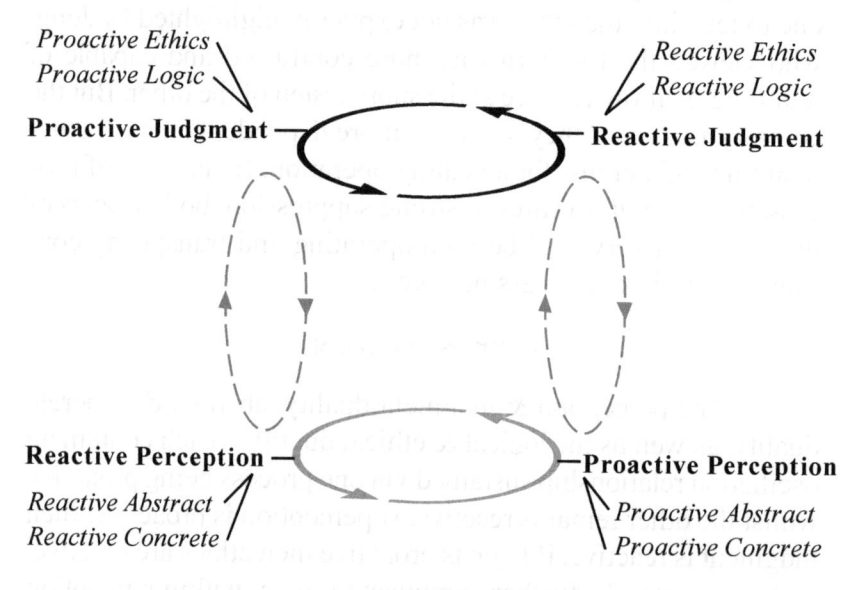

Figure 2

a. Proactive Perception & Reactive Perception

To explain these operations in more detail I'll begin first with perception, as it cycles from extroversion to introversion. As I mentioned earlier in this chapter, the process of perception is preoccupied with the synthesis of incoming information with pre-existing information. The feedback loop begins with the intake of information, which is always done by the proactive perception process. The *seeking-out* of information existing outside of the self – the outer world – must necessarily be done by the proactive process which abandons the subject for its magnetic attraction to the object. I will hereafter refer to this proactive perception as the **Explorer** process.

2. OF CONSCIOUSNESS

Inversely, the role of the reactive or subjective perception process is to seek information within the self; to delve into memory and reference pre-existing perceptions/worldviews – as it is incapable of going outward for its information: it must delve inward. I refer to this process as the **Worldview** process as it supplies a body of knowledge – a tapestry to draw from – for the navigation of the explorer process and the calculation of the judgment processes. Yet I must also make a differentiation between this process and the phenomenon of "memory". It would not be correct to directly correlate the two, as memory exists as a physical entity of the brain's physiology, not as a function. The Worldview process is one which recollects *from* this memory, but the entirety of it is not available to this process at any given time. It is more akin to a librarian than to the library. The manner in which it archives the information and recalls it differs between each of the two worldview processes, but this is the essential role of both worldview functions.

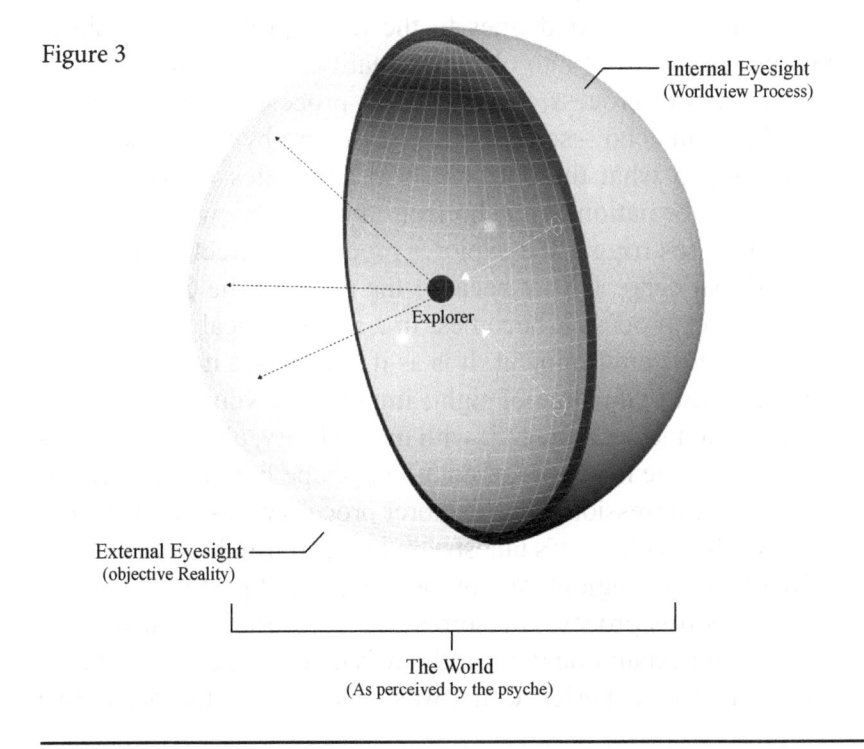

Figure 3

Internal Eyesight
(Worldview Process)

Explorer

External Eyesight
(objective Reality)

The World
(As perceived by the psyche)

COGNITIVE TYPE

However, while the explorer process must seek *outward*, the psyche makes no distinction between the fantasy generated by our psyche – our proxy of reality – and reality itself as it may appear outside of human perception. Thus, in the literal sense, even the exploration of Pe is confined to the mental landscape of the person and will explore the information available within this mental terrain.

The diagram above is a general representation of the operation of the perception oscillation which may help to illustrate. At the centerpoint we have the explorer process, and on the left hemisphere we have objective reality. On the right hemisphere we have the internal world of the worldview process. In other words, the entire expanse of "the world" that the explorer process can see is composed of both the outer world and the worldview. What forms "reality" to our mental sight is never just the retina's present information. The explorer process can glance at memory just as it glances at reality and memory is also treated as a sort of existing phenomenon.

Here the dotted lines to the left represent the explorer process seeking-out into objective reality. With each projection of the explorer process, the worldview process will respond and send back an echo – so to speak – seen here by the dashed line, according to what the data taken in associates to within pre-existing information. An echo from the worldview process will in some cases trigger the explorer process to direct its attention toward that echo. This is because the moment the echo reaches the explorer process it becomes, in a metaphorical sense, a visible part of its environment. It is as if suddenly a new object appeared within your line of sight; impulsively your gaze will be drawn to it and seek to see it with more clarity, although this object may not be made out of color and shape but out of words or intangible impressions. The explorer process will seek to explore parts of the worldview's tapestry to bring to mind a fuller image of reality as a conglomerate of the present and past information.

As this process transpires new memories are also being created and expanding the worldview's tapestry, according to the overall mental experience that was generated by the perceptive processes and judgment processes collaborating. The manner in which these happenings are stored as memories, or rather how they're interrelated, reflects the way in which the two perceptive processes brought them forth into awareness. Hence a very clear imprint of our cognitive functions is left in our memories, as they're encoded in a manner that aligns with them, even though our memory itself is a separate phenomenon from cognitive type.

b. Proactive Judgment & Reactive Judgment

Judgment is the process of deliberation, intentionality, and ultimately of execution. However, there is internal intentionality, and external intentionality. Extroverted judgment is the process that conveys and executes its judgment onto the world. It is also a proactive process which means it proactively strives to align the world to the decisions it arrives to. Proactive judgment is externally-oriented, gauging how to control the outer-world as an extension of one's self. I will refer to this process as the **Articulator**, as this process is not directly motor-movement-based, and its identification can be gauged from one's manner of speaking. Reactive judgment is oriented within, and its control lies in personally held convictions; it is one's ethical or logical **Compass**. Reactive judgment alone is a reasoning process that is satiated when the proper conclusion is drawn from a situation. Proactive judgment is a reasoning process that is satiated when the outer world reaches an arrangement that it believes is reasonable. In this manner, introverted judgment does the same 'controlling' that extroverted judgment does, but internally.

To describe how these functions operate in synch: if for example, the proactive ethical process takes initiative and acts toward an organization of the social world more suited toward Life, then the reactive logical process will dispassionately evaluate the effects of the action taken, and this analysis is available for the ethical process to calibrate its next action. Were the logical process instead also proactive, the individual would be conflicted between two directly clashing positions of how to execute himself outwardly – and be unable to take adequate action of any sort, as no mediating process is available to reconcile the discord.

The compass process calibrates the articulator process and is calibrated by it through comparing its idealizations against the outcomes of the articulator's dynamic movements; movements it can never make on its own to hone in on how accurate its ideals truly are. Thus, more detrimental still than the inability to decide on what course to take, would be if neither process served as the *evaluator* for the other, as each would be unable to receive the position of the other. Individual growth would not occur in the same way we presently understand it if there was such an irreconcilable clash between ethics and logic. Even though the possession of both ethics and logic in a cyclical formation can often still result in an internal dilemma that may lead to a level of indecisiveness, it is of a different sort than the paralysis that would result in the former – as an oscillation would not be established from which the judgment process of either could be recalibrated or refined.

7. THE FOUR FUNCTION OSCILLATION PAIRINGS

The two opposing facets in the judgment and perception oscillations – which multiply to eight facets when we consider the reverse direction of energy flow – are what Jung termed our **cognitive functions**. However they are more accurately viewed as four systems, each with two facets, as it is not possible for one aspect of this oscillation to exist or even operate without the other – both being fundamentally two parts of the same equation. Where one is visually seen, or psychologically identified, the subsequent half is inescapably present. If I am to convey the concepts properly I must first explain them via dualities.

I must also make a few remarks pertaining to the Jungian description of the two processes termed *Intuition* and *Sensing*. I will not be using the words intuition or sensing to describe the differences between these two functionalities, as the term sensation – or data intake through the sensory organs – is an operation which is performed by both abstract and concrete proactive data intake – termed by Jung as *Extroverted Intuition* (Ne) and *Extroverted Sensation* (Se). The process of data intake is performed by both Ne and Se: both seek out information (going away from the self). Ne is thus a sensory intake process, in the literal sense of the word, as it is proactive perception. Inversely, both *Introverted Intuition* (Ni) and *Introverted Sensing* (Si) are worldview processes which draw their "perspective" from within themselves. Both Ni and Si are inward-turned, or introverted, meaning their energy and focus resists/rejects the outer world – and goes into oneself. Because of this, neither Ni nor Si proactively perceive the environment – they perceive the inner world of the self. Hence, Si is less a "sensory" process than Ne, and relies exclusively on an internal tapestry of pre-existing information built from the input of Ne. Ni does the same, being quite similar to Si; the difference lying primarily in the manner in which they catalog information into their Worldview.

Furthermore I must denote that *intuition* is by no means an unconscious process, nor a process so visceral that it necessarily escapes a more concise definition. Perception will always seem less controlled to our awareness than judgment, as judgment is commonly associated with our awareness and choice-making. Because judgment requires deliberation, intent or decision, it often reveals to the mind of the individual the nature of its operation. Whereas, the incidental synthesis of information undertaken by the perception processes lacks deliberation and thus the causality of its influence is less available to the awareness of the individual. However, to say that this inherently makes abstract perception less conscious would be a misconception and a partiality toward the judgment processes. The scope of our consciousness is not confined solely by what thoughts crystallize into words or images within our mind's eye, but also extends to all the visceral information processing transpiring within us continually as we are impacted by the present reality. I would reserve the word "unconscious" instead for the deeper recesses of an individual's psyche, the unearthed landscape of their mind, which is a separate thing than the processing they undertake in real-time to construct a sense of reality, and whose operation may or may not be explicitly apparent to the individual in question.

COGNITIVE TYPE

What we experience as intuition, in the common sense of the word, is the mutual operation of both abstract and concrete perception – synthesis. Keen ability to feel out and intuit the reality around us is something that abstract perception could not do alone, as it becomes delusional and disconnected from reality if left to itself. And concrete perception is no less a visceral and impressionistic process as abstract perception; as the quality of what it perceives registers with thousands of nuanced details – each detail intimately affecting the overall formation of concepts from that data. It is no easier to trace with precision than abstract perception.

a. The Ne-Si & Ni-Se Oscillations

When the explorer process is proactive abstraction (Ne) and the worldview process is reactive and concrete (Si), the psychological approach to information synthesis is prolific; one of plurality. Inversely, the Se-Ni duality has a psychological approach tending toward linearity. If we were to compare the processes via a ratio, the Ne-Si pair generates more connections but with each having a shorter range, while Se-Ni generates fewer connections with each holding a larger range. This key difference in information synthesis is comparable to the dichotomy of *r-selection* versus *K-selection* in animal reproduction strategies. There is often an inverse relationship between how many offspring a species reproduces and how much parental care and time must go into each offspring to reach maturity. Species that follow an r-selection strategy produce a multitude of offspring which require a shorter time until reaching maturity but are much frailer and smaller. Examples of r-selection species would be most insects, spiders, plankton, and guppy fish. Their frailty, short life spans and high mortality rate is compensated for with large numbers, increasing odds of survival and ensuring the perpetuation of the species remains unbroken. K-selection species take the opposite approach and produce much fewer offspring but require more energy and time toward each one to reach sex-

5: On r and K selection, Pianka, E.R. – 1970

2. OF CONSCIOUSNESS

ual maturity. Examples of K-selection species would be whales, penguins, chimpanzees and of course humans. Such species are typically more durable and capable of holding longer life spans. They compensate for their comparatively low population with this durability. Both strategies of procreation are considered equally successful and often coexist in the same habitats.[5]

In extraverted perception, this phenomenon of plurality arises inevitably when we have abstraction – which is the process of interrelating – oriented outward. If we consider the explorer processes' operations, then we understand why it is that when the explorer process is also the abstraction process, many more connections are formed in more rapid succession and of shorter range. It's because the explorer process is real-time, absorbing reality at miniature intervals in order to give us our constant and unbroken sense of reality, and always moving its gaze to new observations. If the exploration process must also be abstract, then the activity of abstracting must keep up with this pace. For Ne, abstraction cannot be a long and premeditated activity, but one which coalesces with, and retains the qualities of its own rapid exploration.

Here we see a diagram that depicts the difference in the process of interrelation as it transpires within the two perception oscillation pairings. As you'll see, The Se-Ni pairing holds its

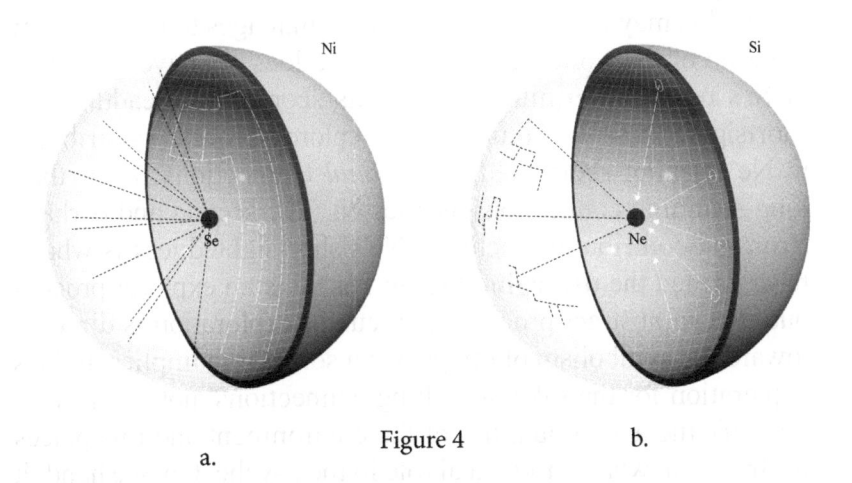

a. Figure 4 b.

abstraction process internally and its concrete process is held outward, thus it never abstracts when coming outward.

Inversely, for the Ne-Si pairing abstraction is done by the explorer process when coming outward. This means that for Ne, the interrelation process happens while fast, multiple/prolific exploration of the environment is taking place, shown here by the interconnecting lines. To elaborate on the precise mechanics of this disposition toward prolific, quick and fleeting interconnections, I would like to describe two factors that strongly affect the attitude of Ne. The first I have termed the **refresh factor**. The perspectives of the two explorer processes are contingent on what is transpiring in real-time, while the worldview processes are constant perspectives not dependent on the present moment. Each time the mind conceives a topic, an event or happenstance, it is recreated by the explorer process as if it was occurring for the first time. The explorer processes by themselves have no precedent, seeing reality anew each passing moment and this is a crucial element of their operation. It is the role of the worldview process to echo back a precedent. The perspective of the explorer process alone would be entirely dependent on the present moment and what can be extracted from it were it not in dialogue with the worldview process. Due to this constant refreshing, Ne's ability to interrelate information is confined to what variables appear in its thoughts at the instance of interconnection. While this may include some of what it manages to receive from the echo of the worldview process Si, it does not have the whole of Si's reservoir in mind, lacking its scope and breadth. This shortsightedness inherent to the explorer process contributes to Ne forming short-lived, *situational* connections rather than long-spanning connections as does Ni. The second and perhaps strongest contributing factor of Ne's shortsightedness is what I have termed the **diverging factor**. As Ne is an explorer process but also an abstract process, its focus in exploration is directed toward the symbolism of things; what something implies. It does exploration for the sake of making connections, not so much to quantify the actual qualities of the environment and this places Ne in a somewhat paradoxical role in the psyche. On one hand, it must assimilate sensory data, but on the other it must disengage from the presently-observed data in order to "leap" its mental or literal gaze to another dataset with which it can make an association. This leads to a natural divergence of attention away from the literal qualities of objects in the outer world at every leap, causing it to lose focus on an object when it ceases to be a source of correlation. That is to say, unlike Se who looks at an object for its qualities, Ne is less equipped to ascertain the literal qualities of an object – as it becomes, almost immediately, a symbol. Indeed, often Ne may fail to truly grasp what it is perceiving as it does not allow itself to linger long enough to absorb its nuance, but is instead diverted immediately into a chain of interconnections spawned from the symbol that the object represents at a very immediate glance.

When Se explores reality it seeks to assimilate a plethora of data as it appears to its senses without any modification, which is then all synthesized with the help of Ni into interconnections. Ne proactively seeks to interrelate elements together, while Ni generates connections reactively from Se observing reality unfold. Hence, as one would expect, the Ni tapestry is much more tied together due to its interrelating transpiring within the worldview process and not the explorer process. Ni is not quite as generous in its interrelations as Ne, as the role of the worldview process is to give predictability to the world. In comparison to Ni, Ne carries an optimism in association-forming – as it makes a point of finding ways that data can fit together, and its talent does not lie in making the data rational within itself, nor is its motivation the creation of a consistent and predictable landscape of reality. It will see no limitations as to what can be interrelated, nor does it seek to hold itself accountable for the interrelations it previously formed, as its own interrelations quickly become obsolete to it when refreshing occurs. Se, also being an explorer process, is equally constantly in an accelerated state of refreshing and absorption, but it doesn't finish absorbing the qualities of an object as quickly as Ne, because it actually is gathering the literal qualities, which are more plentiful than the general symbolic meanings. Se will linger, both mentally and visually, longer on objects in order to receive their literal qualities. And from this large array of "premises", the internal process of interrelating weaves together more encompassing connections retrospectively – having also at its disposal all prior knowledge. In other words, for Se-Ni, each new event is synthesized viscerally with all prior connections, rather than with what is brought to mind in the moment. This is not to say Ni-Se is any more rational or objectively accurate in its approach, although it will most certainly experience its own associations with more certainty than Ne would. This self-persuasion toward surety may ebb across the whole psyche, convincing the individual that certain inevitabilities are at play before any situational grounds exist to warrant such suppositions.

    I would also like to elaborate on the relation the worldview processes have to memory. As mentioned earlier, the worldview process is a function of the psyche that handles the structure of our memory; the way in which such information is stored and recalled. There is a general reluctance existing in both worldview processes towards new information, as new information offsets the worldview and forces reconsideration. The worldview process by itself holds no desire for outside information and would be content holding a perception of reality generated entirely by the data already accumulated. While it will not venture into the external world by itself, it is forced to adjust itself by the intake from the explorer process – and as these readjustments occur it regains *predictability*. While Si accomplishes predictability by storing the real-time associations of Ne as concrete information that can be referenced as static facts, Ni accomplishes predictability through tying together Se's array of static, sensory input into a lattice of directional outcomes. Hence, the tapestry of Si is filled with situational, largely isolated and compartmentalized interconnections which are continually being re-triggered into consciousness by the environment and reordered by Ne through active rearrangement before they re-settle again into a static form. It is necessary for Ne that Si store data as static information, as this allows Ne the freedom to rearrange and selectively connect data clusters into new forms without being restricted by

2. OF CONSCIOUSNESS

the connections they might have to other datasets. The Ni worldview works in an inverse manner, as new data from Se alters its tapestry in such a way that the rearrangement of any dataset affects all other datasets that it may be connected with – as a ripple spreading through an ocean surface. Such interconnection can cause undesired effects, as what might have been a correct perception, initially arrived at from direct Se experience, is altered by modifications to adjacent datasets into something erroneous. And this new perspective is felt with the same level of inevitability that the original perception was felt with, even though it had no direct sensory basis for its newly modified form.

As is no doubt clear at this point, both the Si-Ne and Ni-Se perception oscillations contain logical fallacies in their functionality. The former is prone to fallacies of anecdotal overreliance and wishful thinking, the latter of unwarranted assumptions and an inability to theorize alternatives. It is the task of the judgment functions to weed out these fallacies, but the tendency to make them will forever exist within the corresponding users, as they are a natural consequence of the perception oscillations' normal operation.

b. The Fe-Ti and Fi-Te Oscillations

While the perception pairings viscerally construct a view of reality as it appears in the present, including within it the context attained from the past, the judgment pairings will **register** the meaning of those perceptions according to their criteria of judgment. I will be using the term "register" to refer to the ignition of a conclusion by the judgment processes; the very moment at which the environment is consolidated into a deduction. All variables in the environment congeal into a panorama which the judgment processes can see and, via an application of thresholds, draw lines in that panorama to differentiate substances and situations. The psyche reduces environmental variables by drawing these conclusions, then only consciously manages those conclusions. Without the judgment processes, the causality around you would continue to flow as one endless stream between the present sensory experience and how it triggers previously observed

COGNITIVE TYPE

sensations but with no ability to contrast the two between themselves or to chronicle them properly in space or time.

Furthermore, the rate at which these differentiations are executed is comparable to the rate at which perceptions congeal, making judgment – at its most incremental scale – an incredibly rapid process. Because of this the registration of any single judgment is not always clearly echoed in the awareness of the individual as a thought. One may only become slightly aware that one's disposition toward the environment has shifted to a conclusion. By the time we become aware of a thought and it is clearly echoed through our mind, it is no longer a single judgment but the apex of an enormous architecture; a pyramid built

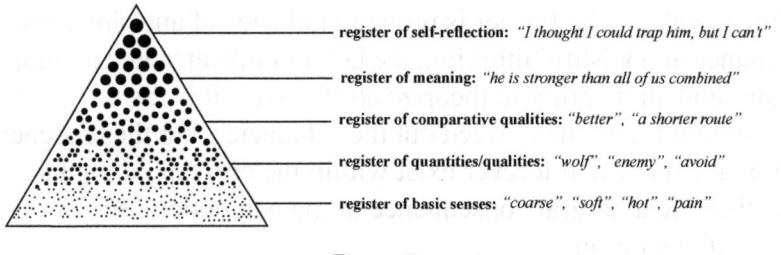

- **register of self-reflection:** *"I thought I could trap him, but I can't"*
- **register of meaning:** *"he is stronger than all of us combined"*
- **register of comparative qualities:** *"better"*, *"a shorter route"*
- **register of quantities/qualities:** *"wolf"*, *"enemy"*, *"avoid"*
- **register of basic senses:** *"coarse"*, *"soft"*, *"hot"*, *"pain"*

Figure 5

from a foundation of hundreds of micro-judgments converging into a broad-reaching conclusion.

Above we have a diagram to help represent this higher and higher convergence. Toward the bottom of the pyramid each dot represents the register of a basic sensory input. As we move up toward the top of the pyramid those dots merge into more complex conclusions that account for more variables, including previously reached conclusions. The convergence to greater complexity happens as a gradient effect, without any strongly differentiated levels; the five sections listed herein are only to give a general concept of the contents that may be contained along various points of that gradient.

Now, the process by which things congeal is what differs between the judgment processes. Each of the four judgment processes has a different way of consolidating this data into conclusions and so data is taken to represent different things. As thousands of minute conclusions converge, the end result contains a very clear imprint of the **methodology** being utilized in processing the perceptive data. It is these methodologies that are the defining attributes of the judgment processes as, when divorced from context, individual judgments coming from various processes can overlap one another. The same conclusion can be reached via different avenues, however the same methodology will never be employed by more than one process.

Economy

I would first like to contrast the consolidation process of Te against Fe. Both of these processes may be described as a registering of, and dynamic execution within, an ethical or logistical **economy**. I use the term economy not strictly in the materialistic sense but to describe a system of managing available resources of any sort and coordinating the distribution of energies. At the smallest scale, this management is done through a continual comparison between one perceivable variable and another, and then arriving at the conclusion that the relation between those two things is either beneficial or detrimental to the desired external arrangement. As such, the entirety of the extraverted judgment (Je) processes' functions take place within an external setting and are related to other external factors. If something is not in the environment or affecting the environmental situation, then it is not considered relevant to their deductions. For Fe, these factors relate to an external management of social economy and to Te this translates to a management of logistical economy.

The economy which Fe registers, and which it manages is one where the emotional states within people are registered as though they were tangible factors in the environment and are manipulated with energy distributions; energy which can be either positive or negative. If Fe registers that there is too much energy in one area, it may siphon it off to another area. If for example someone is gaining too much at another person's expense, Fe may coordinate the translation of negative energies via shame or some other tactic to rebalance the circumstance. It is important to emphasize that these tactics relate to a translation of emotional energies and not necessarily a logistical arrangement. The actual environment may suffer no change as the movement of energies transpires within the individuals involved. If a logistical arrangement facilitates a needed translation of energies, then Fe may arrange the situation but for the sake of making that energy exchange possible. Even so, Fe will not be the most adept process at coordinating a logistical arrangement, and will first and foremost seek to arrange the situation by persuading the parties involved of its reasoning and have a collaborative effort taken towards that logistical aim. Thus, Fe compensates in part for its inability to change logistical causalities effectively by moving people's motivations; by persuading more hands to get involved in the problem in order to bring it to a solution.

Inversely, Te rearranges variables according to where substances need to be placed in order to perpetuate systemic functioning as Te does not manage via the manipulation of emotional states, but by the rearrangement of the environment. While the conclusions that Fe and Te arrive at may sometimes appear identical if expressed verbally, they will differ fundamentally in their implications. What the conclusion means in a practical sense will be very different to each function due to the different methods employed to correct or direct a circumstance. Te is a process which by itself is blind to the effects that its proactivity has on the people involved, unless the effects are so blatant that they immediately become logistical problems, due to its disassociation from the emotional register. Indeed, Te must disassociate itself from the emotional register if it is to gauge a situation objectively. While Fe, as an ethical process, is tended towards anthropomorphizing a situation, Te will tend toward viewing humans as objects no different than mechanical items. It is only in Fi that Te recovers a sensitivity toward the dimension of people, and indeed such sensitivity can be strong when the Fi-Te oscillation pairing is harmonizing. Yet this will not alter its methodology of proactive execution. Instead, a Te user may feel deeply affected by the ethical reality of a situation, and will use that passion as a motivator to channel their focus towards

2. OF CONSCIOUSNESS

finding objective, logistical solutions to perceived environmental imbalances.

Principle

At their most incremental scale, the operations of both introverted judgment (Ji) processes and the methodology they employ to differentiate perceptions compares not one external variable to another, but instead compares all to itself. Both lie at the center of all focus, judging situations and occurrences via a timeless, philosophical sense divorced from the particular dynamics occurring in the present. With this methodology, each individual instance of judgment measures whether or not the matter at hand resonates or clashes with a principle. Therefore, disagreement with a variable happens not by whether the whole situation necessitates a certain disposition, but by how the variable relates to the disposition of introverted judgment. Both Ti and Fi give priority to the internal rather than to how those internal ideas manifest in the outside world. If something ought to be true in principle, the principle is sustained even in opposition to an environment that may make the principle impractical. This is not to say that adaptation of judgment is impossible for Ti and Fi, but for these two processes alteration of a principle happens through a general reconsideration of the underlying reasoning to the principle. Should a shift in its principles occur, it will not only affect the present situation, but the individual's psychic disposition altogether as the compass process strives for convergence; a unification of focus in all of its judgments without any contradiction. The Je processes, in contrast, will feel entirely justified in executing the appropriate situational judgment to accomplish the desired outcome without any regard for internal consistency. "The ends justifiy the means" is perhaps an apt description of the economical thinking that the Je processes utilize when working out of harmony with the compass process.

We can exemplify this difference in functionality by the diagram in Figure 6. The light grey circles represent the individual. The small black circles represent environmental variables. To the left we see an example of the compass operation,

COGNITIVE TYPE

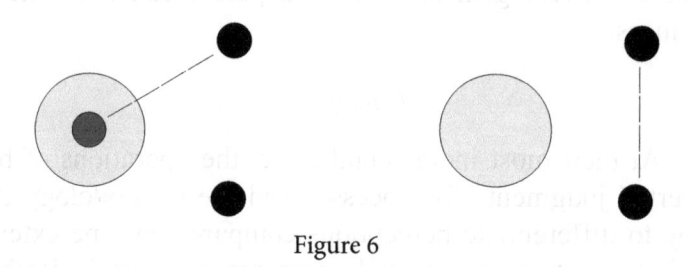

Figure 6

with the central compass process (the small dark grey circle) in the middle of the individual. Notice here how it analyses the top variable in isolation. One by one, the compass process individually compares each variable to itself before going on to the next. The Je process to the right always compares things to other things, and there is no central comparison point, seen here by the absence of the inner dark grey circle.

Now, Fi and Ti differ from each other primarily through the association or disassociation with the emotional register. For Ti, disassociation from the emotional register refers to a lack of consideration of one's own bodily sense. The Ti process is unique in its operation as it is not only disassociated from the object – the external – but also disassociated to a degree from the internal. It is neither connected to the topic of life or death, nor to what is happening in the world. Due to this twofold disassociation, the experience of Ti may be one where the individual experiences themselves as though from a third-person perspective, and while this is surely an illusion – as it is not possible for any psychic process to escape its psychic origin – this disassociation from the self can be a pertinent experience. Being divorced from external happenings, its operation in data discrimination, instead, turns purely to the conceptual. Its impetus drives it naturally toward a convergence of concepts and the formation of a perfect, internally consistent logic. As it removes itself from the material and the personal, it is no surprise then that individuals with Ti often re-discover the philosophy of Zen with every passing generation, as this is a natural mode of operation for this process.

The Fi process, being instead connected to the emotional

register, is in a continual state of sensitivity – registering how a situation strikes their heart. It weighs situations by how they independently benefit or hinder life in whatever way the individual comes to personally define *life*. However, it is not necessary for an Fi user to have complete conscious awareness of their own definition of life – which their psyche may viscerally form through communion with the emotional register – but the effects of that definition will be strikingly exposed when a situation prompts their revelation. Such revelations will nonetheless be indirect, manifesting through another process as Fi itself never leaves the subject for the object. The Fi process is fully capable of registering the emotional truth of a situation, but there will exist a level of blindness as to how to go about moving people's hearts. This ignorance exists because Fi disassociates itself from the outer world and its dynamic operation. It seeks only to internally dissolve dissonance within its ethical principles. However, its association with the emotional register creates a paradoxical situation which I will refer to as **emotional radiation**. Despite not deliberately moving emotional dynamics, Fi users incidentally do so, to some degree, by their own sheer permeability and sensitivity to the emotional. As reality registers very personally for a Fi user, others may see how this impacts them and may be indirectly moved by their internal conviction. Nonetheless there will be an element of privacy and passivity to such radiation. It will differ from the influence of Fe, as Fi's radiation is unintentional and has no dynamic coordination. By itself it cannot select what type of impact to give, or what is appropriate, for the situation at hand; it cannot convey anything other than what the Fi user currently and genuinely feels.

8. THE WHOLE OF A COGNITIVE TYPE

Through this algorithm and its exponential operation, our perceptions and deductions quickly multiply into countless expressions, beliefs and worldviews – each stemming from relatively few fundamental principles working in unison and in rapid succession. Each human possesses one of these two judgment oscillation pairings and a perception oscillation pairings, completing all the necessary functions for cognitive operation. The necessity for the presence of one oscillation pair at the exclusion of the other relates directly to the energetic relationship that defines those pairings. As we have established in this chapter, the operation of Ne-Si, for example, is entirely counter to that of Se-Ni both in its way of perceiving reality as well as in its process of archiving memories. The discord that would result from the presence of both oscillations within the same individual would be an inability to properly record or recall memories, or interpret the environment due to conflicting instructions in the same domain.

The overarching algorithm of cognitive type includes an antagonistic relationship between Te-Fi and Ti-Fe as well as between Ne-Si and Ni-Se. However, because each individual human can only possess one or the other, the final antagonistic relationship of this algorithm magnifies and completes itself beyond the individual level and cannot be understood in whole without an understanding of the collective. As some humans represent one aspect of the equation, others will display the opposite – and thus not only are there internal oppositions within the same individual, but this psychic tension exists also between humans.

a. Hierarchy

There are two factors at play in determining differentiation of types between people: the oscillation pairs that are present within them and their energetic arrangement. We see four general sub-classes of human emerge from the mutual exclusion of oscillation pairings, as Ti-Fe and Fi-Te can exist with either Se-Ni or Ne-Si. These four sub-classes each possess all necessary components for psychic operation, however the energetic arrangement of those processes differs in people. This is because the psyche requires an energetic vector in order to perpetuate the cycling of those processes forward. An individual can either lead with the judgment oscillation pairing or the perception oscillation pairing, and of those two options an individual can either lead with the proactive or reactive function of that oscillation.

The default state of an individual's psyche will rest in the

2. OF CONSCIOUSNESS

primary oscillation pair while the secondary oscillation pair will be supportive and feed the first pair, but its aims will never be pursued outside of their ability to properly aide the prime directive. The primary 'drama' within a psyche is the first oscillation; the attention and obsession of the psyche will be directed toward synthesizing the two polar ends most native to it, and while it will never succeed in fully doing so, via its effort it will generate an ever refining comprehension of the themes it touches upon. If for example we take an individual who possesses the Ti-Fe and Se-Ni oscillation pairs, their core psychological disposition will be either that of judgment or perception. In the case of wielding Ti-Fe as their primary mode of operation they will be lead towards certainty, internal alignment and conclusiveness since both Ti and Fe hold the same decisive disposition and can communicate and compromise with one another even if they disagree on the specific content involved. They strive for accuracy in deduction and require the antagonistic operation of each other in order to do this successfully. They will then use Se-Ni as subordinate processes to aide them by delivering data from which they can draw more distinguished conclusions. The data fed in

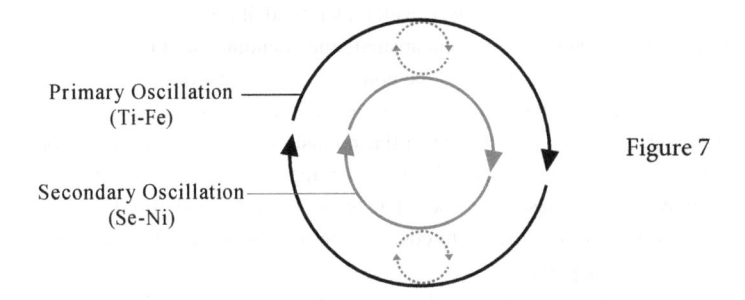

Primary Oscillation (Ti-Fe)

Secondary Oscillation (Se-Ni)

Figure 7

by Se-Ni will be analyzed and concluded upon by the joined effort of the Ti-Fe process.

The diagram above shows a depiction of what this arrangement looks like, via a modification of the diagram on page 16. One oscillation has been expanded, as seen here by Ti-Fe, while Ni-Se is contained within the diameter of the larger oscillation. It is in this sense, also, that cognitive type differs greatly both from type as defined originally by Jung as well as Isabel Briggs Myers. The psyche does not work as compartmentalized bits, nor does it work with percentages of use of each process. It would be simple to say that each function has a general definition and that an individual has 100% of that first function with progressively less amounts of all the rest, as if assuming functions came in quantities. But instead the functions work as a complex system and that system is interwoven by governing dynamics in ways more nuanced than a simple sliding scale of prevalence in the psyche. And so a hierarchical arrangement as described by these principles would not be "Fe > Ni > Se > Ti" but instead "Fe(Ni-Se)Ti" – where Ni-Se is contained within Fe-Ti and the psyche is led by proactivity. If instead the psyche is led by reactivity, then the resulting hierarchy is Ti(Se-Ni)Fe. These two hierarchies are the same fundamental sub-equation, differing only in their overall direction of energy flow, making them closer to one another in functionality and information processing than to any other types. This polarity in energy flow exists for each of the other pairings, leading to the sixteen cognitive types.

I must also make a few remarks pertaining to the Jungian naming of these eight cognitive functions. As Jung himself well understood, it is impossible for a single descriptive term or label to wholly encapsulate the phenomenon it is designed to represent nor is that the intent. One must be content only with holding a convenient shorthand for the concept embedded within it in order to make communication more possible. However, from the time of the initial publishing of *Psychological Types* (1921), a great deal of confusion and misunderstanding has arisen from the terminology chosen by Jung for these processes. The terms "feeling" and "thinking" can apply so generically not only to all eight cognitive processes but to all phenomenon that transpires within the psyche.

The fine distinctions between these concepts and how they stray from the laymen's use of the words were well noted in Jung's Psychological Types, but they have since been misinterpreted by subsequent typological models, and I wish to stray away from having the reader unduly associate my definitions to those of existing interpretations or to generate new misconceptions. In seeking to remedy this difficulty, I was conflicted with the dilemma of assigning new names to something that has already existed and been quantified – although to a different degree. And despite my hesitation, certainly if progress is to be made, a new definition of these processes must be generated. I sought therefore to invent a new terminology for the psychological functions, in which a single word encapsulates the entirety of the

2. OF CONSCIOUSNESS

oscillation-pair, as the two functions comprising a pairing are not a separate concept within Cognitive Type theory. However, were I to decide instead to use another descriptive term, inevitably the new adjective would be given more priority in defining the concept in the minds of people than is appropriate, and once again a distorted view is created of the underlying process.

I reasoned it was best to use either a word which does not itself possess preexisting meaning, or a visual symbol which is not contingent on vocabulary. And the words I have selected are ALE (Ti/Fe), EDA (Te/Fi), M (Si/Ne) and V (Ni/Se) – the creation of which is explained in my chapter titled Terminology at the end of the book. For the sake of not wholly confusing readers who may have come to this book with a Jungian understanding, throughout this material I will be using the two-letter shorthands of Jung's functions interchangeably with these new terms, although I will not be using the longhand definitions to refer to the eight functions.

3
JUDGMENT & PERCEPTION

Experience has taught me that while there are certainly many variations in the expressions of any one individual, each individual has but a limited sphere of expressions which account for the vast majority of their manifestations. The body's disposition, it would seem, prefers a certain rhythm and tempo which complements its psychological disposition. Such a rhythm lies in a sea of circumstantially attained habits which often partially overshadow that rhythm – making it difficult to distinguish from their culturally formed persona – but the traces of this rhythm can never be fully obstructed. This is because our outward persona is itself a creation of the psyche, birthed from the activity of our consciousness, and therefore carries within it the signature of the methodology used for its construction.

Often I have been met with the argument that no feasible way must exist to derive psychic rhythms from facial expressions because, after all, expressions are random and wholly learned from nurture. But it is no easier to feign the activity of your psyche, or its visual expressions, as it is to make a violin sound like a piano even if they're playing the same song. Even the manner in which we learn to express ourselves reveals within it the apparatus of our psyche. If, for instance, an individual with primarily recessive and reactive energy is attempting to convey a proactive persona, such disorientation will show a strain on their body. Their body will appear as though it is in a constant struggle to hide from the world it is so adamantly striving to be engaged with. The psyche cannot hide its energetic limitations and how that generates traces of compensation in the body.

For a vultologist (a practitioner of vultology), this is the key quality that allows for the systematic analysis of psychic dynamics. Were the countenance a patternless assortment of mus-

3. JUDGMENT & PERCEPTION

cle contractions, the systemic identification of principles through its observation would be impossible. But on the contrary, if we observe the countenance from a dispassionate yet receptive perspective, patterns emerge on their own – revealing to us what the psychic dynamics at play are without a dependence on the abstracted *a priori* speculation of any one practitioner. Because of this, the newly emerging field of vultology possesses great capacity to grow in accuracy through collaborative exploration and review.

While the descriptions in the previous chapter surmise the core psychology of cognitive type, it is in seeing it work firsthand that one comes to realize the necessity of these principles and how they flow causally out of the activity of the psyche as discerned through our visage. No amount of language could compensate for the enormity of evidence that is available through firsthand experience. I therefore invite you, the reader, not only on a written journey but on an experimental journey through this book. At every step, I invite you to find within your environment the dynamics described and measure with your own judgment whether such expressions are indeed connected to the real-time disposition of the respective individual's psyche.

Tension

There are many ways to approach the topic of visual reading, but I would like to start with judgment and perception. Judgment is a process that determines where we stand on a matter or belief. It is the realm of conviction, decision-making and execution of those decisions. And because of this, when the body actively makes or executes a judgment, it becomes rigid and defensive of those convictions. There is at once a sense that the person is standing behind their words, as though they have become the physical embodiment or guardian of those ideas. When a person is using judgment in real-time, this manifests in the body being stiffer and the movements of the hands and head being more straight and linear; directional and sharp with well-defined halts. The muscles become tense, primarily around the head and neck, but this may extend to the entire body. The fingers may be-

COGNITIVE TYPE

come taut, whether stretched out entirely or locked in a claw-like posture. The head in particular remains rigid, and when it moves it does so vertically or horizontally with quick, deliberate motions. Were we to personify, for comparison's sake, an individual wholly judgmental, such a person would never move except out of deliberation, their muscles would remain forever tightened and each of their movements would be like a sharp swing of a sword. Their every phrase would be a statement, spoken with a simultaneous rattling of the head up-to-down and left-to-right. And while surely no human is so unilaterally judgmental, the disposition of judgment generates this tendency to varying degrees in all persons. No individual is continually emitting these signals, but at the very moments in which they do, their psychic disposition will certainly be one of conviction and closure. If we compare the words that accompany their expression, we will see traces of that same finality reflected. The correlation between judgment and bodily tension is so consistent that we need only to turn our attention, ever so slightly, to seeing its presence for it to become an unavoidable observation.

Fluidity

The opposite is true of perception, which is an altogether fluid and ongoing experience, both mentally and physically. When the psyche is engaged in absorbing data it is not engaged in rejecting it, nor in selecting away what it finds irrel-

Figure 8

3. JUDGMENT & PERCEPTION

evant. The process of judgment marks the closure of receptiveness to new information, thus causing rigidity in the body as it defends the finite perimeter of an idea, but perception draws no such boundaries, nor is it concerned with standing behind a cause with an unyielding character. As such, when perception is engaged the body's disposition is not restricted by definitive halts or tensions. The body will appear altogether loose, receptive to movements and the whims of the environment or one's own internal recollections. We have all seen someone in our circle of peers whose body sways as they talk, and their head swivels from shoulder to shoulder as their spine collaborates in this dance with a syncopated rhythm. Their words flow as an unbroken stream of thoughts, often with no definite point to get across, but merely the relaying of an experience. To perception, the truth of reality is the immeasurable qualities contained therein, undisturbed and uncompromised, not what might be picked out and considered of most importance. All is of equal importance, and the task is turned toward assimilating it all in unison. For this reason, the flow of a strong perceiver's thoughts will navigate and drift through an untold number of topics without any concern for a destination.

  I must also note that this psychophysical fluidity is not necessarily contingent on motion, although motion certainly reveals this fluidity most strikingly. Even within a sedentary posture, the body of a

a.

b.

c.

Figure 9

41

perceiver will carry the same adaptive quality. To make use of a metaphor, if we liken judgment to a stone and perception to a small plant, then in the absence of wind the plant may be entirely still just as the stone, but it would be far less rigid and solid than the stone would be amidst the wind. The qualities of the plant remain the same, however their revelation awaits an occasion for contrast. It is in the way that the body moves from one state to another that we see the presence or absence of tension.

Face-Centric & Eye-Centric

Furthermore, this division between tension and fluidity alone is not able to distinguish a judgment type from a perception type, as all humans express both attributes to varying degrees, depending on what the situation necessitates and on the development of their processes. The presence of a dominant oscillation can be gauged instead by whether the entire body is steered by the head or by the eyes, what I have respectively termed **face-centric** and **eye-centric**. When we look closer at those who have the strongest fluidity, we see also that their eyes have a powerful influence over the direction of not only their head but their entire posture. It is as though their eyes are the focal point of their body; the origin of their fluid movements. Their eyes will move first and the rest of their body follows, trailing behind by only a fraction of a second, in a manner reminiscent of a cobra or the path of a fish. Oppositely, when we look closer at those who have the strongest rigidity of body, we see that their eyes are often neglected or rejected, while their posture is dictated by the uniform presentation of their countenance. As the information of the eyes, which are the most notable indicator of perception, is rejected by judgment, they become altogether of lesser importance in the overall countenance of the individual. They occupy a secondary place, while all other facial muscles cooperate to form a cohesive accentuation that corresponds to the convictions held. If the eyes move to the sides the whole head will feel no obligation to follow them. Instead the head will remain where it is and the eyes will soon return to the direction that the whole face is facing. In other situations, the head may even move to a

3. JUDGMENT & PERCEPTION

new direction first, and the eyes will follow it some time later.

In this way we can gauge which oscillation pair takes priority in the psyche of the individual. Those with perception as their priority cannot reject their external or internal eyesight or the manner in which it affects their entire being. They are drawn to those perceptions and consumed by their influence over them. The judgment type is not subordinate to those perceptions, nor the eyes (which are their origin), but instead is able to take in that information as if it was only a passing suggestion, rather than a consuming vision.

In Figure 10 we have a metaphorical representation of this difference. Imagine that the grey lines inside of these two men were semi-flexible metal wires which restrict the movement of their spines. Each also has a pivot point that dictates the way in which the head can move. On the left (judgment) the pivot allows for the head to swivel left-to-right and hinge up-to-down;

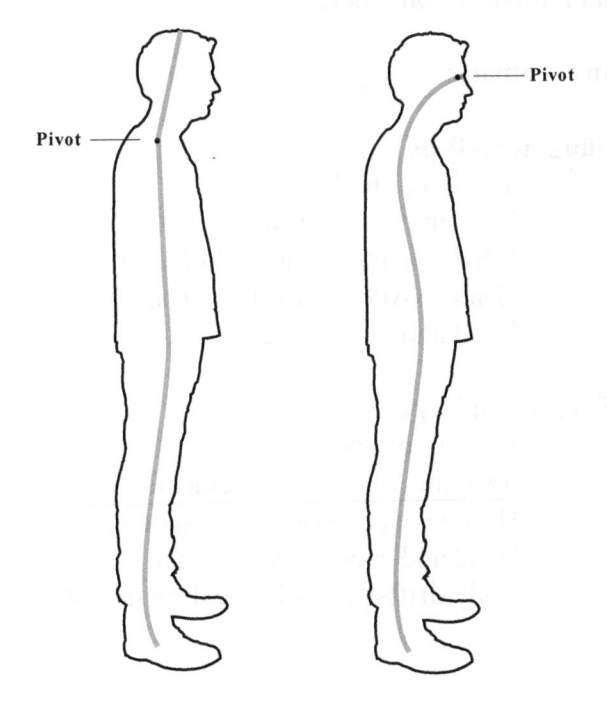

Figure 10

yaw and pitch. On the right (perception) the pivot allows for the head to roll easiest from ear-to-shoulder, but turning left-to-right is more difficult without moving the entire body in that direction. This is a good way of illustrating where the constraints in both body types lie. Naturally every human is capable of using both styles of movement, short of a legitimate anatomical impairment, but always one style will be predominant in an individual.

It might be worth noting that the silhouettes of both these men are deliberately left identical to emphasize that the difference between these two types is not in their manner of standing but in their patterns of motion. The judgment type does not necessarily have *good* posture, nor is the head necessarily more erect, and the perception type does not necessarily have *poor* posture nor a neck that leans itself forward further than the judgment types. These are habits independent of the body-steering effect that I am describing herein.

In Summary:

Judgment-Type
    Tension of body
    Exacting, angular movements
    Head swivels left-to-right (yaw)
    Head swivels up-to-down (pitch)
    Head and eyes move independent of eachother

Perception-Type
    Fluidity of body
    Swaying, ongoing movements
    Head swivels shoulder-to-shoulder (roll)
    Head and eyes move together
    Body drifts/glides in the direction of the eyes

4

THE ENERGETIC QUADRANTS

For those following the content of this book in accompaniment with a visual observation of those in your surroundings, it may be worth noting that the optimal circumstance from which to gauge these signals in people is in an interview-like format. The psyche's activity is gauged most clearly when it is actively creating its concept of reality. We are able to see the genesis of a thought, expressed through the face, most clearly when there is no time given for premeditation. In such a situation, the new question must be absorbed, compared against previous perceptions, weighed against one's internal compass, and then a position articulated via proactive judgment. All of this happens most strikingly during the first seconds, or fractions of a second, following the initial question.

It is also best, especially for those learning these concepts for the first time, that the dialogues take place one-on-one. Interviews where multiple people or crowds are watching encourage an overuse of the persona and will make it more difficult to decipher how natural a certain expression is to the person.

1. COMPASS AS THE LEAD PROCESS

Momentum Halting

As we observe judgment types more closely, we begin to see that their rigid expressions will oscillate continually between the exertion of an exacting motion, and intermittent moments where the body will halt in a suspended or frozen state until the next exertion is delivered. Of the judgment signals previously outlined, the Je processes are responsible for these outward motions while Ji is primarily seen by these abrupt halts in motion. When the Ji process is engaged the body remains rigid, tense, and

COGNITIVE TYPE

calculating, but also withdrawn, recessive and motionless. This is because no reactive process ever seeks substances away from the self, and for judgment that is introverted, this is no different. The result is a conservation of that rigidity but with no exertion of energy forward; instead the energy goes away from the world and into the self. It would appear as though all energies, resources and focus were being directed, by some emergency, into a very intense internal dilemma. When the body is actively engaging the compass process, at that very moment the body will seem to freeze, halting the momentum of the extroverted processes. And in the same way that the signals of judgment and perception will mirror the psychic state of the individual, when this freezing occurs the quality of a person's thoughts will follow from that place of internal conviction. Suddenly the psyche is turned to assessing whether the situation at hand has some internal inconsistency with one's own ethics or values.

Eyes Disengage Down

Furthermore, the process of Ji, being both judgmental and introverted, has a twofold resistance against the perception of the outer world. While judgment itself is pivoted against perception in such a way that the eyes take a secondary role, the compass process retracts its energies so completely from the external world that the eyes will disengage from the environment. In these moments, it is of no

a.

b.

c.

Figure 11

4. THE ENERGETIC QUADRANTS

relevance to the psyche what the environment appears like – as its entire focus is being channeled toward the elimination of internal contradiction, the refinement of conviction, and often the pinging of the mind or heart for a previously formulated opinion. Here, the eyes will drop downward, accompanied by the top eyelids, often nearing a complete closing. In Figures 11.a and 11.b we see examples of this disengagement. It will often be the case that in these moments the fingers will stretch and freeze in a particular posture for the duration of the disengagement.

A secondary form of disengagement that occurs is excessive blinking, being yet another way to disconnect from perception and withdraw energies internally. Disengaging downward and excessive blinking will often appear together with the activation of the compass process, although disengaging downward will be a more persistent signal in types that lead their psyche with Ji. Blinking in excess is an altogether more brief disengagement, as the psyche quickly pings the compass process before resuming its composure without needing to halt the momentum of the entire body.

Exerted Push

When a Ji lead type tries to articulate and project an idea, there will be a very notable struggle in the body, as if their entire posture were battling to give birth to their idea. The body's tension will grow strongly as it starts to make the transition from introversion to extroversion, pushing out their articulation with effort. This is because the energetic transfer of an internal conviction to an extroverted form (Je) is initially very strenuous and unnatural. A type that leads their psyche with Ji will experience this constant battle to express their ideas via Je, while their body continually hides under a rigid and self-kept posture. Additionally, immediately following each one of these *pushes*, the body will deflate and withdraw. The voice and appendages will fade, like a tide returning to the ocean, with a level of softness and passivity. This signal is a result of the effect that Ji has upon Je, and not the result of Ji alone, but it is nonetheless a signal that identifies the process of Ji even though the push itself is ultimately caused by Je.

2. ARTICULATOR AS THE LEAD PROCESS

Gesticulation

The articulator process, being the proactive expression of judgment, demonstrates itself through accentuated motions of the head and body from a place of rigidity. The body will jitter as an autonomic response to the verbal delivery of a judgment, however slight this jittering may be. Head shaking, head nodding, raising eyebrows, chopping hand motions and head pushes forward are the most notable expressions of this activity. Regardless of whether the individual has had any formal training in gesticulation, at the time of this process' manifestation there will existing a strong tendency to move the appendages – in whatever way possible – to the rhythm of their face and mind when conveying a conviction. Often times the forms the arms, hands and fingers take, in the struggle to exhale these convictions, are forms the person has never before utilized – yet the impulse to gesture them prevails. The hands will twist and bend in awkward ways, as if struggling to give tangible form to their ideas. Facial emphasis, such as accentuating with eyebrows or widening the mouth when speaking, equally stem from this impulse to manifest that conviction.

It is important for me to emphasize that this tendency, or perhaps it is better described as an *urge*, to accentuate speech is not contrived by culture, although its specific execution is indeed susceptible to cultural influence. That is to say, the urge is innate, while its specific manifestation holds a level of variation among societies. It is, by default, more difficult to refrain oneself from utilizing some form of projection when articulating a conviction than to allow one's body to find its own avenue of expressivity.

Both extraverted processes, Pe and Je, are marked by a proactivity in the body; motion. However, Je delivers motion from an origin of rigidity, while Pe delivers motion from an ori-

4. THE ENERGETIC QUADRANTS

gin of fluidity. To use an analogy, we can contrast the two forms of motion as follows:

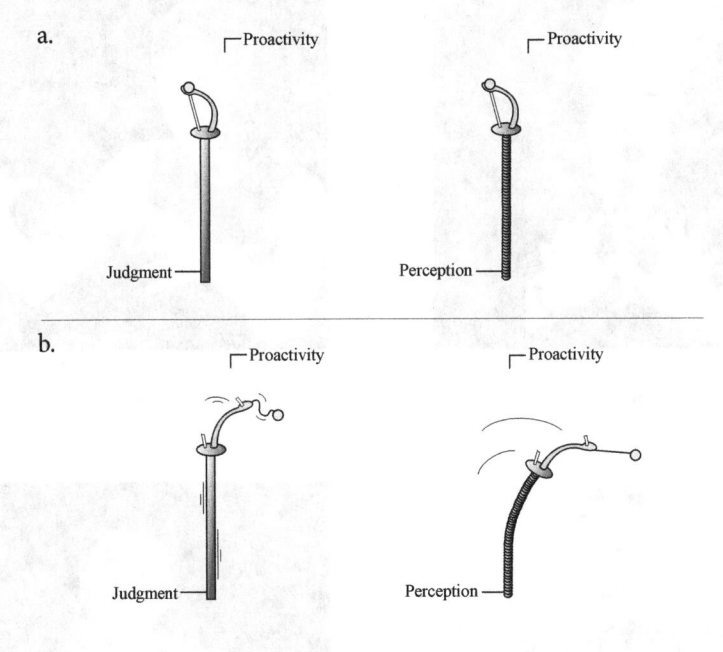

Figure 12

Here in Figure 12.a we see two rods, one made from a solid metal (judgment) while the other is made from a spring (perception). At the top of both of these rods is a small catapult with its cargo attached to it by a rope, so that upon releasing the catapult the cargo will be yanked back by the catapult. In Figure 12.b we see the catapults released and the effects that the yanking has on the two rods. In both, the catapult represents a proactive motion, while the rod represents the way the body responds to the movement. For a Pe type, their own motions will give momentum to their fluid body; the motion of the catapult will drag the whole body with it, swaying it in that direction with energy. For a Je type, their body will jitter as a result of the cargo's momentum being abruptly stopped by the rigidity of the body. As tension is still sustained throughout the body for a judgment type, Je's exacting motions act only as a temporary release of

COGNITIVE TYPE

a.

b.

c.

d.

Figure 13

that tension for the sake of projection, before the body returns again to its default composure.

Deliberation

The motions of Je can take a large variety of forms and this is because, unlike all other processes, Je has a level of deliberation that is inherent to its nature. It is the *intentional* (judgment) delivery of motion (proactivity), for the sake of managing external causalities. Now, this does not make its signals *false* because they are consciously controlled to some degree; it is an entirely expected part of its functioning as both a deliberate and proactive process. The articulator process exhales itself through the mannerisms of the person, utilizing whatever forms they know how to use to convey meaning in gestures. And if no forms are known then they will still generate movements with no particular premeditated coordination. Gesticulation, as a whole, can be called the practice, refinement and systemization of the articulator process. It is the means by which humans convey conviction and meaning to one another. This is also why I call it the articulator process. While Je can be used without communicating with another human (for example by simply deciding to move some physical objects into a different organization) its signals show themselves when conveying meaning to another person. The physical, mechanical movement of objects is not itself evidence of Je operating, but the decision to do so does call forth the Je process.

Often what people imagine when they argue the legitimacy of a correlation between facial/body expressions and cognition is that because expressions can be controlled, there is no validity in what they convey. Such an argument is only considering the deliberating process of Je, which is but a sliver of the whole expression of a person, and ignoring all else that transpires in the body. Not all expressions are under conscious control, and even those which are still reveal striking qualities about the psyche of the individual in question. Along the same lines, a common misconception is to believe that if there was a correlation between the psyche and expressions, it would appear as an unambiguous one-to-one connection between a static signal and a single mental experience. That is to say, if we were to photograph a single posture, disconnected from all context, then we ought to expect that the person making that posture would be having a certain psychic experience at that moment. But naturally, we won't always be psychologically experiencing the Je process simply by arranging our limbs in a posture resembling a Je signal. An expectation for such a binary correlation would automatically make it impossible to identify whether or not there may also be a different reason for making those muscular contractions in different occasions. It would wholly close off investigation into the nuanced ways that humans carry themselves and what may be motivating them to act as they do at different times. If indeed gesticulations were a result of Je's cognitive processing, then it would need to be true that muscles can be used for locomotion as well as for expression, and the layered existence of both doesn't automatically make one or the other invalid through some imagined mutual exclusivity. Muscles can be used both to mechanically posture oneself in certain forms, as well as convey the activity of Je and other processes.

3. EXPLORER AS THE LEAD PROCESS

Alert Eyes

As previously mentioned, the activity of the perception processes has a strong influence over not only the gaze of an individual, but the manner in which that gaze directs the head and body. For a type that leads their psyche with proactive perception (Pe), this entails a proactive exploration of the environment through environmental **tracking**. A Pe lead type will be in a constant state of alertness, as their eyes are consistently engaged with some aspect of the environment and being lead in its direction in order to absorb its information. This will show itself in the contracting of the center of the orbicularis oculi to better expose the eyes. While other types may hold a more casual demeanor to their eyes, Pe types will appear to have a level of excitement always about them. There will be a quickness in their observation, as they promptly notice changes and visually respond to them.

4. THE ENERGETIC QUADRANTS

Now, having alert eyes does not necessarily mean that Pe types have strong *focus*, if we take focus to mean an unbroken attention span. Pe types will have strong focus and alertness towards what they're observing at any specific moment, but they are also equally prone to divert their focus to something else which catches their attention anew. Because of this, ironically, Pe types may even be seen as unfocused, inattentive, and non-perceptive.

Darting Eyes

Along with giving the user an alert look to their eyes, Pe is responsible for making the eyes **dart** in a couple different ways. The first is as a response to physical changes in the environment; the diversion of attention to other stimuli. However, the second is an automatic effect that is entirely independent of external environmental stimuli. We've often seen how the eyes of another person fly around in seemingly random directions, or toggle from one place to another very quickly, while they are clearly not gathering information from their physical surroundings; instead their environment is wholly ignored. Yet if we look closely, this seemingly random activity happens most often when a person is seeking to find a way to say something, envision/imagine something, or recall an idea. It is as though their eyes are mimicking the physical activity of *searching*, in the external environment, when they are doing a similar investigation internally. This is because, to the cognitive process

a.

b.

c.

Figure 14

of Pe, there is fundamentally no difference between darting eyes for tracking aspects of the physical environment and for internally exploring the tapestry of Pi.

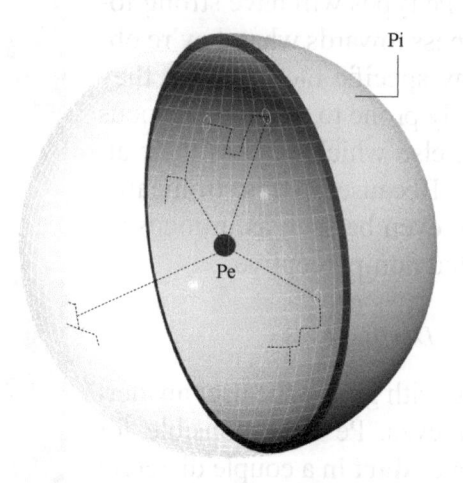

Figure 15

In the figure above, we see the explorer processes (the black sphere in the center) exploring the tapestry of the worldview process, where information exists that is not in the physical view of the individual. The left, transparent, hemisphere is objective reality, while the right hemisphere is reality as it has been approximated in our worldview function. Because the psyche makes no distinction between the fantasy generated by our psyche (Pi) and reality itself as it may appear outside of any human perception, the entirety of "the world" that the explorer process can see is a panorama composed of both parts. What forms "reality" to our eyesight is never just the retina's information. The explorer process can glance at memory just as it glances at reality, and memory is also treated as a type of existing phenomenon. It diverts its gaze from one to the other continually in its process of exploration; it explores both the present and the previously archived, in an attempt to piece together a richer mental image of the reality of the present moment.

I must also make a distinction between this form of ex-

4. THE ENERGETIC QUADRANTS

ploration and the echo of the worldview process. Data recall is fundamentally an activity of the worldview process, and the explorer process does not receive the information of the worldview's tapestry without collaboration with the worldview process. The explorer process pings and an echo is received. Visually and cognitively there is a striking difference between data recall when it is initiated by the explorer process and when it is initiated by the worldview process. When the explorer process initiates, the eyes will retain their alert focus as well as toggling eye motions while their upper eyelids and brow will be marginally affected by the Pi processes to integrate the signals of Pi. These signals will be additional but not central to their expression, which is altogether more animated and prone to transitions according to the person's thoughts. Inversely, when Pi recalls of its own accord there is far less animation and the eyes will not intermix the signals this heavily.

Momentum

Now as a proactive process, similar to the articulator process, Pe generates movement and excitation; it carries an impulse towards *initiation*. However, all of this energy is not restricted by a rigidity of a judgment type's body. The articulator process clamps down a proactive movement after its initial expressing, essentially resetting its movement to zero, but because the explorer process does not clamp its own expressions, new energy is amplified by previously generated energy – giving rise to **momentum**. This momentum is amplified according to how much stimulation the environment offers (not forgetting that memories and abstractions can also provide stimulation). For a Pe type, their energetic movements will emerge from a place of *intrigue*. Their body will have a fluid energy, often causing their posture to sway playfully and perk up when there is a spike of stimulation in the environment.

In extreme cases, Pe can manifest as restlessness and an inability to sit still. However, not all Pe types will be so restless or continually mobile, nor should this be used as a definite criteria for Pe. Many Pe types may live quite externally uneventful lives, yet they will nonetheless be continually finding some source of stimulation in their lives. There are entire worlds to explore inside books, games and fantasy. The mind of an explorer type can easily be captivated by these forms of stimulation - absorbing mountains of data from them - and yet externally appear to be a reactive type. However, there will exist always a *bubbling* current of energy running underneath the being of a Pe type, independent of which lifestyle they've chosen. Even when we find them in a sedentary posture, it will appear as though their body is suspended, ready to move at any moment and move quickly should it be prompted. Other types, such as Ji leads, will seem entirely static in their energy and be continually deflating into inaction. Instances of movement quickly die down without savoring their opportunity. For the explorer process, instances of movement are reveled in by the body, and slow down very gradually as momentum is naturally lost.

4. WORLDVIEW AS THE LEAD PROCESS

Inertia

The Pi process, being likewise fluid, does not subscribe itself to the rigidity that the judgment processes produce, yet, due to being a reactive process, it reduces activity in the body. This fluid reduction of momentum leads to a type of density in the body that may be best described as **viscosity**. It does not produce a sudden halt in the body, but instead the body drifts heavily with the **inertia** of the explorer process and its energy. For a Pi type, the most typical pattern of movement begins with an initial excitation from the explorer process (in the form of a perk-up, body sway, or eye-diversion) and then the body lingers in the movement's aftermath while steadying its gaze upon a fixed point. Such excitations are much less energetic than those of Pe lead types, and far less frequent.

The words *momentum* and *inertia* are not only analogous to the quality of movement these two types produce, but also of their psychology. The Pi process, as an object locked in Newtonian motion, retains its direction and nature until disturbed by an outside influence or catalyzed by the momentum of Pe. In Pi,

4. THE ENERGETIC QUADRANTS

this resilience to change is not due to an argument or principle that acts as the guardian against reconsideration, but simply due to the familiarity and affinity that the mind has to its existing mindset. A tendecy will exist to assimilate new data with pre-existing data; to keep the worldview map mostly unaltered and simply increase its size. This tendency will be unintentional; the psyche will effortlessly gravitate towards explaining the present through the lens of the past and in this way, Pi succeeds in retaining its shape, as much as possible, while also avoiding loss of predictability of the world.

Fixed Gaze

Like the Pe process, the worldview process is directly involved with the activity of the eyes. Yet, unlike Pe, it does not go outward for information. This creates a paradoxical situation in which Pi autonomously engages the eyes in the typical activity of perception while the mind's focus turns inward. This leaves the eyes fixated upon some point in the external environment that they only appear to be focusing on, while the actual object is being rejected. This differs distinctly from the Ji process, which disengages the eyes wholly from the outer world in order to go inward. For Pi, the eyes still remain open and connected to the outside world due to it being a perception process, but its attention leaves the external and searches inward for a specific dataset in the person's memory.

The user may be looking directly at a person, for entire minutes at a time, while their mind's attention is doing nothing but drifting through internal landscapes, hopping from one dataset to another. An outside observer may register a distinct impression that the Pi type has utterly lost touch with the outside world, or with them, and is now lost chasing a trail of ideas that have been previously interconnected. This tendency in Pi types is so common, that I often refer to it as **Pi rambling**. When this occurs, especially when accompanied with little or no Je gesticulation, the mind's motivation turns entirely to the conveying of experience and not to any singular point. The Pi type may relay all that he or she knows about a certain topic, simply because the

COGNITIVE TYPE

a.

b.

Figure 16

4. THE ENERGETIC QUADRANTS

information is connected, without any direct or practical application to the situation.

Eye-Drifting

While a long, fixed gaze may represent an unbroken span of worldview accessing, a less pronounced expression of Pi appears through **eye-drifts**. Pi types will commonly reference their Pi for brief moments by drifting their gaze to their left or right side, lingering for a moment as they recall the necessary information, then returning again to the person or focus of the discussion. This pattern appears more commonly in those with proper development of their judgment processes, where the Pi type will alternate between worldview accessing and gesticulation. Yet the prevailing dynamic will be the eyes and their dominance over the face and body. The eye-drifts will often carry the head and body with them, casually swaying the person's posture in that direction, then return again to the audience with the delivery of a gesticulation.

Scowling

In the emotional sense, scowling is an expression used with several feelings such as anger, pain or shock – each of which carries within it an element of rejection, or defensiveness against some element of the world. It is also used, for reasons not entirely unrelated to the former, to block out sunlight and to focus the eyes more intently while searching for an object in the environment. Now, as my focus is not in deciphering emotional expressions (I would refer the reader to the works of Dr.Ekman for such an explanation) but rather in deciphering higher cognition, the latter use is what will be relevant to us here.

As yet another example of the psyche's intimate connection with the face, and of the automatic crossover between it and the use of facial muscles, we see the action of scowling also performed when a person is more deeply and intently searching the bowels of memory. Now, scowling would not aid whatsoever in looking for a specific thought, memory or idea, as such things cannot be found in the outside world. The tendency to scowl is instead the eyes' natural response to intense perceptive focus – whether internal or external. It is a sort of vestigial activity of the eyes, a byproduct of an otherwise more directly advantageous gesture. When Pi is heavily accessed, scowling will accompany eye-drifts and fixed gazes, intensifying and relaxing depending on the obscurity of the recollection. And in other cases where the Pi process is exceptionally pronounced, the user may have a permanent scowl on their brow, accompanying their countenance in all manner of cognitive activity.

***

These four categories may be viewed as **energetic quadrants**, as they describe not what functions constitute a person's type, but the energetic direction of their psyche. And as a person's cognitive type is the combination of their intrinsic functions and their energetic direction, this constitutes half of a person's nature.

In this chapter I expressed these signals as they would appear in those who's primary nature corresponds to these processes, in order to isolate and better describe these otherwise heavily interwoven expressions. As each human possesses a Pe, Pi, Je and Ji process, rarely does a person display little more than the signals of one process, and such a person will quickly reveal a mind that is just as heavily imbalanced as their signals. More commonly, humans alternate between these four modes of expression. In conversation, at one moment they will divert their gaze to the side, scowling as they search for a thought, then return again to you with a head nod and rigid hand gestures. Then they may disengage their eyes downward as they process their internal position on a matter, and then strain their body to bring the conviction outward. Yet, it is also rare to find a human who is entirely balanced in these four modes of expression, making it very possible to identify which quadrant a person corresponds to from these signals alone.

4. THE ENERGETIC QUADRANTS

In Summary:

Compass Type
    Momentum Halting
    Body Freezing
    Eyes Disengage Down
    Excessive Blinking
    Exerted Push

Articulator Type
    Gesticulation
    Abrupt Jittering
    Head Shaking
    Head Nodding
    Eyebrow Raises
    Exacting Hand Gestures
    Head Pushes

Explorer Type
    Widening of Eyes
    Environment Tracking
    Diversion of Focus
    Eyes Darting & Toggling
    Fluid Body Swaying
    Momentum of Body
    Bubbling Energy

Worldview Type
    Inertial Energy
    Viscous Swaying/Leaning
    Density of Motion
    Fixed, Unmoving Eyes
    Pi Rambling
    Eyes Drifting
    Concentrated Scowling

PART II

FUNCTIONS

PART II

FUNCTIONS

5

Fi

REACTIVE ETHICAL JUDGMENT

Fi is a function that is intimately connected to the emotional register; to the limbic system and its somatic experience of emotions. It directly associates itself with the body and this connection is automatic. For better or worse, an Fi user cannot disconnect themselves from this influence any more than a Ti user could associate themselves to it. Fi users will continually feel a low-key emotional energy inside of them which will also be seen affecting their countenance at all times. While all human emotions can be felt by everyone, the muscles used to display emotions of *weeping* and *sadness* are always in a semi-contracted state for Fi users. These muscles are the levator labii superioris, levator labii superioris alaeque nasi, zygomaticus minor [1][2] and to some degree the depressor anguli oris – seen below in Figure 17. They surround the nose and, when fully contracted, elevate the upper lip towards it.

This **Fi tension** will often create a *pained expression* on the face, but the internal experience of Fi is not always negative. While for others these muscles typically contract due to emotional pain, for an Fi user they better represent *deep feeling*. They may contract heavily even when no pain is being felt, but instead simply as a side-effect of internal resonance with their compass process. Pinging their compass process causes these types to have more pronounced tension, and those who are primarily Fi types will have the heaviest dose of it.

1: The mechanism of human facial expression, pg.81, Duchenne de Boulogne translated by R. Andrew Cuthbertson – 2006
2: The artist's complete guide, pg.137, 141, Gary Faigin – 1990

COGNITIVE TYPE

Levator Labii Superioris
Alaeque Nasi

Levator Labii Superioris

Zygomaticus Minor

Depressor Anguli Oris

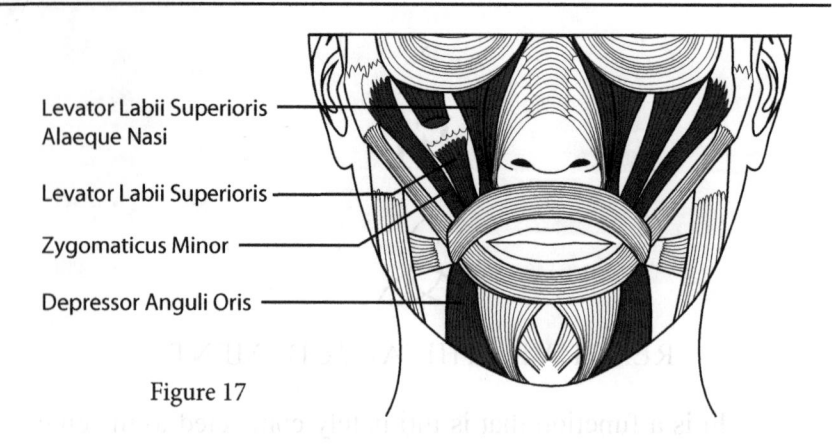

Figure 17

    I should also note that the precise visual identification of Fi can be challenging since there are many factors that affect the overall appearance of Fi tension. Natural differences in skeletal structures, age, levels of facial fat, and the presence or absence of certain muscles contribute to the variations of Fi we see in persons. Chapter 30 is devoted to addressing these nuances, and to establishing a proper method of practice for vultology. Here I wish only to provide an introduction to the concept in the clearest form possible so that exceptions can be understood from a general reference point. In Figure 18 we see Fi at various levels of contraction. The first row demonstrates Fi's tension initiating a smile, the second row demonstrates Fi's tension in a partially opened smile and the third row demonstrates Fi in a fully contracted smile; what I refer to as the **Fi Snarling Smile**. As seen here, when the muscles around the nose fully contract, their collision within such a small area causes a protrusion to form. The cheeks bulge near the nose and a distinct *stretching* occurs between the nose and the cheeks. These *taut cheeks* are seen primarily in those who have Fi-Te as their primary oscillation, but may appear in other hierarchies as well.

Asynchronous Snarling

    Since the levels of contraction that occur relate directly to the internal consultation of the compass process, Fi will cause various levels of contraction unintentionally as it is pinged even

5. Fi | REACTIVE ETHICAL JUDGMENT

a.

b.

c.

Figure 18

COGNITIVE TYPE

Here we see examples of micro-snarling while articulating within a time span of 5-10 seconds.

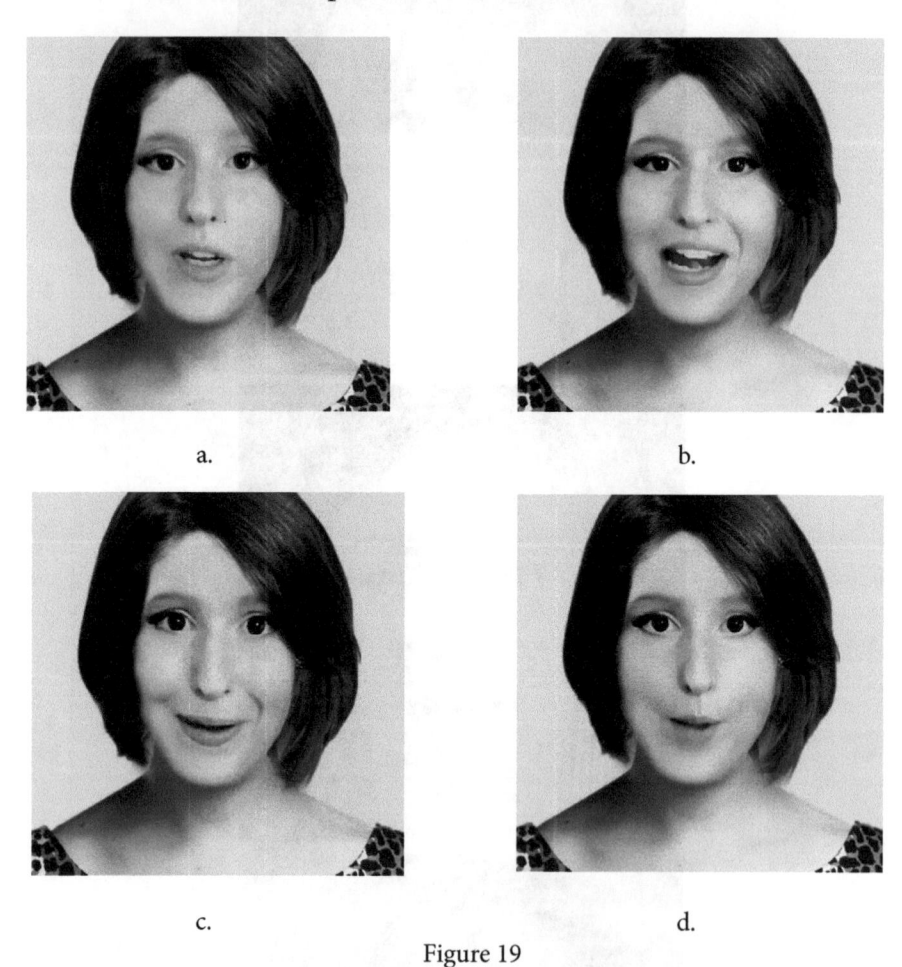

a.

b.

c.

d.

Figure 19

a) Asymmetrical tensions up-left & down-right
b) Asymmetrical tension down-left with snarling smile
c) Giddy smile with concave lips
d) Pursed lips surrounded by taut cheek area

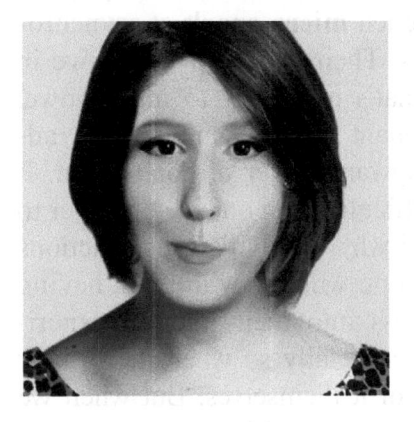

5. Fi | REACTIVE ETHICAL JUDGMENT

e.

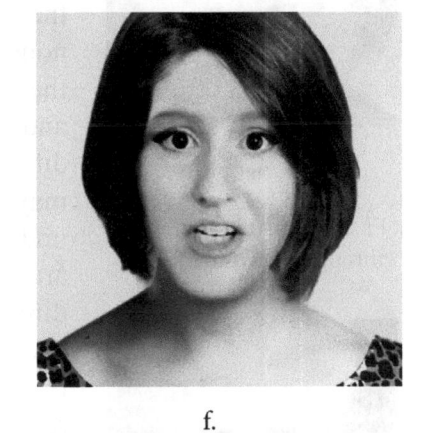

f.

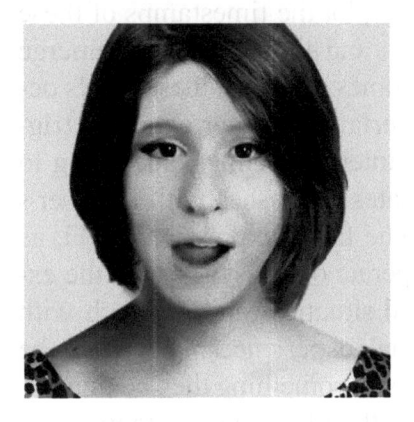

g.

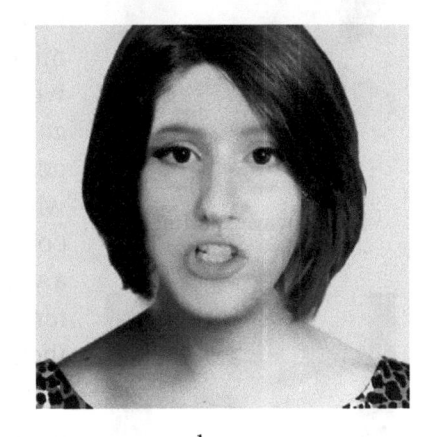

h.

e) Asymmetrical tension up-left, with pursed lips
f) Snarling tension with convex lips
g) Concave lips with tension up-right & down-left
h) Snarling tension with convex lips and tension down-left

COGNITIVE TYPE

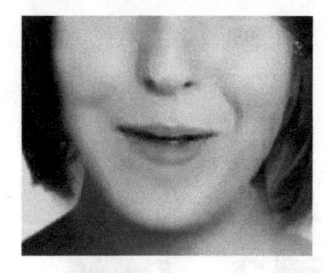

a.

Fi snarl starting midway through the word "feel"

b.

Fi concave snarling

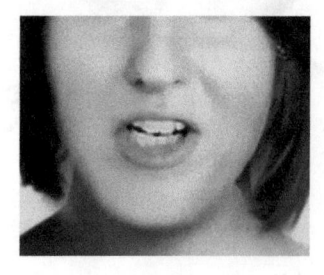

c.

Fi convex snarling

Figure 20

midway through a word or conversation. That is to say, while in dialogue with an Fi type, one will notice that as they speak they will elicit **micro-snarls** at asynchronous times. Their upper lip will move in the way that's necessary to make vowel and consonant sounds, but with an additional, upwards layer of contraction. It may be difficult for an outside observer to understand why these micro-contractions are happening when they are, not having direct access into their internal experience, and especially so when the Fi user is unaware of it themselves. But when we record a single one of these sentences and meticulously plot the timestamps of these micro-snarls and the words they emerge with, it becomes clear that these snarls occur when certain words or concepts trigger deeper internal feelings, according to what resonates or clashes with the user's compass. The facial expressions of Fi, as a whole, operate out of synch with the external social situation, and in synch with their internal experience. They may be speaking about something they adamantly adore, while their face may be contracting in the manner typical of the expression of disgust. At other times they may directly communicate strong affinity for someone while their expression remains largely unchanged. Since Fi on its own has no mechanism to coordinate itself to the outside world, it requires the effort of Te to create a managable social persona, but even then the off-beat nature of Fi's expressions will show through.

5. Fi | REACTIVE ETHICAL JUDGMENT

All of these Fi snarls can also take two different forms: **concave** or **convex**. So far as I can tell, these two forms don't differ in their psychological effects, but relate instead to the physiology of the individual. In Figure 20.b we see an example of a concave snarl, where the edge of the upper lip is turned outward and away from the face. In Figure 20.c we see a convex snarl, where the edge of the upper lip is turned inward and partially hidden inside the mouth. The muscles around the nose contract at different levels to produce these variations.

Airy, Sprite-like Voice

The articulation of an Fi-Te user will always emerge primarily from Te, which has a nasal and monotone pitch. But in cases where Fi is strong, its emotional influence will deeply saturate the user's otherwise dispassionate voice, giving it a breathy, sprite-like tone. It's difficult to convey this sound through text, but for a clear example of it, I refer the reader to the late singer and artist Michael Jackson or the young actress Evanna Lynch. In these cases, the voice comes from the stomach, and air is exhaled as a continuous stream without obstruction of the air passage. It may manifest in some as a form of wheezing and in others as a drawn-out whisper. The larynx takes the necessary form to make its sound and air simply passes through it.

In contrast, the voice of Fe types comes directly from the throat and is projected outward in specific bursts, not as a continuous stream. There is a deliberate, emotional push in the articulation of each syllable. As a general rule, the voice of Fi-Te will be diaphragmatic (Fi), nasal (Te), or a mix of both - depending on what the balance is between the two processes - but it is rarely tracheal.

Giddy Giggle

Fi further affects the individual's expressivity by giving a distinct quality to their laughter. If we consider that laughter is an elated release of emotional energy, then we understand why it is that Fi users each possess very unique laughs. In these moments, the laughter is utterly genuine and emanates unbridled from an inner joyfulness as a vibrating giggle. In some the voice will vibrate rapidly, while in others it will vibrate slowly, but in both cases one giggle will lead into the next with the same continuous, diaphragmatic openness that is heard in Fi's airy voice. In tandem with this giggling, the body will curl inward on itself; the head may be leaned back, the chin may be retracted inward, and the hands may be brought towards the torso. A strong snarling smile will accompany this expression, and the volume of the laughing itself will be unordinary. As with all other Fi expressions, the giggling will not subscribe itself to the social parameters in the environment – leading it at times to be uncommonly loud, sudden, or long.

Asymmetrical Smile

An asymmetrical expression refers to the contraction of a muscle on only one side of the face. Through the works of Dr.Ekman[3] and later through activists like Pamela Meyer[4], the signal of **contempt** has gained a wide consensus as being the only exclusively asymmetrical expression. For the expression of contempt, a single corner of the lips is pulled upward towards the nose and inward, appearing as a *half-snarl*. This expression reveals an emotional experience of moral superiority, self-righteousness and dismissal of the other party's importance.

While all types display the signal of contempt, asymmetrical expressions of various sorts appear far more frequently in Fi types than others. Two factors affect this imbalance the most; the uncoordinated nature of Fi expressions, and Fi's private sense of morality. Fi's lack of coordination causes the muscles of the face to often contract at different paces, not as a collaborative unit geared towards delivering a presentation, as is the case with Fe. This causes asymmetry in the face, which can appear in any of Fi's expressions – whether they be joy, contempt, sorrow, etc. The second factor relates to Fi's constant sense of moral

3: Telling Lies, Paul Ekman – 1985
4: Liespotting, Pamela Meyer – 2010

and emotional privacy. Being an introverted process, Fi holds its own morality in favor of the views of others, and in many cases wholly dismisses outside input. This emotional disposition will trigger the contraction of contempt on the face and continually cause asymmetrical snarls, smiles and grimaces. But this needn't be taken as a sign of ill will, as Fi's morality, however independent, may still have the others' best interest in mind.

Autistic Spectrum

Through my personal experience and dialogue with Fi types, I have been stricken by an all too clear pattern of psychiatric diagnoses ascribed to these unique individuals. Especially in cases where Fi is strong and not properly synchronized with Te, these are often classfied in some region of the **autistic spectrum** as defined by the DSM-5. Mild forms of autism are described by symptoms such as[5]:

Social (Pragmatic) Communication Disorder:

1. Deficits in using communication for social purposes, such as greeting and sharing information, in a manner that is appropriate for the social context.
2. Impairment of the ability to change communication to match context or the needs of the listener, such as speaking differently in a classroom than on a playground, talking differently to a child than to an adult, and avoiding use of overly formal language.
3. Difficulties following rules for conversation and storytelling, such as taking turns in conversation, rephrasing when misunderstood, and knowing how to use verbal and nonverbal signals to regulate interaction.
4. Difficulties understanding what is not explicitly stated (e.g., making inferences) and nonliteral or ambiguous meanings of language (e.g., idioms, humor, metaphors,

5: Diagnostics and Statistics Manual of Mental Disorders V, 315.39 (F80.89) pg.47-48 – 2013 multiple meanings that depend on the context for interpretation).

These symptoms overlap heavily with Fi, as Fi has no built in structure for understanding social dynamics. Without a proper harmonization with Te – its method of understanding the dynamics of "the world" (and by extension people) – Fi is left unaware of how to interface with the social landscape. Add to that Fi's innately off-beat disposition – as expressed through the above signals of asynchronous mouth movements, unmatching relation between inner feeling and outward expression, and unordinary giggling – and what results is an individual who is quite socially peculiar. This is especially so if the individual is a young proactive type with Fi, vividly expressing him or herself for the first times.

Now it is certainly not my intention to undermine the whole of the autistic spectrum, but perhaps to help contribute one opinion for how we may better define the criteria we give certain diagnoses. What is now known as the autistic spectrum has undergone many revisions over the years as we struggle to understand where to draw the line between a natural level of variation in human expressivity and some legitimate anomaly. And this confusion is no doubt amplified by the absence of a serious consideration of type in these criteria. I believe many mild, and some moderate, diagnoses emerging from the DSM can be attributed wholly to improper development of the eight cognitive functions and their resolutions lie not in some medicinal regime, but in a proper psychotherapy.

In the same vein, **alexithymia** (which is a personality trait characterized by a deficit in the cognitive processing of one's own emotions) is common in cases where Fi is underappreciated in the psyche of an Fi type. There will be a "difficulty identifying feelings and distinguishing between feelings and the bodily sensations of emotional arousal"[6]. While it may seem contradictory that an Fi type, being so connected to the emotional register, would have difficulty understanding their own

---

6: Disorders of Affect Regulation: Alexithymia in Medical and Psychiatric Illness, Taylor, Graeme J. – 1997

5. Fi | REACTIVE ETHICAL JUDGMENT

emotions, when the process is not properly consulted, or is repressed for conscious or unconscious reasons, the psyche has no measure with which to weigh its own bodily experience. Unlike Fe, Fi depends on its ability to hone in on bodily experience both for insights into oneself as well as all of humanity, causing an utter disorientation in the whole of the emotional dimension when this internal connection is damaged.

The Seelie & The Unseelie

In all four judgment processes, there exist themes of right and wrong, of correct or incorrect, as data always falls on either side of judgment's sharp blade. In the case of the two ethical functions, this becomes a matter of *good* and *evil*. These two themes are our memetic reinterpretation of what is *conducive to life* (the somatic) and what is *destructive to life*. They are, in essence, a sophistication of the basic instinct and bias for survival. However, the topic of good and evil quickly becomes complex, as often times what is most conducive towards life is the death of another life. In the animal kingdom we observe that the ethic towards life will lead an animal to destroy that which is threatening, and so, ironically it will fulfill its purpose as an *advocate of life* by bringing another death. Here we see quite clearly that the ethical process must handle both the decision to give life and to take it away, if it is to be comprehensive. Because of this, Fi and Fe each carry a light and dark nature – having both creative and destructive abilities, according to what is necessary for the overall protection of the principle of life.

As I examined the characteristics of light and dark Fi, in relation to culture and mythology, I was stricken by its immense correlations with the *fairies* of Scottish folklore (a topic I address more extensively in Chapter 31). But briefly, what are known as the **Seelie** and **Unseelie** fairies, as described in Anglo-Saxon mythology, are a perfect anthropomorphization of the light and dark duality of Fi. The seelie fairies are very private and independent creatures, but not necessarily unsociable. They are whimsical and flighty, yet emotionally sensitive and deeply in touch with nature, love and beauty. They show themselves to humans only if they fancy them agreeable, which they might if the human possess a reserved and contemplative nature as well as a generous heart and the ability to keep the fairy's secrecy.[7] Fairies are also very just creatures, always considering it a duty to repay a debt, whether that means repaying a deed or avenging an insult. When repaying a deed, they may silently fill a human's vase with meal or bring them luck in wagers. When avenging an insult they may rearrange a room to confuse the human, fill their shoes with mud, or do all manner of other subtle things to pester them. However, unseelie fairies are only ever troublesome. They are bitter, misanthropic and destructive creatures. Similar to seelie fairies, their methods can be tricksy, causing ill will through indirect means. A pan may start leaking from a freshly carved hole, or a cupboard might be found emptied. At other times they may be more direct; killing livestock or hovering above the earth and dragging unsuspecting men into the ground. In all of these characteristics, we see the traces of an introverted, ethically independent, life/death-oriented existence. We see a fictional race that is very reserved, emotional, and logistically minded when it comes to executions in the outer world, which they perform in a self-righteous manner. These characteristics precisely reflect the disposition of Fi and how it executes its internal feelings through Te in privately charitable or malicious ways.

The Fi process, when *seelie*, as we may call it, is sensitive, sprite-like, in tune with the individual's inner feelings, and radiates an innocent emotional energy from the person. It is effeminate, both in males and females, causing a very delicate voice and demeanor. Vibrating, bashful giggles abound and their snarling smile rises high upon the face, threatening to overtake the eyes. When Fi becomes *unseelie*, it can become deeply misanthropic and cold. The voice ceases to have its unhindered, airy disposition – reverting to an injured, nasal tone. Vibrating giggles become rare. Te is used much more heavily, causing an emotionally tense, sullen yet aloof communication style. It will be sassy, passive-aggressive, and righteously uncharitable.

Fi can neither hide its joy nor its sorrow; it emanates

7: An Encyclopedia of Fairies, Katherine Briggs, pg.353 – 1978

5. Fi | REACTIVE ETHICAL JUDGMENT

without warning out of the person's internal experience. Unlike Fe, Fi has an inability to hide its emotional radiation, nor can Te properly compensate for this. While Fe can transform an emotion with other emotions, those with Fi-Te can only conceal emotions with the cold shell of Te, creating a calloused demeanor. But the person's heart will always seep through this coating and show on their countenance – revealing their true internal disposition.

In Summary:

Fi Vultology
- Tension Around Nose
- Snarling Smiles
- Asynchronous Micro-Snarling
- Signals of Contempt
- Asymmetrical Smiling
- Accidental, Offbeat Expressions
- Unbridled Emotional Energy
- Airy, Sprite-like Voice (Seelie)
- Sassy, Nasal Tone (Unseelie)
- Giddy, Vibrating Giggle (Seelie)

6

Ti

REACTIVE LOGICAL JUDGMENT

Out of all eight cognitive functions, Ti is the most distant, being disconnected not only from the objective world but also from the subject themself. It has no passion for proactive expression, nor for emotional conviction or involvement. Because of this, Ti has a uniquely **lifeless** disposition. When Ti is engaged, all tension leaves the cheeks, causing them to be entirely relaxed and **flat**, especially in the regions between the eyes and the corners of the lips. In Figure 21.b we see an example of a Ti face at rest. Notice also how the unsupported weight of the cheeks causes the corners of the lips to turn slightly downward. For some, this effect may cause them to appear frustrated or annoyed, when instead their internal experience will be entirely dispassionate.

It is somewhat difficult to visually identify Ti, owing to its innate lack of expressivity. However, this very lack of expressivity, and how that interplays with other processes, will reveal several other signals through secondary effects.

Neutralization

As is true for either compass function, the act of engaging Ti calls energies away from the objective world and into a private, internal focus. But for Ti, all energies retreat into this lifeless and dispassionate center, causing far heavier momentum halting than with Fi. The face experiences a **complete neutralization** as all muscles suddenly relax, even if moments before the user was engaged in very charismatic expressions. The body becomes inflexible, freezing in its current position as the eyes

6. Ti | REACTIVE LOGICAL JUDGMENT

Figure 21

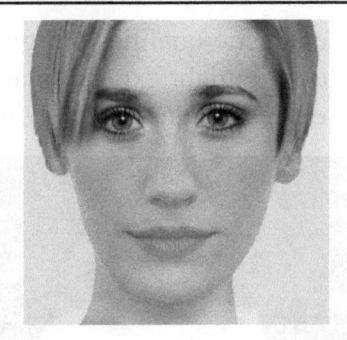

a.   b.

disengage downward. The voice will trickle into a whisper or halt altogether for the duration of this neutrality. These almost robotic pauses differ in their quality from Fi, which never entirely halts the body's flow of energy since one's emotional energies remain engaged. When Ti is especially heavy, the user's whole demeanor continually dwindles into inaction, appearing almost *fatigued*. In these cases, neutrality will take its residence as their default body rhythm, and any proactivity (with Pe or Je) will provide only a momentary break from this flatness, which they will return to quickly yet gently.

Stop-Start

When Ti is a less pronounced function, and proactivity is the default, neutrality demonstrates itself only through momentary pauses. For a split second, the person will halt and neutralize their face and body while their energies remain *suspended*, then after the compass has been checked, the body will resume its activity at the same level of enegy that it halted at. This signal is what I refer to as the **stop-start** nature of the Ti-Fe oscillation. The articulation of Fe is continually being interrupted by these moments of suspension, while the articulation of Te-Fi is far less affected by moments of compass checking. The energy of Te-Fi never ventures to such extremes. Te, despite being a dispassionate process, is still nonetheless strongly *invested* through an objective connection to the world, and Fi, despite being a reactive process, is still emotionally *involved* in how the situation impacts it personally. For Ti-Fe, both of these *invested* and *involved*

COGNITIVE TYPE

energetic qualities are given to Fe, and none to Ti. The result, as we might expect, is an abrupt shift between being strongly expressive and suddenly wholly inexpressive.

a.   b.   Figure 22

Puppeteer Hands

When neutralization occurs during Fe gesticulation, the hands will also freeze in specific ways. The fingers will be meticulous, stretched taut, and strangely delicate. The wrists will also bend, often slightly downward while the fingers bend slightly upwards. This creates an appearance reminiscent of a **puppeteer's hands**; of the sort that pulls a puppet using individual fingers. In Figures 22.a and 22.b we see examples of this. The opposing muscles in the forearms contract to create this isometric pull on the fingers, which is itself caused by the tension of judgment on the body. This occurs more commonly when the individual is struggling to translate the logical precision of Ti into accurate articulation through Fe. The delicacy of the fingers is a reflection of the psyche's struggle to precisely bring reactivity into objectivity. As this dynamic requires participation of both Ti and Fe, it engages the entire oscillation and places the body in a heavier state of judgment. It is not such a prevalent signal in types who lean much more strongly on only one of these two functions.

Placid Fe Smile

6. Ti | REACTIVE LOGICAL JUDGMENT

A strong Ti user's attempts to show Fe expressivity will often be lacking; coming across as *false* or unconvincing. One such example is a Ti type's smile. The smile of this type will spread itself widely through the zygomaticus major muscles, but as the upper cheek muscles don't participate in this expression, the smile will remain flat in the areas below the eyes. It may seem as though it was created by lifting the bottom of a curtain through two points of contact. The flatness of the cheeks weighs on the rest of the smile, causing a more mild, courteous and **placid** appearance than a full Fe smile.

Like in Fi types, there is inherent difficulty in communicating one's internal state. But unlike Fi types, whose facial expressions often don't synch with the intended emotional implications, a Ti type will succeed in conveying the proper or expected expression but lack vitality and energy in its execution. Ti types have a fair sense for what emotional dynamics are occurring in their environment, via Fe awareness, but they may fail socially due to a lack of participation and animation. For such types, sustaining an emotionally engaged persona for long periods of time will lead to physical and social exhaustion.

a.

b.

c.

Figure 23

Zen

The internal experience of Ti is a deeply paradoxical one. Due to the combination of dispassion within an introverted function, the process of introspection leads the individual into a realm where *absence* is found at the very center of its existence. There is a feeling of deeper separation from the self, proportional to the level of internal intimacy one achieves. It would seem, to a Ti user, that at their very soul there is fundamentally only nothingness; the Śūnyatā of Zen Buddhism. Similar to how Anglo-Saxon mythology is, in many ways, an expression and anthropomorphization of the character of Fi, we may consider Zen Buddhism to be a philosophy fundamentally generated by the process of Ti. The whole of its spirituality is that which naturally emerges from, and most cohesively aligns with, the psychology of Ti. While I feel that several volumes could be dedicated just to this topic alone, I will briefly mention some prominent expressions of this philosophy here.

The cause of suffering is attachment.
(The Second Noble Truth)

The philosophy of Zen notes that the origin if suffering is attachment to the world and a relinquishing of all *striving* and *grasping* is the key to achieving separation from suffering. While other doctrines and philosophies may teach that the proper avenue to approach the suffering innate to existence is with vigor, preservation and righteous avoidance of sin, Zen teaches that such approaches can never properly lead to contentment and that **dispassion** alone can unravel suffering since it's caused *by* passion; the yang assertion of agendas and needs. Here we are immediately stricken by the exaltation of a logical disposition and approach to life. Furthermore, this dispassionate methodology is practiced through reorganization of internal content; by **introspection** or meditation (Zen), and not by any organization of the external world.

Kamabhu Sutta: With Kamabhu
(On the Cessation of Perception & Feeling)

6. Ti | REACTIVE LOGICAL JUDGMENT

> "When a monk has emerged from the cessation of perception & feeling, three contacts make contact: contact with emptiness, contact with the signless, & contact with the undirected."[1]

Signless (void of associations and symbols), empty (void of passion and identity), and undirected (void of proactivity); these three *contacts* elegantly capture the three single qualities of Ti. Remembering that judgment is eternally pivoted against perception – in a constant struggle to clarify and dismantle all the information it brings – an intense immersion into introverted judgment will cause a near-complete cessation of the perception oscillation. In such a state, judgment remains empty, undisturbed and still. From this passage we gather than Zen Buddhism calls upon the complete and pure experience of dispassionate introversion, at the removal of all other interferences. It halts not only feeling (the emotional register and ethical function) but also perception, and the person is immersed into a singleness of process.

Godatta Sutta: To Godatta
(On Awareness-release)

> "Passion is a making of themes, aversion a making of themes, delusion a making of themes. For a monk whose fermentations are ended these have been abandoned, their root destroyed, made like a palmyra stump, deprived of the conditions of development, not destined for future arising. To the extent that there are themeless awareness-releases, the unprovoked awareness-release is declared supreme. And that unprovoked awareness-release is empty of passion, empty of aversion, empty of delusion." [2]

In this and many other passages we see a disposition towards a disassembly of delusion, of schemas in all their forms,

1: http://www.accesstoinsight.org/tipitaka/sn/sn41/sn41.006.than.html, par.18
2: http://www.accesstoinsight.org/tipitaka/sn/sn41/sn41.007.than.html, par.10

and bias towards (i.e. passion) or against (i.e. aversion) things. There is neither desire for nor in opposition towards any element of reality. The quenching of desire speaks once again of a logical process, while the dissipation of schemas/themes speaks towards a depreciation of *worldview*. Here again we see the abandonment of perception; of precedent and preconceptions.

> **Suñña Sutta: Empty**
> "The intellect is empty of a self or of anything pertaining to a self. Ideas... Intellect-consciousness... Intellect-contact is empty of a self or of anything pertaining to a self. Thus it is said that the world is empty."[3]

Ti alone has no capacity to create; it has only the power to deconstruct. And it deconstructs logically, leaving behind only negatives – only what things are not, without having any avenue from which to measure what things or reality are. Interpreting reality through this singular function generates a vacuous, *empty* perspective precisely like the one above. And likewise the quest to identify the *innate self* leads the person to the conclusion that there is no self to be found, nor can the existence of anything in reality be substantiated. The *void*, we might say, is what lies at the very end of Ti; an utter stillness that invites one into a strifeless nothingness where there is only a purity of awareness.

***

It is no surprise that Ti, being such an intimate and internal processes, has at times been associated with the very *essence*, or *center* of human's existence. The compass process is readily recognized, even if unconsciously, as the seat of nobility, self-perfection and self-mastery. But while it represents a significant and indispensable part of the equation, it alone cannot lead to actualization or self-mastery. There is as much truth to be found in identifying what reality is not, as identifying what it is. A keenly developed perception oscillation, used in tandem with

---

3: http://www.accesstoinsight.org/tipitaka/sn/sn35/sn35.085.than.html

a sharp discernment oscillation will lead to greater insights than what any function could achieve alone.

In Summary:

Ti Vultology
  Flat, Relaxed Cheeks
  Lifeless Disposition
  Complete Neutralization
  Stop-Start Fe Gesticulation
  Puppeteer Hands
  Placid Fe Smile

7

Fe

PROACTIVE ETHICAL JUDGMENT

The four proactive processes are easier to identify than their counterparts, given how they make themselves apparent by their functionality, but Fe in particular *requires* recognition to accomplish its aim. The whole of its operation is geared towards an emotional visibility. It coordinates the muscles of the face to align with the emotional impact it wishes to impart, and this is the main avenue with which it moves the social economy. Because of this innate control of expressions, identifying Fe is more a matter of gauging whether the individual has deliberate **coordination** of their **emotional presentation**, than it is about identifying any one specific muscular contraction. And while Te can also coordinate a presentation, it will not be infused with emotional investment like Fe, being a much more distant and dismissive process. For Fe, every gesticulation is an emotional undertaking; an attempt to channel one's convictions onto the audience, and because of this it is marked by an *exertion of effort* that is wholly absent in Te.

Fe Smile

The smile of an Fe type will primarily use the zygomaticus major muscles, causing it to stretch widely from ear to ear as seen here in Figure 24. This smile, as well as the rest of Fe's expressions, will be **on-beat**; their timing, duration, and execution will align with the expected, or desired, impact. As a consequence of this muscular use, individuals who are primarily Fe types often possess strong muscle tone spanning diagonally from the ears to the side of the lips. However, in all Fe-Ti users

7. Fe | PROACTIVE ETHICAL JUDGMENT

Figure 24

Zygomaticus Minor (light use)

Zygomaticus Major (heavy use)

a.

b.

the area spanning from the eyes down to the lips will remain neutral at rest. Now, I should note that the zygomaticus muscles can be consciously controlled by any person, whether they are an Fi or Fe user. However, the authentic smile of an Fe type will still primarily use the zygomaticus major muscles, while an authentic Fi smile cannot be created without also contracting the muscles around the nose associated with deep feeling. In this way we can differentiate Fe from Fi in all but the rarest cases.

Now, the zygomaticus muscles are used in Fe types not only to convey joy, but also to convey **upset** and other negative emotions. If, for instance, there is some frustration preventing the Fe user from moving social dynamics properly, the lips will become slightly pursed with the corners slightly tilted downwards, while the zygomaticus muscles remain taut, but not elevated. We see examples of this in Figure 25. It would seem, in this position, that the muscles of the lower part of the face are collaborating to produce an invisible *arrow*, or point of convergence ending at the mouth. This *forwardness* will perfectly reflect their forwardness of thought and intention.

COGNITIVE TYPE

a.

b.

c.

d.

Examples of Fe Smiles

Figure 25

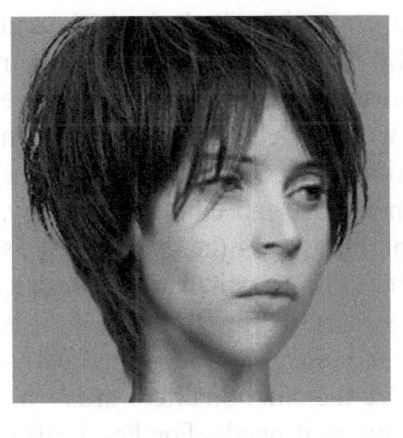

7. Fe | PROACTIVE ETHICAL JUDGMENT

e.

f.

g.

h.

Examples of Fe Upset

COGNITIVE TYPE

Fe Warm Swelling

Now, when preparing to gesticulate, both the body and voice of the Fe type will begin by *building-up* energies for their moment of impact, and this build-up will culminate right before the climactic delivery. In other words, there is a *delay* between the initial ignition of a gesticulation and its peak, and during this period the individual embeds their *tone* and emotional energy. Here in Figure 26 we see a graph that shows the rhythm of Fe's gesticulation. There are two parts to Fe's gesticulation; *swelling* and *neutralization*. While it lags in delivering the motion, it is very fast in halting it. The opposite is true for Te, which delivers quickly, but does not neutralize the emotion afterwards – allowing it instead to linger as long as it needs. For Fe-Ti, after a gesticulation is delivered, energies recede into dispassion for a short time. The fingers dwindle softly and the cheeks relax around the eyes. Gesticulations are given in bursts, and each of these bursts is not sustained for long, even though they may be followed soon enough by other bursts. Notice also how there is a complete neutralization after the first gesticulation (where the dotted line drops to the bottom of the graph). This demonstrates the *stop-start* signal of Ti, and these intermittent pauses are a standard element of the Ti-Fe communication style.

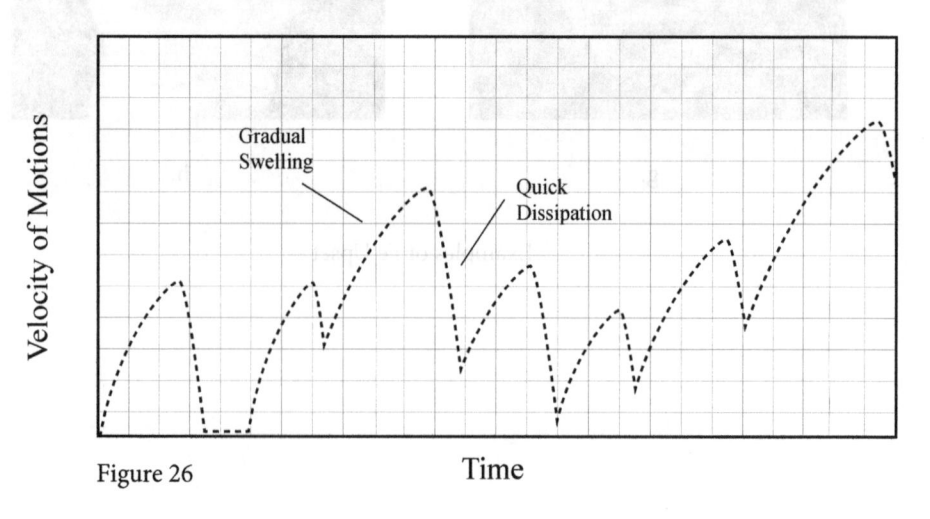

Figure 26

7. Fe | PROACTIVE ETHICAL JUDGMENT

Figure 27

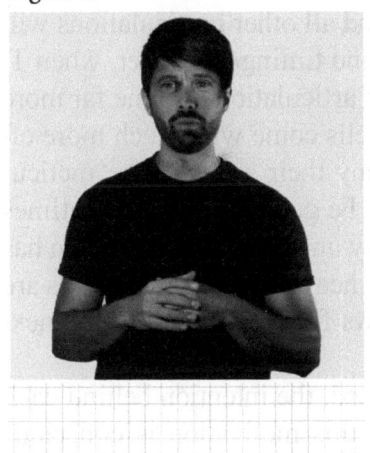

a.
To demonstrate this swelling, here we begin in a resting state. The body remains rigid, the hands remain meticulously folded and recessive.

b.
Then the hands, influenced by Ti's delicacy, begin to nurture a delivery in synch with the mouth. The tone of voice participates, slowly *building up* for the emphasis.

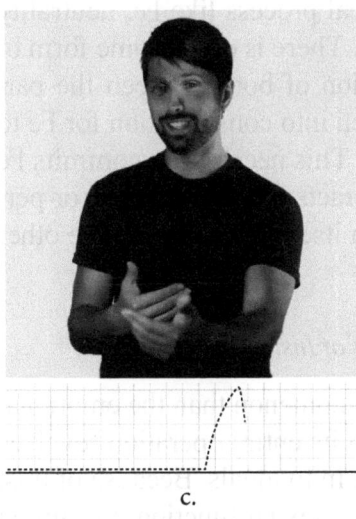

c.
The hands come to a halt with an exacting emphasis, as if delivering emotion directly *to you* with a coordinated tone, motion, and facial expression.

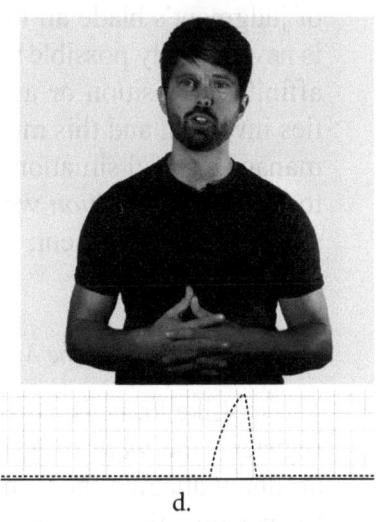

d.
Right afterwards the hands re-fold into a meticulous posture, their enegry recedes as they prepare for the next gesticulation.

These exacting hand motions, head shakes, head nods, shoulder shrugs, eyebrow-raises and all other gesticulations will carry the same *swelling* property and timing. However, when Ti is strong in the Fe user, the halts in articulation become far more jittery, sudden, and prolonged. Swells come with much more effort, and stuttering may accompany their speech. The meticulous nature of Ti transforms these Fe gesticulations, sometimes restricting or delaying their delivery until internal evaluation has completed. But if Fe is particularly heavy in the person, halts are less frequent, and articulation flows from one word to the next without such a pronounced rest.

Now as previously mentioned, the intention behind each of these gesticulations – whether this motivation is conscious or unconscious – is to deliver an emotional influence on the receiving party. This is regardless of whether that influence communicates camaraderie, opposition, shame, submission, or some other relationship between both parties. This is because Fe is incapable of interacting with other humans without establishing a *dynamic*. A situation must fall on either the left or right side of judgment's blade an for an ethical process like Fe, neutrality is never wholly possible to achieve. There is either some form of affinity, opposition or a combination of both between the parties involved, and this must be taken into consideration for Fe to manage a social situation properly. This necessarily commits Fe to create a *disposition* when it interacts with an element or person in the environment; to position itself in relation to the other entity in some way.

The Management of Instinct

Like Fi, Fe is a different phenomenon than the emotional register – the *locus of instinct* – but its entire operation revolves around managing those instincts in individuals. Because of this, the persona, the ego, the shadow, the sexual function, the anima and animus concept, the mother and father concept, and their resulting emotional experiences are the domains of Fe's concern. If the development of the Fe user is typical, then from countless micro-judgments spanning across many years of life, the

7. Fe | PROACTIVE ETHICAL JUDGMENT

individual will have a general, intuitive understanding of how these instincts interact in a real-time situation. Early in life, the Fe type will be struck by these instincts and work to coordinate them into optimal arrangements, often developing systems in which they could be managed within a broad population. Control of pride, control of fear, regulation of praise, distribution of attention, application of shame and the like are considered in order to address the human condition. Every culture is, in some way or another, an attempt to address human instincts and coordinate a way to live with them. In this way, Fe is also a culture-creating process.

The Methodologies of Fe

There are countless methodologies that Fe users can implement in order to coordinate and manage emotional dynamics. However, I have found certain strategies so consistent and persistent within these types, that while they do not exclusively belong to, or confirm this function's presence, they are certainly worth mentioning as examples of the tendencies, approaches and reasoning of this process:

a. Fe Disclaimers

During a real-time conversation, as words first coagulate into the consciousness of the Fe type, immediately Fe will execute a dynamic judgment to determine how the delivery of that idea would affect the surrounding atmosphere. This takes into consideration wording, the audience and their attitude, vocabulary, status, as well as many other factors – to gauge how successful their intended meaning will be received. If, during this realtime *troubleshooting* endeavor, a fatal misconception is anticipated, an **Fe disclaimer** is the result. The first sentence is delivered, followed afterwards (or sometimes beforehand) by a sometimes exhaustive clarification.

"First I should clarify that you did great..."
"But I don't mean to say things are gonna stop being..."

"And don't get me wrong, I love them but..."
"And this doesn't mean I'm jealous, I'm just..."
"And it wasn't one of those sappy poems, he was very.."
"Not that I couldn't do it myself, but we agreed he'd..."

The above are some examples of what such disclaimers may look like. They are, in essence, expectations of the audience's perception and preemptive attempts to *steer* them away from those perceptions. They offer extra information which, were it not for the Fe type's sense of being misperceived, might otherwise be unwarranted. The underlying motivation for such phrases may be to circumvent embarrassment, avoid overstepping a social boundary, sidestepping perceived sensitivities or taboos, preserving a certain self-image, and so on. Notice, however, that none of these underlying motivations are exclusive to Fe types – they are the result of *human instinct*. All humans are capable of disliking embarrassment or desiring to preserve a self-image. It is instead in the method of managing those instincts that we see the hand of Fe.

b. Adaptive Fe

The ability to calibrate one's persona to circumvent negative experience can take an even more pronounced form. At times the whole of an interaction may be treated as an endeavor to harmonize with the audience, leading to a constant **emulation** of the other's peculiarities. In such times, the mind of the Fe type is in a stressful hyperalert state. Psychic energies are channeled towards solving an evolving puzzle, exhausting all available information to dynamically readjust one's disposition and retain alignment. Here the *persona* wholly overshadows the self, yet this act of creation is itself a legitimate byproduct of the operation of the self. It is as much an authentic part of an Fe type's identity to calibrate oneself to their environment, as it is to be themselves; the two are ultimately one and the same. Now, this accommodation of attributes doesn't necessarily lead to a positive or friendly persona. In an atmosphere where there is a callousness to feeling – to positivity or good-will – such attitudes

7. Fe | PROACTIVE ETHICAL JUDGMENT

may be suppressed to sustain a more aloof and distant persona. Sensitivity or strength, passivity or aggression, either may be favored by Fe depending on the social bias of the environment. Indeed, an Fe type may appear paradoxical or fickle to an observer if they witness them use multiple strategies in different settings. This accommodative strategy is more common in Fe users who lack a personally-created ethos; a system of ethical judgment. It may be that feelings of uneasiness or fear will perpetuate a defensive methodology – one where the self is *camouflaged* and hidden – in the absence of well-defined ethical stances. Thus, adherence to an existing ethical system or established protocol is typical in those with an adaptive Fe.

c. Directive Fe

Directive Fe takes the opposite attitude. While adaptive Fe yields to the ethos of another, directive Fe will **push** its own self-created ethos onto others. Fundamentally, in both of these cases, Fe is operating identically; it is ascribing to a system of judgments and adjusting the relationship between the elements at play towards alignment. Whether the arrangement necessitates that they adjust themselves to the protocol, or that others adjust to it, then becomes simply a situational question. Nonetheless, due to this adherence to a self-created protocol, these types may appear **out-of-protocol**, indifferent or imperceptive of social dynamics; traits that may be seen as contrary to Fe. Such a type may in fact see very clearly what social dynamics are at play, but choose not to tailor themselves to them. But this decision to stray from an existing protocol will not be impartial; it will carry within it a keen antagonism. This is because directive Fe cannot be truly impartial or dismissive like its couterpart Te. When the emotional environment does not align with Fe, it will *pull* on Fe's ethos, forcing it to pull *against* that ethos if it chooses not to subscribe to it. It must manifest as *opposition* or some other defensive attitude. In all its dealings, Fe will still be manipulating emotional energy; concerning itself with the *victory over hearts*, continually recalibrating its directivity to better suit that aim. A Te type, on the other hand, may be oppositional and even at times simultaneously emotional, but they will not shepherd the emotional causality of others methodically towards their ethos.

Fe and Cultures of Honor

When we consider the fundamental properties of Fe, and collide those properties – as one would mingle chemical constituents in a laboratory – with human nature and the logistical reality of our world, the result is always similar. There will always be multiple persons and egos, while simultaneously there will be the impulse towards connection. Always more hands on a task will be better than one, and always tasks will need to be accomplished for the sake of survival. But always egos will differ, and there will always be a need for a way to coordinate egos; to designate the *coordinator* and the helpers. The formation of culture is an entirely causal, predictable phenomenon, and when Fe is more heavily represented in a population, that culture will likewise take a predictable shape. It will become, as I call it, a *culture of honor*.

So far as my experience has taught me, every culture possesses both Fe-Ti and Te-Fi in the population, but in a culture where Fe heavily predominates, tasks will be done not only for the accomplishment of some logistical aim, but for the achievement of some **social standing**. And **honor** – because the culture as a whole values it as such – is made to have a legitimate, logistical weight. Honor becomes translatable into favors, support, and therefore ultimately logistical power. Dealing in honor is therefore not fundamentally different from dealing in money; it simply has one extra (or perhaps one less) layer of *conversion*. It is a successful and alternative avenue of managing reality; one that accounts for and includes the human emotional center into the equation. Cultures such as the Korean, Japanese and Hispanic, which carry a system of **honorifics**, are profoundly marked by the presence of Fe, both visually and psychologically. In such cultures, economic success is near-inseparably tied to social success. These cultures present a heavy contrast to those of the U.K., U.S.A., Australia and other neoliberalist cultures which do

7. Fe | PROACTIVE ETHICAL JUDGMENT

not marry the two facets; allowing instead for one's economic success to depend solely on their financial competence.

In Summary:

Fe Vultology
    Diagonal, Zygomatical Smile
    Diagonally Toned Cheeks
    Fe Upset
    Fe Warm Swelling
        Exacting Hands
        Head Nods
        Head Shakes
        Eyebrow-Raises
    On-Beat Gesticulation
    Stop-Start Gesticulation
    On-Beat Voice Tone
    Fe Disclaimers
    Fe Adaptability/Emulation
    Fe Directivity/Shepherding

8

Te

PROACTIVE LOGICAL JUDGMENT

Te as a process is simultaneously proactive and dispassionate; it is a marriage between two seemingly contrary dispositions. While it exerts energies outward in a passionate form, this passion is cold and disassociated from emotional concerns. The combination of such forwardness with absence of feeling creates a very *crass* function. Without the consultation of neighboring processes, Te deduces, differentiates, and organizes mechanically and insensitively. However, its omission of extraneous emotional factors is what primarily facilitates Te's ability to be **faster** and more **efficient** in its execution than Fe. Te will cascade from one relational deduction to the next with far more ease, and this is because it remains unhindered by the ambiguity that often surrounds ethical considerations.

While both Fe and Te track and adjust to dynamic variables, Fe's process is slowed by the methodical consideration of each environmental variable's real-time position and relation to human instincts. Whether or not the topic at hand directly involves emotional causalities, at the very least, Fe will *always* execute an additional layer of processing to ascertain that indeed the topic has no social impact on the parties involved. Te follows a far more acute, linear and logistical deductive route which does not have a social apparatus native to its operation. For Te, social adaptations, or the implementations of conduct, arise from an understanding of their logistical sensibilities rather than from an inborn urge to personally touch and shepherd another person's emotions.

8. Te | PROACTIVE LOGICAL JUDGMENT

Snippiness

As a direct reflection of Te's streamlined psychological attitude, its gesticulations are equally marked by *briefness* and *quickness* of execution. They will carry a different tempo than Fe's gestures, being **snippy** in their delivery and earlier in their repetition. Each gesture escalates to high velocity very quickly, and sustains this velocity until another gesture of equal velocity shifts its trajectory, or its momentum gradually dissipates without interruption. Below we see an example of Te's rhythm of gesticulation.

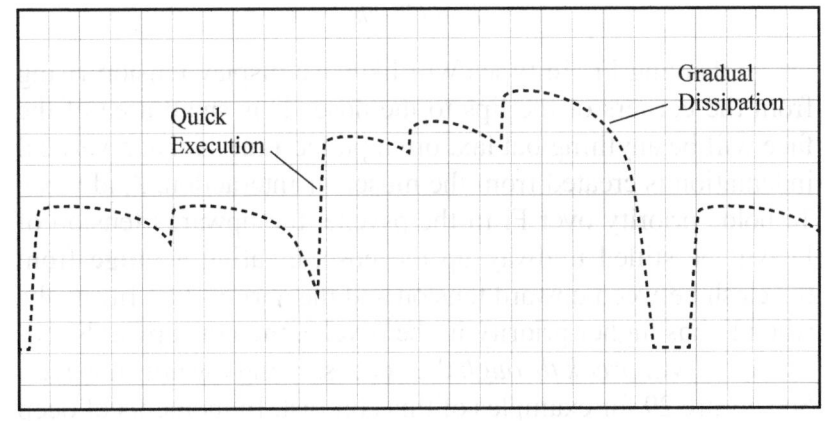

Figure 28

As you'll notice, every motion has a steep acceleration curve, a plateau in which it retains this acceleration, and a gradual fall. In some cases the rigidity of judgment may abruptly stop motion altogether; giving the pattern a sharp rise and sharp fall with a steady plateau in the middle. This is opposite of Fe's expressions which have a definitive peak/climax to each motion, rather than sustaining gestures at high velocity for a prolonged span. During this plateau period, the Te type may rattle their head back and forth quickly and continually, shrug their shoulders or raise their eyebrows in the process, as their articulation delivers a stream of expressions with little, if any, intermission. When unseelie Fi is heavily influencing the emotional disposi-

COGNITIVE TYPE

tion of the Te type, this snippiness will tend towards a **sassy** and passive-aggressive attitude. The emotional *independence* of Fi combines with Te to give expression to its disapproval, but this disapproval will be conveyed through the snappy articulation of Te as an acute and brief distaste. Oppositely, when seelie Fi is strongly present, a Te user's snippiness can be significantly reduced, leading to a soft and liquid flow of articulation. It will nonetheless retain its cascading and unbroken *flow*, transitioning from one deduction and expressive motion to the next with a nearly uniform velocity, whether that velocity is fast or slow. It will not oscillate between halt and push as Fe-Ti does.

Taut Cheeks

Having Fi, Te types will likewise display tension rising from the corners of the lips to the nose. This small area of the face will be anything but lax, often pulled **taut** so that a vertical indentation is created from the muscular interaction. And when Te holds priority over Fi in the psyche, the upwards tension of Fi will be stifled midway up the nose, creating a **bulge** from the clash between upward tension and the abrupt stop. Inversely, when Fi has higher priority in the psyche, then the upwards tension of Fi will *break through* the cheeks, rising towards the eyes. See Figure 29 for examples of this contrast. In moments of deep feeling, a strong Te type may also display this breaking effect, but for the largest part their emotional expressions will not reach the eyes.

As an additional byproduct of this muscular clashing, when Te is very strongly represented there may be a **split** between the cheeks stemming a few centimeters horizontally from the corners of the lips, as is visible in Figure 29.c. This subtle indentation is a further effect of the conflicting muscular pulls going vertically across the face. This signal is not always visible in Te-Fi users, but its presence is a definitive marker of this function's existence in the psyche. The tension that occurs in Fe-Ti users in this specific area of the face will never be pinched in this manner. Instead the skin will be creased vertically and pushed like a curtain diagonally toward the ears.

8. Te | PROACTIVE LOGICAL JUDGMENT

a.

b.

c.

Figure 29

Nasal Voice

Being void of a certain *pathos* which creates delicacy and earthiness in articulation, Te's voice will instead carry a **nasal**, pinched and often piercing intonation. Its words will be spoken with the same directness as its gesticulations and will avalanche forward with the same uncompromised ease and momentum. Even at a very early age, a high Te child will have no trouble articulating, doing so seamlessly as the environmental causality registers mentally as quickly as it registers vocally. Additionally, this nasal voice will tend to be **monotone** due to the absence of a swelling, emotional emphasis. However, because of how one's intonation is influenced by the language native to the person, this signal must be understood relative to the baseline intonation of the spoken language.

Te Overbearing

For a primary Te type, it may be difficult to properly coordinate all of the *yang* energy that naturally emerges from their process. This yang energy is not only distant and insensitive, but it's also **off-beat** due to Fi's influence. As with Fi, the tone, duration, and volume of their speech may be unordinary and stronger than may be expected. Often a Te type will not know where limits lie in a social setting, and thus come across much more harsh, cold and forceful than they may intend. This is not to say that Te is any more predisposed to cruelty or ill will than Fe. But despite that, however sincere, generous, and well-intended Te may be, there will come with it an inherent difficulty in monitoring one's brashness against other people's sensitivities; a difficulty that is only abated with practice and many years of developing tact. Fortunately, Te is a process that is well equipped to develop methodologies for managing environmental variables – of which people are one. Should an interest arise in the individual to coordinate themselves socially, they need only to direct their logistical thinking to cultural adaptation to produce a functional approach.

8. Te | PROACTIVE LOGICAL JUDGMENT

Te Humor

Naturally, the specific approaches used for interaction vary greatly between persons, but it has been my experience with Te types that their methodological approaches in societal affairs are quite often **indirect** ones. It would seem that Te-Fi prefers to operate in an emotionally self-contained form, and *grease the wheels* of conversation using partially disconnected, yet engaging means of interacting such as knee-jerk **humor** and irony. Quick and witty responses to conversational scenarios and anecdotal stories allow Te types to capitalize on their speed of logistical thinking and produce relevant, yet unexpected conversational material. In this way, the Te type secures a form of interpersonal connection while retaining an uncompromised self.

The psychological keystrokes that play upon the humor sense in humanity are identified and exploited far more easily than other dynamics of the psyche. Humor carries none of the confusion and difficulty that surround emotional hurdles, or matters of intimate connection. At the same time, humor invokes a positive emotional experience, requiring no pathos to play upon its strings. It is easy to see, then, why this approach would be so alluring to Te types (though this approach is by no means exclusive to Te). However, as convenient as such a method may be for establishing the beginnings of interpersonal connection, a Te type that scarcely interacts outside of this single methodology displays a characteristically underdeveloped Fi process. In such cases, never is the compass truly examined or reflected upon to consider the impacts of one's social interaction. Instead, all interactions are treated either as purely logistical matters or matters of recreation; avenues of comedic gain. As the Te-Fi pairing is properly balanced, more direct methods of emotional interaction will begin to emerge.

Te and Instinct

Now, despite being a dispassionate process at core, when this function combines with the rest of the psyche, as it inescapably will, it cannot operate entirely dispassionately like its counterpart Ti. Due to the *proactive* properties of its function, it must call upon some purpose or **driving factor** of humanity which acts as the *catalyst* for its direction. In all humans, the driving *impetus* to organize reality stems always from the instinctual center; from the **libido** and the specific way that it manifests in the person. Therefore, it would not be entirely correct to say that a Te person's actions themselves are dispassionate. Having said that, Te's methodology is one that weighs the relationship between elements at play and discriminates based on logistics alone without factoring in the dynamic flow of emotions. It acts from emotion, but acts through a dispassionate methodology, to the end aim of that emotion. The aforementioned tendency toward humor is one such example. It is important to recognize this in our evaluation and analysis of people's types. Without factoring in this reality, one would find few people who completely qualify as dispassionate, regardless of their logical preference. As with Fe, we must detangle impetus from method. We must accurately differentiate the driving psychic forces behind an act and the manner in which the act is being executed. Only with this distinction will the differentiation between Te and Fe become entirely clear.

8. Te | PROACTIVE LOGICAL JUDGMENT

In Summary:

Te Vultology
    Quick, Brief Gesticulation
    Snippy Movements
        Fast Acceleration
        Steady Plateau
        Gradual Deceleration
    Jittery, Bobble Movements
    Cascading, Unbroken Flow
    Taut, Buldgy Cheeks
    Horizontally Split Cheeks
    Pinched/Nasal Voice
    Monotone Voice
    Off-beat Fi Energy
    Overbearing Energy

9

Si

REACTIVE CONCRETE PERCEPTION

Si, as a perception process, is intimately connected to the eyes as well as the muscles surrounding these organs; the obicularis oculi, corrugator supercilii, frontalis, as well as a few other minor muscles. I should mention early on that the difference between the eyes of one type and another is not a matter of anatomical size, but of the shape produced around the eyes by different levels of muscular tension. Different muscular tensions will indicate different attributes of *focus* and purpose for the eyes. As an example, the eyes of Se types carry a high level of muscular tension and focus, having the eyelids peeled back and exposing more of the eye. But Se requires such alertness to fulfill its purpose as a literal absorption process and keenly register as much information in the environment as necessary. For Si, which is not a data absorption process, this is not the case. The eyes resist the information of the environment, although they remain open. The attention of the mind is turned inward, into internal perception and precedent while the eyes partially simulate real-world observation as an automatic effect of perception. But since the eyes of Si ignore the environment, there will be a distinctly *dulled* feeling about them. The eyes of Si will not track objects in the environment, remaining instead fixed in a steady stare forward for the duration of the Si recall.

Confused Expression

The dullness of Si's expression arises from a contraction of the obicularis oculi immediately above the eyeball by the pretarsal region, with a complete relaxation of the obicularis oculi

9. Si | REACTIVE CONCRETE PERCEPTION

Obicularis Oculi

Orbital : lax
Preseptal : lax
Pretarsal : taut
Preseptal : lax
Orbital : lax

a.

b.

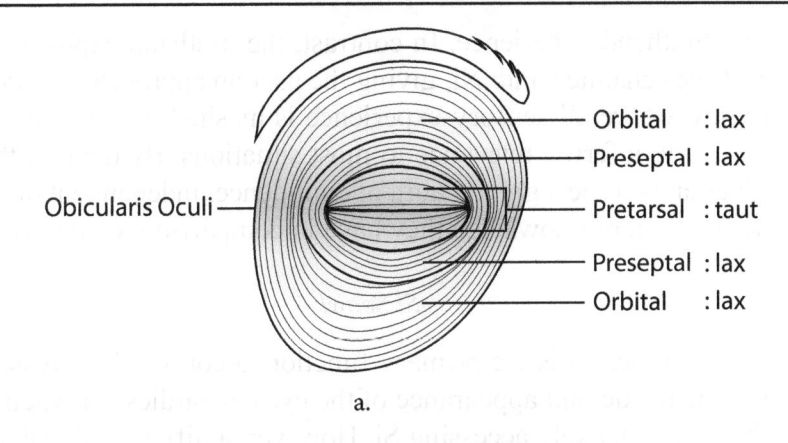

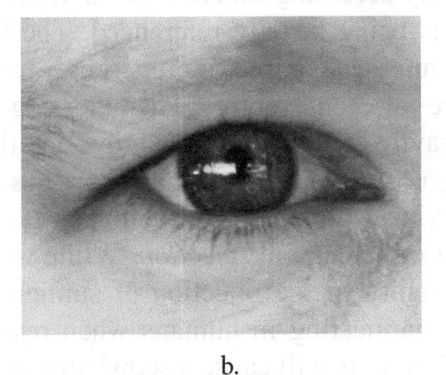

Figure 30

in the remaining areas. This gives the eyes an *awake but unfocused* quality. The bottom edges of the frontalis muscles contract slightly, creating a downward slant toward the outer edges of the eyes and an upward slant toward the center. The combination of these contractions generates what may be considerd a **confused** expression, while in fact the Si type may experience quite the opposite; a level of certainty and clarity as they recall their worldview in a definitive way. At other times this may represent legitiamate confusion. When we consider that the Si-Ne pairing has a less cohesive worldview than Ni-Se, inherently filled with many more information gaps which its Ni-Se counterpart fills using the interconnectivity of its abstract worldview, we see how Si-Ne types are more predisposed to appear uninformed and bewildered when touching upon a topic that does not directly relate to a firsthand experience. In contrast, the firsthand exposure of Se types channels into Ni, giving the user an approach of *generalities,* where all sensory experience is meshed into a web that has some inferred relevance to most situations. By default, this gives an Ni type a greater aura of confidence, independent of the actual level of knowledge they have in comparison to an Si user.

Si Scowl

When Si is the primary function, a confused expression will be the default appearance of the eyes, regardless of whether the user is actively accessing Si. However, a different signal appears when Si is being heavily referenced. The bottom edges of the frontalis muscles contract more strongly, creating an inverted curvature for each eyebrow. The outer edges of the eyes will be more heavily concealed by the brow, and the corrugator muscles may also contribute, creating an elevated **scowl** between the eyes. As previously noted, the phenomenon of scowling is an automatic effect of perceptual *rejection*. While we see its more obvious functionality in the rejection of sunlight, we see the same principle manifesting in humans when rejecting data of any sort. The Pi process will cause a scowl around the eyes as a resistance to the data absorption of Pe. In these moments, data is primarily being recalled from precedent, and the heavier the recall is, the stronger the scowl becomes.

Also, the transition period between the confused expression and an Si scowl causes what I refer to as an Si **dancing brow**. The scowl will begin at the outer edges of the eyes and wave forward until it peaks at the center, remaining elevated. You can see an example of this motion in Figure 31.c. While the wave-like motion is not always this pronounced in all Si-Ne types, the appearance of this signal is a definitive indicator of Si-Ne's presence in the psyche. As Si types toggle between Ne exploration and Si recall, the brow may continually dance in this way. This dancing will be especially pronounced when Si-Ne is the primary oscillation pairing.

9. Si | REACTIVE CONCRETE PERCEPTION

a. Regular Expression

b. Si Scowl

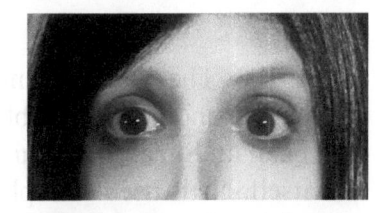

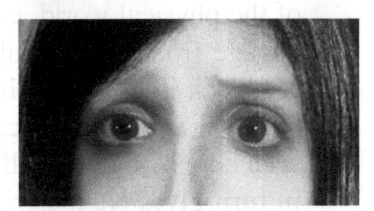

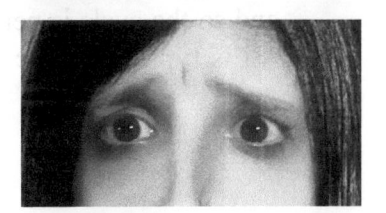

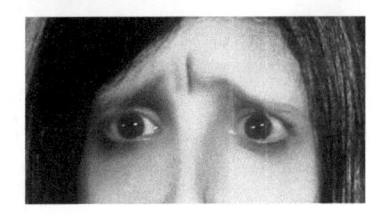

c. Dancing Brow

Here in Figure "c" we see the progression of the eyes and brow from an alert, Pe expression down to an Si scowl. The brow is gradually inverted from an upward arch to a downward arc. The eyes will retain an awake and wide-eyed look, but will be overshadowed by the concentrated scowling of Si. Surprisingly, this scowl may revert itself back to normal just as quickly as it formed with none of the emotional toil that the brow's appearance may suggest.

Figure 31

Si Ramble

The habitual and prominent use of the Ne-Si pairing causes another noticeable signal to arise from these types; what I call an **Si ramble**. During an Si ramble, perception loops in on itself. Ne is used to explore the terrain of Si's worldview instead of the physical world, causing both perception processes to disengage from actual reality. To visualize this, in Figure 32 we see black lines, indicative of Ne, exploring the internal tapestry of Si. As exploration occurs, Si datasets echo back into thought, seen here by the white lines that are returning to the center. This in turn gives Ne material to make its next round of association – and so the cycle is perpertuated endlessly. Now, the operation of Si is typically static – limited to the parameters of the data

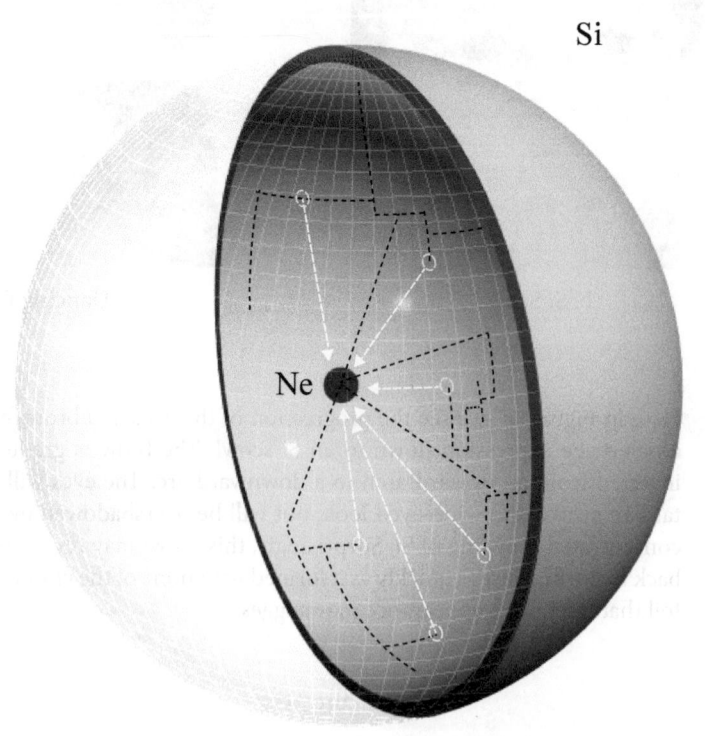

Figure 32

9. Si | REACTIVE CONCRETE PERCEPTION

it holds on any given topic – but when it combines with Ne in this way, it forms an interconnected *chain* between these static datasets, together building a more dynamic strand of otherwise isolated recollections. When this happens during conversation, the Si type will reach a dataset relevant to their line of thought and verbally convey it to the audience, however, as they extract this information, Ne is also actively leaping from one dataset to another using its associative property. What results is a continual topic-hopping effect; first one topic is exhausted using particular details and then another marginally related one begins with no definitive 'point' or cohesive direction to these interconnected topics. When Si is heavy in a type, a tendency will exist to talk from a place of precedent whenever any information in the environment eludes to previously stored concepts or experiences. During this activity, the type may become unaware of their surroundings even though, perhaps ironically, they are heavily engaging both of their perceptive processes. The quality of Si ramblings will always be shown by a narrow focus on the static qualities of one topic, and the detailing of the data therein, cradled in subtle buoyancy as they leap into other, somewhat related topics. In this sense, their quality will differ from Ni's rambles, which will have broader focus, less attention to the particulars, and far less, if any, topic-hopping.

Si Drifting

As with Ni, moments of heavy Si access will be marked by the eyes drifting diagonally to the sides. Often times, as the Si type is articulating, their gaze will sway, along with their whole head and neck, off toward some otherwise irrelevant location on the floor or background. It will remain there, fixed steadily, for the duration of their recall and then their eyes will reconnect with their audience after the information has been gathered. This results in a **back-and-forth** pattern where the type is constantly taking intermissions and breaking eye-contact to go into Si recall. But unlike Ni, during these drifts the eyes of Si will truly appear to be looking at the floor or the object they are facing rather than looking beyond it. Si's drifts may even appear to

COGNITIVE TYPE

a.

Figure 33

b.

be looking closer than the object their eyes are facing, as though they were staring at something invisible right in front of them.

These head motions will also lead the whole body's direction and tempo, subtly affecting their posture as a wind-rocked tree. The body-swaying of Si will be viscous and relaxed, but slightly less so than that of Ni. This is because Ne's buoyancy will influence the energetics of Si, giving it occasional excitations of spriteliness even in the heaviest Si types.

9. Si | REACTIVE CONCRETE PERCEPTION

In Summary:

Si Vultology
- Si Dulled Eyes /Awake But Unfocused
- Si Confused Expression
- Si Scowl
- Si Slanting Edges
- Si Dancing Brow
- Si Back-and-Forth Eye-Drifts
- Si Concentration / Near Focus
- Si Body-Swaying with Ne Buoyancy

10

Ni

◯

REACTIVE ABSTRACT PERCEPTION

Ni, as a perception process, is intimately connected to the eyes and the muscular tension that surrounds them. However, being a recollection process and not a data absorption process, the ocular tension it exhibits does not relate directly to any active engagement with the landscapes or objects in its line of sight. Instead, the quality and *focus* of Ni's eyes directly relates to the quality of the recollections that are happening during a specific moment. The eyes of Ni will neither engage nor track the environment, remaining open yet wholly unattentive to its movement.

In this lack of attentiveness, Ni runs parallel to Si, however the specific appearance of Ni in the eyes is a direct inversion from that of Si. For the eyes of Ni, the pretarsal region of the obicularis oculi is relaxed while the preseptal and orbital regions are pulled taut, as see in Figure 34. This causes the top eyelid to rest more comfortably over the eye and the eyebrow to arch upward slightly. This arching effect will often be heavier toward the outer edges, giving Ni types a far more forward and **intense** stare. The lowered eyelid, hovering above a steady stare, will then give Ni's eyes a distinctly **unimpressed** appearance. In a general sense, the default expression of the eyes can best be described as *bored* or *uninterested*. In some situations, Ni's gaze may even seem annoyed or irritable, independent of the user's actual emotional experience.

Hypnotic Gaze

At times when Ni is pronounced, the eyes will produce

10. Ni | REACTIVE ABSTRACT PERCEPTION

Obicularis Oculi

Orbital : taut
Preseptal : taut
Pretarsal : lax
Preseptal : taut
Orbital : taut

a.

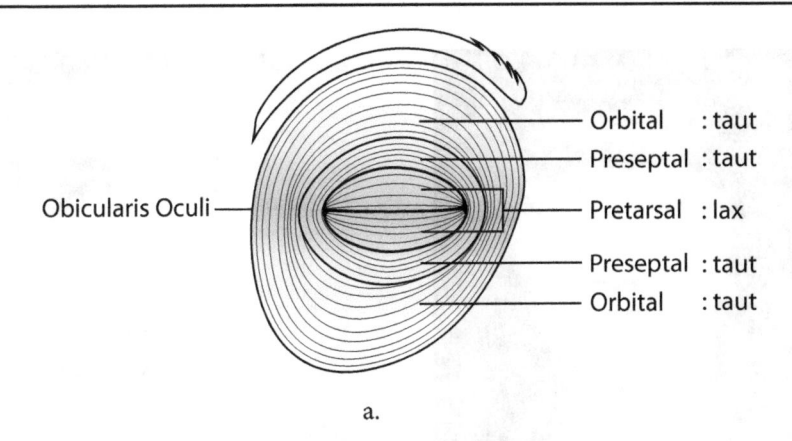

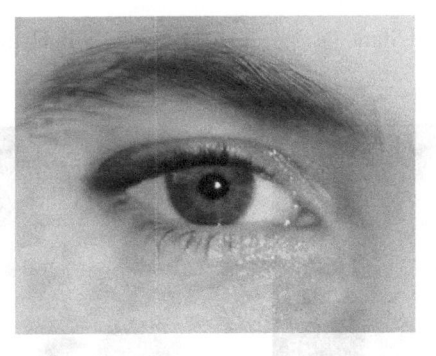

Figure 34

b.

a **trance-like** effect, due to the manner in which their stare can be sustained for far longer stretches of time than Si. The stare of Ni is not broken as often as Si's since Se fixates on subjects for longer periods than Ne. Si-Ne as a whole is less visually steady, even though Si by itself would remain wholly steady if it could. The Ni-Se oscillation, and especially Ni, can carry an almost **permanent stare**. The combination of this uncompromising gaze with the relaxation on the upper eyelid creates a distinctly **zoned-out** effect. The eyes of Ni can remain fixed in this zoned-out state even while they talk, in which case the audience may feel as though they are looking *through* them, and not at them. It may appear as though the Ni type monologues to some divorced aspect of reality, and the conversationalist has become a mere spectator. Indeed, this may be precisely the case, if the Ni type has drifted away into the waves of their own worldview; flowing

COGNITIVE TYPE

a. Unimpressed Stare

b. Hypnotic Gaze

c. Faraway Zone-Out

d. Faraway Zone-Out

Figure 35

Figures "c" and "d": Si has a *near-focus* zoneout, while the Ni has a *far-focus* zoneout. The eyes of Ni will appear to be looking at a point far off in the distance.

10. Ni | REACTIVE ABSTRACT PERCEPTION

through the interrelations they have formed in a manner comparable to Si's rambles.

Ni Rambles

As with Si-Ne, Ni can enter into a perception loop in which Se navigates the terrain of Ni, rather than the outer world, creating a complete disconnect from the environment. When a type heavy in Ni speaks from this place, their words will be very linear in their direction, and yet will often avoid drawing definitive conclusions. While Ni follows one impression or rather **narrow** line of thought, sometimes beyond its natural scope, it will differ from a judgment process. Ni will not be the psychic process axiomatically opposed to alternate ideas or interpretations; it will simply not see them by itself. If told "well it could play out this way too" they may nonchalantly shrug, while their head tilts to the side and they leap back on their linear track through some other entry. There will exist a tendency to run away with one's own cascading sense of inevitability. Even if they may be unsure of what the definitive outcome may be, a casual reluctance will still exist to notions too divorced from their impressions, even if such notions may seem to them as being more logically or ethically founded.

I must also take a moment and differentiate this process from the influence of *fear* in the psyche. The natural reluctance Ni has toward certain trails of thought, or its heavy gravitation toward a small cluster of interpretations is not the result of denials or paranoias. All persons can become resistant to certain interpretations of data and fixate or narrow their scope of possible outcomes based on a desire not to believe in directions contrary to their sense of safety. For Ni, such motivations are entirely unrelated to the manner in which it processes perceptions. It would be more correct to say that Ni is often *unaware* of alternatives, than to say that it filters out incongruent information to sustain a singular path. For the same reasons, Ni is a different phemonenon than the adherence to a philosophical or religious schema, which can take one's life experience and interpret it all from one unified framework. For Ni, there is no cohesion in its framework save for what is incidentally, and sometimes even irrationally, sensed about things. An Ni type may be entirely passive and undecided about many aspects of reality, having no definitive position or stance, but only abstract impressions as persistent to them as the information received from their eyes. These impressions are formed independent from how they may come to judge such a sense.

Ni Cryptic Information

Another quality of Ni's ramblings is its **cryptic** conceptualization. When Ni speaks and transitions fom one abstraction to another, it does so from a web of associations created uniquely by them and which may make little sense to others. The Ni user alone holds the **decryption key** to this web of connections, which contains many hundreds of strands built atop one another and which will influence their response to even the simplest comment. Their audience may become confused by seemingly ambiguous, acausal or unclarified statements. This is not something so prevalent within Si types because for Si, the 'key' to a conveyed experience is in the experience itself. Considering datasets are static and interconnections are short-hops; associations are less expansive, which makes them easier to trace individually, even if there are plenty more of them. The way that Ni leaps through so many wide-ranging ideas is not at all visible to others, thus the ramblings of Ni are more bewildering in a general sense. Even when the root experiences that lead to their impressions are properly conveyed, the audience may not feel they are enough to warrant the conclusions drawn. Unless the judgment processes become keenly involved in quantifying these abstract impressions, Ni's worldview experience will remain, for the most part, hidden from their audience.

Ni Intense Scowl

When Ni is being heavily accessed for the purpose of recalling a specific association, the eyes will mirror the process of tactile searching by furrowing the brow into a scowl while the

10. Ni | REACTIVE ABSTRACT PERCEPTION

a. Ni Intense Scowling

b. Ni Intense Scowling

Figure 36

119

eyes search inward into memory. During this activity, the outer edges of Ni's brow will rise up even further and the corrugator muscles will contract in the center of the brow. The preexisting sharpness of Ni's eyes, caused by the tension of the orbital region of the obicularis oris, will be amplified by this additional contraction, generating a far more striking, and perhaps intimidating, complexion than Si's scowl. Ni's scowl will also be elevated above the eyes, while Si's scowl will more commonly compress the eyes, weighing heavily over them and obstructing them to a degree.

Ni Drifting

Ni's intense scowling will occur in small bursts of strong concentration, while a far more typical and casual use of this function can be observed through its **drifting**. When drifting, the viscous body of an Ni type will sway and lean loosely in the direction of their gaze. During dialogue, the gaze will transition from the audience to some unrelated point in the environment, then back, allowing the mind to *glide* through the vast expanse of its inner world and find whatever information may be necessary in that moment. Unlike Si, which has a near focus, the eyes of Ni will carry a **faraway focus** during these drifts as seen in Figure 35.d. The eyes of Ni will appear to see *beyond* the subject, as though they were attempting to see past the earth's horizon.

In Summary:

Ni Vultology
    Ni Unimpressed Appearance
        Lowered Eyelids
        Elevated Brow
    Ni Hypnotic/Zoned-out Gaze
    Ni Permanent Stare
    Ni Rambles
    Ni Cryptic Information
    Ni Intense Scowl
    Ni Far Focus Drifting

Ne

PROACTIVE ABSTRACT PERCEPTION

Of all four perception process, Ne is the most internally divided. Its entire operation revolves around the assimilation of new information, however, the information Ne collects from the environment will never fully represent the actual objects observed. This is because Ne's abstract nature holds no interest toward the environment as it truly exists, but only in what it can infer from it. Its eyes will focus on an object so long as that object is a means to create abstract, *situational* associations. If an object carries no novel or abstract qualities which Ne can extract and correlate to other datasets, the object becomes a vague, peripheral impression, void of any relevance. The eyes of Ne will then **diverge** their focus to another mental or literal object with the intention of finding another association, ad infinitum.

For Ne, the information it registers from a literal object will not be exhaustive or detailed, but be a **caricature** of it. Iconic qualities are emphasized while nuance is omitted, making it easier to mentally manipulate the object spatially and relationally. Two unrelated objects may be mentally associated or combined when details such as scale, shape or material are omitted; details which might make the association wholly implausible if they were considered. But by being lenient with this information, Ne succeeds in generating many more hypothetical arrangements between things than it ever could do otherwise. And as a perception process, the viability or legitimacy of these associations is not the domain of Ne's concern. It aims only to bring forth information in the form of potential arrangements from which the judgment processes can discriminate.

COGNITIVE TYPE

```
Obicularis Oculi ─┐           ┌─ Orbital    : lax
                  │           ├─ Preseptal  : lax
                  └───────────┼─ Pretarsal  : taut
                              ├─ Preseptal  : lax
                              └─ Orbital    : lax
```

a.

b.

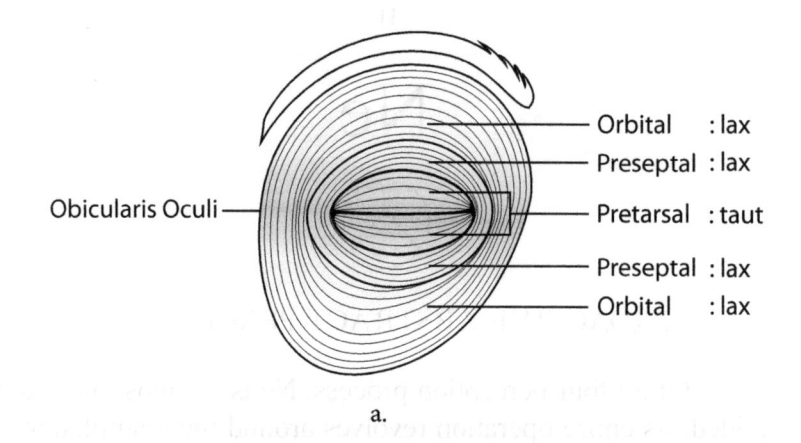

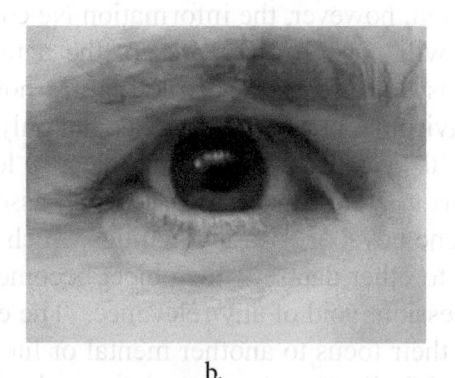

Figure 37

Ne Naïve Eyes

Due to this lack of interest in details, the eyes of Ne will be far less strained for visual input than Se. Ne eyes will never fixate on the object of its focus, seeming instead only to be casually or passively glancing at it. While the eyes may indeed open widely by contracting the pretarsal region of the orbicularis oris, the orbital region will not be taut, but almost entirely relaxed. The area immediately surrounding the eyes will be soft, holding the eyes within a gentle embedding. This will give the eyes what may be called a **naïve** or childlike appearance.

11. Ne | PROACTIVE ABSTRACT PERCEPTION

Ne Eye-Toggling

The internal division in Ne between visual engagement and diversion will demonstrate itself through an **eye-toggling** effect. The eyes will quickly and casually wander about, moving in their sockets while not heavily steering the rest of the head in their direction. As with all perception processes, the head will indeed follow the eyes, but only when a strong enough interest is taken toward a certain direction. Otherwise the eyes will simply toggle effortlessly between various elements of the landscape. In Figure 38 we see various examples of what this toggling may look like.

Additionally, this eye-toggling will also happen when Ne scans the internal world of Si. As mentioned in Chapter 9, Ne-Si often becomes looped in on itself, engaging its proactive association with the static datasets that have been archived by Si. As this occurs, the eyes will simulate real-world exploration, searching Si's mental landscape while **darting** casually in their sockets. This will give Ne eyes a distinctly **scattered** quality, as eye-toggling occurs far more strongly and often in Ne types than Se types. This is because for Se types, associations can be generated viscerally and gradually over long periods of time by Ni without any distinctly proactive expressions. In contrast, Ne carries the responsibility of creating the mind's conceptual associations in these types, which can only be generated through real-time cross-contextualization. An Ne-Si type must engage the explorer process in order to interrelate their sense of reality, which will result in the aforementioned scatteredness being a standard quality of their eyes.

When Si becomes even more heavily involved in Ne's exploration, a variation of this signal can be seen. Toggling will happen underneath the hood of an **Si scowl**. When Si lead types reference their Si, toggling is not a common occurrence, but in types that prioritize Ne over Si, scowling rarely occurs without eye-toggling. Since, for Si types, recall is effortless and natural, it requires no intense involvement from other processes. But Ne types don't access their Si effortlessly, causing instead a heavy

COGNITIVE TYPE

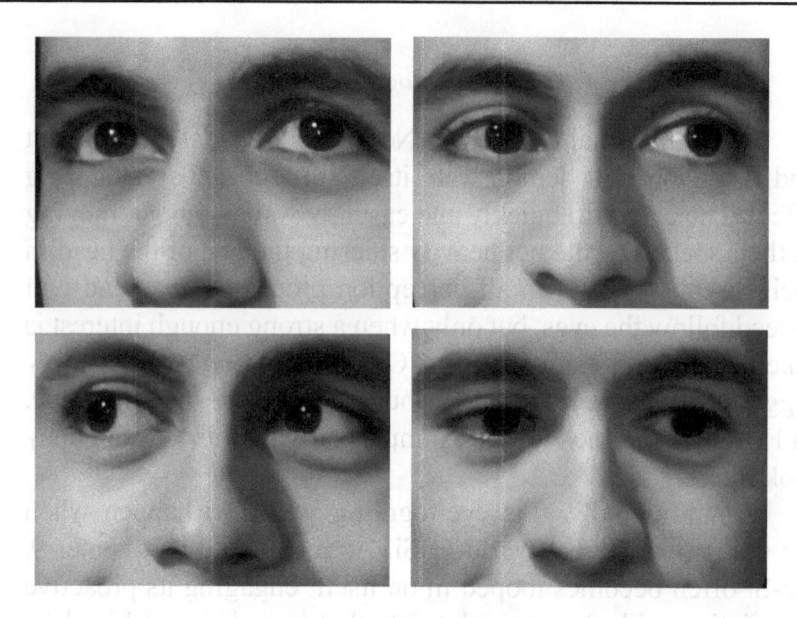

Ne Eye-Toggling

Figure 38

concentration on the recall. Here, the brow weighs heavily over the top part of Ne's eyes, partially breaking the gentleness of the eyes.

Ne Buoyancy

Along with the scatteredness of the eyes, Ne produces strong *momentum* in the body. It will carry a natural level of excitation which, in pronounced cases, may manifest as **restlessness**. The eyes and body of Ne are always eager to proactively intake information, causing alertness to the environment – despite the lack of any *specific* point of focus. Subtle **swaying** and body jittering is common in these types, often syncopated at different latitudes in the spine. This proactive process is not restricted to rigid movements like Je, allowing instead for energy to flow loosely without any coordination. Like the movements of its eyes, Ne's energy will be spritely, spontaneous, and quick to shift trajectories, giving it a type of natural **buoyancy**. One

11. Ne | PROACTIVE ABSTRACT PERCEPTION

a.

b.

c.

d.

Figure 39

might feel a sense that this type could move at any given moment; even when their body remains still, it will merely appear suspended between one movement and another.

Ne Parody

It's been my experience with Ne types that their net psychological activity will also produce certain consistent behavioral patterns which may be worth noting. Often times the momentum of their associations will not confine itself to their mind. Excitation and proactivity will intermingle themselves with these playful associations, causing them to be extroverted. The externalization of Ne's associations will not be dialectic or resolute, but expressive; a direct translation of the unguided impressions at work. They will manifest as a **parody** of the hypothetical situation that exists in their mind at the time; a miniature enactment of the drama or novelty of the interrelation. Personifications may be created using body language, facial exaggerations, voice modulations, accent imitation, and the like. These mini-skits can be as brief as a split second and dissipate as quickly as they arrived. When Ne is especially heavy, parodies will be very common and may even become the person's most typical form of interaction with the world.

In Summary:

Ne Vultology
    Ne Naïve Eyes
    Ne Engagement-Divergence Duality
    Ne Eye-Toggling in Sockets
    Ne Eye-Toggling Scowl
    Ne Buoyancy
        Spritely Body Swaying/Jittering
    Ne Parody

Se

PROACTIVE CONCRETE PERCEPTION

Out of the four perception process, Se is the only one which directly absorbs literal information without intentional modification. We might say that none of the other seven cognitive functions are as deeply connected to reality as this process. Se will thirst for richness and nuance in data – gravitating to information which is subtle, layered, as well as raw in format. Unlike Ne, which extracts caricatures from its surroundings, Se invests the time needed to observe the particulars of a situation for what it displays void of alterations. Because of this, Se is also less imaginative – that is to say, it does less imagining, inferring, or letting extrapolation compensate for data which it can more easily encounter firsthand.

This focus on the **existing** – the present – will demonstrate itself through a **sharpness** in the eyes, and an alertness to the environment. The eyelids of Se will often be peeled to the brim of their sockets, with the pretarsal, preseptal and orbital regions of the orbicularis oculi muscles pulled taut – making Se's sharpness span from the very edge of their eyelashes up and beyond their brow. Se requires such alertness to fulfill its purpose as a literal absorption process and keenly register as much information in the environment as necessary. The only exception to this sharpness might occur when heavy Ni use causes the upper eyelid to rest gently over the top of the eye, but even in such cases the bottom eyelid will remain pulled taut. At its strongest, a parallel connection will exist between the objects in the environment and the eyes, with the eyes being **locked on** to their position, varying little in their quality or motion. And while

COGNITIVE TYPE

```
                            ── Orbital    : taut
                            ── Preseptal  : taut
Obicularis Oculi ──         ── Pretarsal  : taut
                            ── Preseptal  : taut
                            ── Orbital    : taut
```

a.

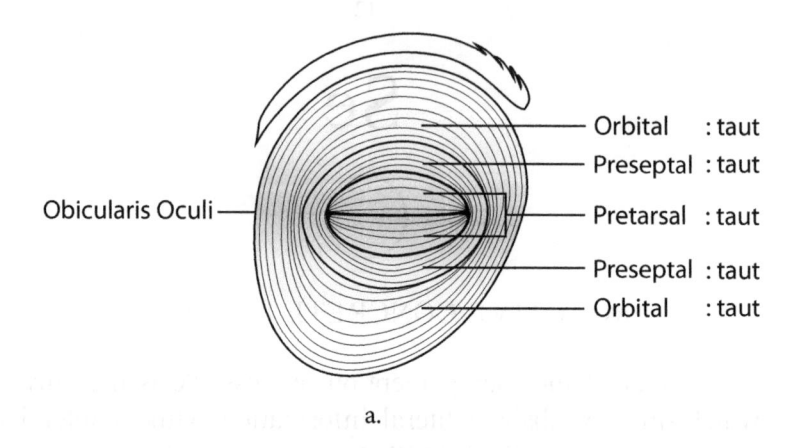

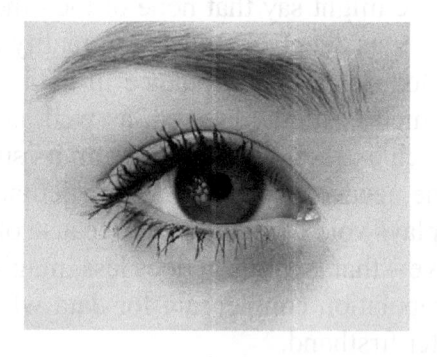

b.

Figure 40

the eyes of Se will eventually leap to another object of focus, they will lock onto this new object with the same level of focus as the last.

Se Tunnel Focus

The eyes's *field of vision* is approximately 120 degrees wide, and is divided into two primary areas; the foveal and peripheral regions[1]. The foveal region is the very center of our eyesight, roughly two degrees wide, where we see the sharp-

1: The perceptual span and peripheral cues in reading, K. Rayner – 1975

12. Se | PROACTIVE CONCRETE PERCEPTION

a.

b.

c.

d.

Figure 41

COGNITIVE TYPE

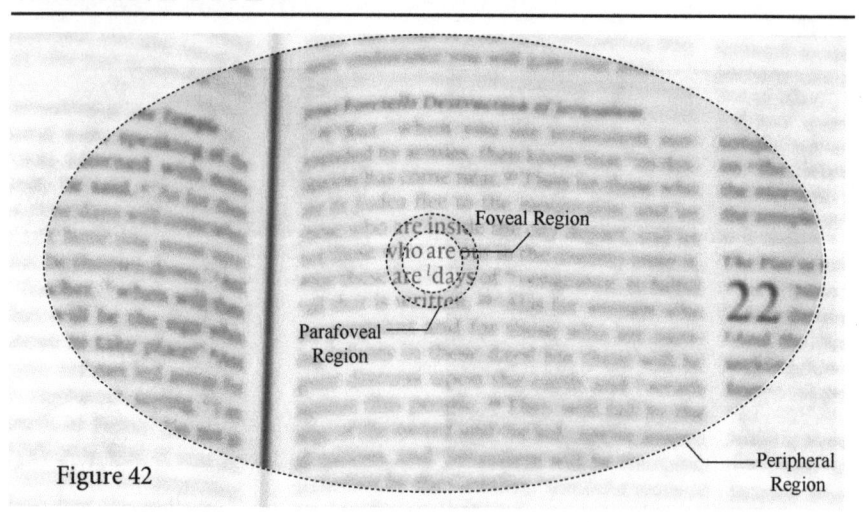

Figure 42

est amount of focus, due to a higher concentration of cone cells in the fovea of our retina. The peripheral region accounts for everything outside of the foveal and parafoveal region – which together cover only five degrees of our field of view. This leaves the remaining 115 degrees to peripheral vision.

As we gaze at our environment, we move this single focal region, sometimes referred to as the *perceptual span*, across objects and piece together a sharp image of the landscape by hopping from one fixation to another. The leap of motion between one fixation and another is called a *saccade*; more commonly referred to as a *toggle* in this book. For Se types, toggling primarily involves a series of very short-distance saccades revolving around their center object of interest. This allows for a thorough mapping of their focal point. The saccades of Ne will be far more sporadic, covering wider distances and staying connected for a shorter duration.

The concentration with which Se views the environment therefore creates what is known as the **Troxler Effect**. This is a curious phenomenon where a person's peripheral vision dissipates out of sight if they remain fixated on a single point for a long period of time. Ne types will have a far more active and

2: The role of fixational eye movements in visual perception, Susana Martinez-Conde – 2004

12. Se | PROACTIVE CONCRETE PERCEPTION

discernible peripheral vision field due to their lack of fixation and their constant diversion of focus – both of which prevent the Toxler Effect from taking effect. Se types will have a less active peripheral vision due to their longer fixation periods and less pronounced toggling, causing a **tunnel focus** effect to manifest.

Se Stimulation

Both explorer processes have at their core a propulsion toward a specific experience or point of gratification. For Ne, unbridled speculation is most gratifying and enchanting because it is *vision*; abstracted. Ne will feel stimulated and energized by the formation of new datasets from the rearrangement and reconnecting of existing sets. For Se, vividness is cherished and sought for most keenly. Riding each moment seamlessly, with an amplification of sounds, colors and sensations brings about the same, or higher, degree of stimulation. Here, realism is taken over idealism or speculation. And in the same way that Ne becomes uninterested when associations aren't possible, Se gets equally bored without stimuli.

Se Sensitivity

Yet this same receptiveness to direct stimulation can turn into undesired overwhelm. This happens most commonly in types with a polar Se, which threatens the tranquility of a primary Ni process. Se's absorption presents such a direct channel into the psyche that a little physical discomfort can be highly amplified. Should the environment be unwelcoming, a far more jarring experience is registered.

This is further aggravated by what I term the Se-Ni *persistence effect*. In times when a situation feels bleak or uncomfortable, Se will unintentionally reinforce this reality with each new loop or refresh in perception. For this type, there is often no escape from the perspective of their Ni-Se worldview, which perpetuates the sobriety of the situation. While Ne can reexamine an input and find a new angle to look at it from ("look at the bright side") which downplays the bad by omitting detail, when Se does a second take it often perceives the situation as still just as troubling and insurmountable. This is because the reality of the unpleasant situation has not shifted, and Se observes it directly without extrapolating alternatives. This causes Se-Ni types to be more serious and affected by matters, while Ne-Si types can more easily entertain alternative optimistic perspectives – notwithstanding the potential lack of legitimacy or accuracy of such perspectives.

In Summary:

Se Vultology
    Se "Presence"
    Se Sharp Eyes
    Se Locked-On Eyes
    Se Tunnel Focus
    Se Sensitivity
    Se Stimulation
    Se Persistence Effect

PART III

TYPES

PART III

TYPES

A Note

Up until now I have attempted to explain the signals belonging to the eight functions using as little behaviorism as possible; describing specific behaviors only where I found doing so inescapable to the proper explanation of the function. I would otherwise run the risk of misleading the reader by associating certain actions or habits to the functions or energetic quadrants, when habits and behaviors are, for the most part, situational manifestations. Thus, Section II presents as direct an image as I could convey of the isolated traits belonging to each process without tying them down to particulars.

Yet matters of the psyche are rarely so directly compartmentalized, and information that exists in a sea of overlapping layers is just as legitimate and relevant as that which marks itself distinct or easily identified. In taking this isolated approach, much of the richness and nuance of these processes, which have overlap with other aspects of the psyche, has been lost. I find it also necessary, then, to reinsert this overlapping information and bring it into view – in full acknowledgement of the risks implied – understanding it to be indispensable to a full understanding of the functions.

There is no better place to learn about the nuanced workings of these functions than where the overlap actually happens; in the cognitive hierarchies of the types. For that reason, the following sixteen chapters will delve into how these functions come together to form behavioral patterns in individuals. I have further divided each chapter into what I consider the most typical modalities of the types. I call these modalities "subtypes"; they are descriptions of personality that are not themselves definitive categories, but modes which a person may travel between, given different lifestyles and external factors The subtypes aim to capture the essence of a modality – which is usually a type's reliance on a certain function – through its most distinctive behavioral qualities. From these subtypes we get some idea as to the full range of the type's expressivity, but many people will fall somewhere in the middle; having little bits of all their subtypes but in reduced quality. I call this intermediate development *standard*, with other developments being noted by name.

When aspects of a person's own psychology have not been explored intently, nor the question of the self in general, many aspects of personality will be far more culturally defined. Two people with standard development will often share lifestyles, beliefs, goals and habits despite belonging to different types. They will not embody any particular subtype strongly in part due to a lack of differentiation from their social sphere. Hence, standard development will often signal a pending individuation process whereby contrast is created between an individual and their cultural nativity.

If instead an individual has a very concentrated expression of various subtypes, especially from their primary and polar functions, I term the person *balanced*. A balanced person will have easy access to all four functions, but will express the qualities of their primary oscillation most strikingly. They'll have several behavioral overlaps with their polar type and may compete effectively with them in the same fields.

Quick Tip

No two faces are identical. Even among the same type, the structure of a person's face (due to ethnicity, bone structure or facial muscle count) can vary greatly. And as cognitive type is not a physiognomy, every time a visual reading is attempted, it's important to first start by creating a brand new *baseline*. Take into account the individual's natural facial features – such as genetically high cheekbones, flat cheekbones, small eyes, large eyes, or sagging eyebrows due to old age – and have those qualities signify nothing whatsoever. Then begin the reading afresh; identify gestures and contractions in relation to this baseline.

If even with this resetting of the baseline, they prove to display significant muscular tensions belonging to a certain process or type, that will give you a clearer indication of their cognition.

Figure 43

FiNe

EDAMIN

The FiNe type emerges when the Fi-Te oscillation is primary and lead by Fi, while supported by the Ne-Si perception oscillation. Having Fi as the leading process will tend the FiNe toward accidental radiation of emotional energy, accidental facial expressions and a softness in demeanor. The tension rising toward their nose may be strong, often remaining permanently present. And when combined with the naïveté and confusion of their Ne eyes, what can often result is a pained or *wounded* facial expression, independent of any actual discomfort. Their eyes will scan the environment as they rest casually in their sockets, having a tendency to toggle and drift about lightly. As a compass type, their energy will be low-key, albeit emotionally active to some degree at all times. But when Fi is consulted more intently, they will disengage their eyes down as they process their judgments, pausing to reflect on their internal contents before delivering their stance. During these moments their snarling tension may increase due to a pinging of the emotional register. The FiNe will have a very personally-crafted aesthetic and ethical framework which can form through a myriad of subtle conclusions – some outside of their own awareness. When Fi has yet to translate its framework into language through collaboration with Te, it will be felt as endless visceral emotional repulsions or attractions to concepts, ideas and objects. These judgments will be kept private and their external execution may bear no difference until an occasion presents itself which requires that they move logistically. At that time they may object to certain actions which may appear trivial or unimportant to others but which violate some unspoken principle to the FiNe. If the FiNe's motives are not well explained to others, they may be seen as needlessly difficult and fussy about such matters.

COGNITIVE TYPE

a.

b.

c.

d.

Figure 44

While the FiNe female can express a more fairy-like appearance, the FiNe male can often carry a gnomish appearance, especially if they're heavier in weight. We may be reminded of the dwarves from Disney's *Snow White* classic or of Bilbo in Jules Bass' 1977 adaptation of *The Hobbit*.

13. FiNe | Edamin

The FiNe's momentum halting will not be quite as pronounced as we see it in Ti lead types, due to the cascading nature of Te's gesticulations which require less accentuated intermissions. Upon a gesture's delivery, they may display a level of snippiness in their body as well as a rattling of the head. This type's voice is almost always memorable, each one having an unordinary pitch or tempo. In those with an open and sensitive channel to their own emotions, this voice will be breathy and have a sing-song quality. In those whose Te is used as a protective membrane between them and the world, it will be nasal and pinched in a rather wounded way.

1. THE SEELIE FAIRY

When the Fi and Ne processes are especially heavy, Ne's buoyant energy will augment their already ephemeral and sprite-like character, creating an *unreal* aura unrivaled by any other type. The Ne process tends the user toward the imaginary and the possible – rather than the actual – and when this already disconnected perception combines with the emotionally charged idealism of Fi what results is a distinctly **dream-like** effect. As Ne's abstract perceptions emulate Fi's already elusive framework, they create a far less anchored demeanor than what we see in other judgment types – earning this subtype the name of Seelie Fairy. More than in any other type, this subtype's Fi will carry a whispery, bashful tone and giddy character. We find examples of this ephemeral quality in the young FiNe Liza Minnelli, as well as in FiNe Evanna Lynch. The latter's role as Luna Lovegood in the *Harry Potter* movie franchise presents a decent, albeit limited, representation of this subtype. When interacting with these individuals, one may be stricken by the feeling of suspension that surrounds them, as though they were interacting with a floating, magical entity. While this description may seem wholly fantastical, it's no exaggeration to say that FiNe types can manifest in such ways. We owe this type's fictional associations to European folklore, which carries in it heavy influences from this subtype. In Western mythology, the FiNe type is commonly used to represent the *anima* spirit of the culture: the concept of *female* as seen in the male soul. Being itself a demographic heavy with these four cognitive functions (Fi-Te & Ne-Si), it is no surprise that we see the compass process Fi represented in their mythology in like manner as Ti exists at the heart of many Eastern philosophies.

2. THE SCIENTIST

Not all FiNe's subscribe to a fairy-like demeanor. In other manifestations, the Te process can weigh far heavier in the psyche, leading this type into a deep interest for empirical study. As a polar process and companion of Fi, Te can play a critical role in the FiNe's concept of reality. It is the primary way in which this type comes to form a dynamic understanding of how their world operates, and it can provide solidity when their Fi and Ne processes cannot. However, the FiNe type will prefer to pursue these empirical investigations from the comfort of a conceptual setting, naturally leading to *the scientist* subtype. Contrary to many descriptions of types by professors such as Beebes and Myers, it is not the TiNe type that can claim the title of the secluded scientist or physicist: it is in fact the FiNe that is most suited to that title. The TiNe type has no exceptional talent for understanding dynamic elements of logistical reality. Their talent lies in giving clarity and systemization to matters of social dynamics, better placing the TiNe's talent in the domain of psychology and philosophy.

Additionally, it is a heavy misconception to consider the FiNe type to be gifted with any exceptional degree of dynamic emotional intelligence. As noted in previous chapters, it is the Fe process that excels at matters of tracking social dynamics, while Fi types can often struggle in such fields despite their strongly ethical presence. Hence, the social awkwardness often attributed to the TiNe type is likewise better represented in the FiNe type. Having Fi as a lead process does not make a type any more talented at matters handled by Fe, and having Ti as a lead process does not make a type any more talented at matters best handled by Te. Instead, a type relies always on their Je process, whichever it may be, to pursue interests of external *causality*. As with all *delta* types (types with Fi-Te and Ne-Si), FiNe's are **empiricist**. Their Ne-Si oscillation operates by conceiving isolated datasets, while their Fi-Te process gauges the manner in which those datasets dynamically interact. We see examples of FiNe scientists in Nobel Prize laureates such as Edward Witten, Neils Bohr, Bruce Beutler and Charles Kuen Kao. Another example of an FiNe in this shade is scientist Brian Cox, who has a well-rounded development and a capacity to convey his Fi sentiments to the general public using his gentle and alluring voice. Almost always the level of breathiness in an Fi lead's voice will be indicative of their non-reliance on Te in matters of personal principles. Heavy Fi types will also tend toward organic frameworks, honoring the mysteries of the soul and approaching human matters differently than logistical ones.

We see an example of this in an interview by Wim Kayzer with the exceptionally whispery Edward Witten. Notwithstanding a firm background in physics and a fundamentally empirical approach to knowledge, when speaking about the private and subjective, Witten defensively states:

Witten: What it is we're experiencing when we experience consciousness, I see as remaining a mystery.

Kayzer: Forever?

Witten: That's what I tend to believe. I tend to think that the workings of the conscious brain will be alucinanted, to a large extent. So I tend to believe that biologists and perhaps physicists contributing will understand much better how the brain works. But why something that we call consciousness goes with those workings, I think will remain mysterious, and perhaps I'm mistaken. I have a much easier time imagining how we'd understand the big bang, even though we can't do it yet, than I can imagine understanding consciousness.

For Witten and surely for other FiNe scientists, the domain of the human heart is not compromised or subjected to the reductionist and objective thinking of Te. Priority is still given to the complexity of human nature even though a keen interest for the logistical may exist. This is not always the case when Te is prioritized above Fi, encouraging types to diminish the personal as "merely subjective" and sometimes irrelevant to life's dynamics. Naturally, each FiNe's framework will hold its own particularities, but a general reverence for the soul, however it's come to be defined, will always persist.

3. THE SENSITIVIST

At other times, we see Fi being heavy while all other processes still remain lacking in their expression and development. Such types will be deeply affected by their own internal causalities, as prompted by their internal or external environment, and unable to coordinate those inner impressions. We see a particularly moving example of this FiNe portrayed by Joaquin Phoenix as Theodore in the 2013 film *Her*. Theodore, a kindhearted recluse whose job requires composing tender letters for strangers using his own emotional landscapes, represents the paradox between this subtype's deep feeling yet stark disconnect from people. We see in him the affection of Fi and what a powerful influence it can have in their life while giving little capacity for connectivity although it births a great capacity for empathy. This disconnect is by no means intentional, but a consequence of lacking a *proactive* channel for interaction, whether it be their Ne or Te. Theodore's breathy voice, difficulty conveying his thoughts and his passivity all reflect an absence of Je. It's been my observation that these types can suffer great depressions due to having a distinct need for the emotional connections they find so difficult to attain.

But there is a sister iteration of this subtype – the social sensitivist – wherein Fi remains strong but not so inwardly directed as to render relatability and interaction impossible. This FiNe is surprisingly influential and able to resonate with others in transformative and sobering ways. They may invest a lifetime in understanding humanity, but do it from the inside-out. While many Fe types approach the question of humanity from the outside-in (by how visibilities and experiences prompt an occasion for contemplating human dynamics and structures), the FiNe discovers what it means to be human by inner searching and searching also within those closest to them. From this personal understanding, a philanthropic philosophy can often emerge. Because of Fi's non-economical thinking, emotional reciprocity is not the primary motivator behind their own Ji beliefs and attitudes. As such the FiNe sensitivist, when very seelie, will manifest in highly *altruistic* forms. The social sensitivist may become involved in political activism, charities and awareness-raising despite the social challenges they may confront by being in the spotlight.

For a complete account of this type's vultology, we can look at interviews of the following FiNe public figures:

Name	*Development*
Edward Witten	Scientist/Sensitivist
Brian Cox	Seelie/Balanced
Neils Bohr	Seelie/Scientist
Linus Torvalds	Scientist
Liza Minnelli	Seelie Fairy
Joan Baez	Standard
Evanna Lynch	Seelie Fairy
Meredith Godreau	Standard
Regina Spektor	Standard
Aurora Aksnes	Standard

Figure 45

146

FiSe

EDAVIN

The FiSe type emerges when the Fi-Te oscillation is primary and lead by Fi, while supported by the Se-Ni perception oscillation. With Fi as the leading process of the psyche, this type will tend toward an accidental radiation of emotional energy and facial expressions. With supportive Se, this will be accompanied by a sharpness and steadiness in the eyes, but these eyes will not be heavily engaged in exploring the environment. They may look in the direction of the face due to their steadiness, but will not steer the body's direction. Body movements will arise from the FiSe with a gentle intentionality and poised composure. However, due to the gravitas of Se, the ephemeral levity of Fi is more predisposed to become grounded rather than remaining suspended, as we see in the FiNe type. Even so, the FiSe type can hold a very ephemeral, light and *seelie* character as we see in FiSe's such as Marilyn Monroe, Michael Jackson and the young Audrey Hepburn. Their voice will carry a breathy, receding tone, which compliments their delicate mannerisms and harkens back to their inner privacy. In other examples, such as FiSe Kanye West, we see a more *unseelie* manifestation of this type. A *sullen* disposition weights upon their face as Fi's tension spans from their nose down below the corners of their lips and into a light frown. The eyes then cast a dissatisfied glare reminiscent of the NiTe type.

The body of an FiSe type will be rigid, continually and inescapably receding back to a self-kept posture after each gesture. Their Te's articulation will often be overtaken by a coating of Fi's energy, causing it to be slowed down in accordance with the tempo of their emotions. Yet it will still remain unbroken, albeit elongated, in its tone and rhythm. These articulations will carry a private *investment* in them that does not push outward

COGNITIVE TYPE

a.

b.

c.

d.

Figure 46

as we see in Fe types, but instead leaks out in a veneer of silent sobriety.

While this type draws its understanding of the outer world from a literal and proactive perception process, it is primarily governed by Fi, which is a subjective process. Therefore, the ultimate result of this type's internal experience will be one somewhat divorced from the world or its reality. It will remain tinged with one's own interpretation of causalities. Life becomes first and foremost a matter of personal emotional concern, and secondly a reality that flows sensationally and is understood by sensational influences. Yet, this divorce from reality is not at all like the *dreamlike* effect of Ne. The FiSe type will not default to imaginary or extraneous ideas, but simply respond to their reality based on externally unavailable causalities. These causalities do stem from the events and happenings of the reality around them, but are the internal responses caused by the external world. The sensational dynamics of their inner world can become prevalent topics of heart, often leading to an exploration and expressivity of these sensations.

1. THE INDIE ARTIST

The FiSe type, along with the TeNi type, share the curious phenomenon of being simultaneously the clearest expressions of the human emotional register, while also often being quite unaware of the magnitude or nature of their own expressions. Paradoxically, it is this very lack of conscious awareness of the emotional register, and therefore control or alteration of its expression, that facilitates such raw expressivity in Fi lead types. Were the emotional world at the conscious control of manipulation, as it is with Fe types, the information elicited from this type would not be quite so telling of the universal themes within humanity.

As a Ji type, the FiSe is keen to its compass, following a private, self-created aesthetic and flow, which often leads to the embodiment of off-beat, indie lifestyles. While culture and fashion shifts in and out of endorsing off-beat lifestyles, for the FiSe type – now and throughout history – the indie lifestyle is a native and natural result of their own psychology. Practically speaking, this can manifest as having very long or very short hair (independent of gender), cross-dressing, transgenderism, bisexuality, staunch celibacy, or a myriad of other things. This is not to assert that FiSe types have a higher percentage of variation in gender orientation than any other type, but only that their constant pinging of their compass will lead them to embrace their sexuality honestly far more commonly in situations where other types might suppress their own less popular sexual preferences.

We see examples of this subtype in musicians such as FiSe Enya and Björk, who touch deeply on themes of the heart through sensational videography, eccentric attire, and heart-opening lyrics delivered through a delicate, yet strong, spritelike voice. When asked about her attire choices in a 2002 documentary titled "Inside Björk", Björk expresses that a feeling of uneasiness exists in her which abates itself only by the alignment of the external form to the internal world. Such is a perfect metaphor for the psychic relationship within the FiSe type. Björk offers her listeners a window into the potentialities of humanity by the creation of songs emerging from unconscious, or commonly ignored, emotional terrain. We see the polar, and more devious, reflection of Björk in TeNi Madonna, who captures another dimension of this function combination. Types with these four functions, sometimes referred to as *gamma* types, have an internal fervor to give tactile form to the private aesthetic of their Fi, which expresses itself most obviously in the transformation of their self-image. The late FiSe Michael Jackson presents another fascinating case of delicate independence, childish eccentricity and controversial appearance. In opposition to years of harassment and defamatory rumors, Jackson continued to make decisions about his appearance which won him little rest from the criticism of the public. Both Björk and Michael Jackson are strong Fi users, as can be seen by the prevalence of Fi signals on their face and in their voice, which accounts for the uncompromising directness of their expressions. While this serves as an important contrast and extreme to measure against, I should note that few FiSe take their expressions to such lengths, and the artistic preferences of FiSe's are certainly not *required* to fall into fringe categories. Naturally, it is more conceivable that a fair percentage of them would, if only by chance, align with contemporary beliefs and taste.

2. THE "VEGETARIAN"

The selectiveness of Fi's morality will span from the smallest daily decisions to the broader concepts of life and death. Often Fi will lead its user to deeply consider questions of life, its fundamental value, and its varied forms of expression. It is no surprise, then, that this type may come to deeply empathize with forms of life other than humans, due to a reverence for a *life* principle, disconnected from any particular species. They may take the position that animal life is of no less value than human life and should be treated with equal respect. Such an attitude naturally leads to **vegetarianism**, which is a very common lifestyle among many Fi types such as Mohandas Gandhi, Jane Goodall, Natalie Portman, Kate Bush, Madonna, Janet Jackson and Chris Martin. Now I term this subtype *The Vegetarian* due to the overwhelming gravitation toward this topic in the FiSe type, but this thematic tendency to find a point of protest is not exclusive to the topic of meat consumption. Other topics such as women's rights, abortion, the oppression of minority groups, child labor and more obscure topics will lead the FiSe type to take rigid stances for or against a side. Far more often, Fi lead types will opt for positions that revere the ability for personal liberty of choice rather than for ethics that reduce the power and freedom of individuals for the sustainment of ideologies or societies. Uniformity, even to ethically founded ideals, may be disquieting to FiSe types, which often value personal choice just as strongly as correctness in other ethical matters.

3. THE UNSEELIE HAUGHTY

Ethical topics may become strong points of friction between the FiSe and their friends and family as the FiSe will not be so keen to relinquish their positions. Due to the heavily personal premise of their choices, topics inescapably become personal;

the morality and character of others is gauged by where their stances fall on a given topic relative to where the FiSe's stances are. From this information they may decide to distance or disassociate themselves from those who represent the opposite of their morality. Indeed, when an FiSe is unseelie, they may utterly resent or ignore strangers or casual acquaintances on the single premise of believing, or suspecting, that they conflict in values. Since an FiSe lives as an embodiment of their values, often the assumption is made that others are also representations of their beliefs. This leads FiSe types to be as keenly opposed to others as they are to the ideas they hold, perhaps not properly factoring in the degree of seriousness/triviality with which others hold their views. In more haughty manifestations, the unseelie FiSe will interact with humanity preemptively anticipating foul character. When Ni's worldview becomes too heavily involved, generalities are used to gauge matters rather than person-specific judgments, leading to unfair accusations and prejudice.

Undeterred by the darker parts of human nature, the unseelie FiSe also navigates without reservation into the oppressed and demonized elements of society. More than a few FiSe artists are producers of gore, violence and terror; not so much from a sadistic psychology but from an inner calling of the raw and primal soul. The surreal, haunting works of FiSe Zdzisław Beksiński perfectly capture this flavor of expressivity. Beksiński was a reclusive fellow who paid little heed to the affairs of others, immersing himself in the transcribing of sensations which emerged unsolicited from him – out of some melancholy and musical impulse. Having never titled any of his works, Beksiński worked with no thought of an underlying theme or expected reception. He expected his art to be misunderstood and always worked under that assumption.

4. THE HARMONIOUS SEELIE

But if the FiSe is not so focused on his own convictions, perhaps respecting the opinions of others as part of their sacred individuality, he will integrate far more gracefully into his social setting. Despite a seemingly self-oriented emotionality, the

14. FiSe | Edavin

FiSe can, like all human beings, feel very nervous about a lack of acceptance from others. Especially when their off-beat nature sets them far apart from their peers, this disconnect may cause strong feelings of unrest. Fortunately, the FiSe's literal tracking of the physical environment will lend a degree of natural understanding of social dynamics; a sense that is not always registed as easily by the FiNe. The FiSe's desire to be an unbridled self then finds a way to *harmonize* with those they care most about, although not necessarily with their entire culture. While the specific emotional shifts leading up to people's behaviors may elude them, they will understand the general protocols in place and aim for an ethical code that ensures a reverence for everyone involved. They may become the understanding teacher, the school counselor or ministry leader.

For a complete account of this type's vultology, we can look at interviews of the following FiSe public figures:

Name	*Development*
Jacqueline Kennedy	Seelie
Marilyn Monroe	Seelie
Audrey Hepburn	Seelie
Janet Jackson	Indie Artist
Michael Jackson	Indie Artist
Bjork	Seelie/Indie Artist
Kanye West	Unseelie
Princess Diana Frances	Unseelie
Sonny Moore	Indie Artist
Liv Tyler	Harmonious Seelie

Figure 47

15

TeSi

EDAMER

The TeSi type emerges when the Te-Fi oscillation is primary and lead by Te, while supported by the Si-Ne perception oscillation. Having Te as a lead process, the TeSi type will have a noticeable presence, often speaking their mind directly alongside snappy gesticulations, a rigid posture and a *matter-of-fact* voice. However, by far the most pronounced visual quality of this type will be their mouth, which will be peculiar in the diverse expressions it makes and the extent to which these expressions are generated. As an Fi type, the TeSi will be subject to accidental and asymmetrical muscle contractions as they speak but, being a type which articulates often, these asymmetries will be commonplace. Their mouth will fall into peculiar shapes, tensing near the nose and sometimes creating a horizontal splitting of the cheeks. In many TeSi the continual vertical stretching of Fi causes their facial muscles to create a *taut square* effect in the area around their mouth, as seen in Figure 48.d. The depressor angili oris muscles, which pull the corners of the mouth downward toward the chin, are directly opposed to the levator labii superioris muscles which pull the corners of the mouth upward toward the nose. When both are engaged, this creates the four points of the taut square. This effect can appear in others with Te-Fi as a primary oscillation, but is perhaps most noticeable in this type.

The TeSi, like the SiTe, has a bit of a droop to their eyes. Having Si leading over Ne, their brow will often become upward turned at the center of the eyes and slant downward at the outer edges of the eyes. Occasionally, their eyes may become naïve and childlike as they toggle lightly across the environment, but will usually remain unchanged and focused forward with a dullness about them. As a judgment type, their body will not be

COGNITIVE TYPE

a.　　　　　　　　　　　　b.

c.　　　　　　　　　　　　d.

Here in Figure "d" we see the taut square most clearly. The four black dots around the mouth represent the corners of this square; caused by upward and downward pulling.

Figure 48

156

steered by the direction of their eyes, but instead their head and body will move as a cohesive entity, independent of what the eyes may be glancing at.

The TeSi will be an expressive type, yet their expressions will be cold, suggesting a sort of mechanical indifference on the surface, while thinly veiling many private feelings and vulnerabilities. Emotional energies, such as sorrow or anger, may be present in them but these feelings will seep out of their voice sporadically instead of through a deliberate coating of pathos over certain words. Indeed, their emotions may be far more discernible through this rawness than through a coordinated effort. Special training or a position as a spokesperson may lead to the development of some elongation of sounds for emphasis, but always their voice will lack the sensitivity of an ethical process such as Fe. An element of rigid calculation and sharpness will triumph over their speech. We will often hear a nasalization of the voice; a *pinched* tonality that runs opposite to the breathy tones of Fi. This tonality will be accompanied by many snippy gestures such as head shaking, head nodding and shoulder shrugging. Often their trademark nonchalance will be accompanied by a snappy sense of humor; one that aims to take material consequences to their natural conclusions in the most sarcastic or self-depreciating way. Having Ne, this sense of humor can become very unconventional or quirky and perhaps even enjoy the reactions of being seen as bizarre.

1. THE ENTREPRENEUR

The TeSi is a curious creature, containing gifts both for vast innovation but also practical application. The energies and possibilities seen by Ne-Si are channeled through the practical filter of Te, simultaneously supplying and endless stream of potential arrangements and weeding them down to only those that jive with the way of reality. Because of this, one of the major subtypes for TeSi is *The Entrepreneur*. While the NeFi type is more suited to the initial generation of a concept or invention, the TeSi is capable of developing the idea to further lengths by being able to listen and resonate with the optimism of another Ne type's abstractions (particularly when other practicalists would not) and by applying Te toward their manifestation.

We see a classic example of a TeSi entrepreneur in James Cameron, who has not only created a vast array of imaginary worlds through film-making, but has invented many of the needed technologies for those films himself. He is also one of the only human beings to have manned a scuba tank to the bottom of the New Britain Trench, and is also an avid fantasy writer on the side. TeSi are individuals who not only have multicolored interests, but who often pursue many of them to mastery or high proficiency. Their logistical methodology and naturally proactive energy will generate and endless assignment of personal projects or goals. In many TeSi, this talent for productivity, once recognized, will be firmly associated to their ego identity. Objective and functional achievement then become synonymous with personal success; creating a self-made standard that demands of the TeSi an unreal level of output. This mindset will transform many a TeSi into an overachiever or busybody, and if the TeSi is not careful, they may place an unjust amount of stress on themselves, which will be amplified even further if a disconnect exists between their Te and their Fi's bodily sensibilities.

Another expression of the prolific TeSi can be seen in the the exhaustive writings of TeSi J.R.R. Tolkien, who created an entire fictional world history of more than 3,000 years with internal consistency, while also being a polyglot fluent in more than 15 languages and a full-time teacher at the Oxford University. Yet, despite this immense imaginative capacity, a TeSi will far more often view themselves as a realist and dislike attempts by others to take imagination as anything more than a recreational act. The energies of Ne are seen as an asset to their overall psychology, rather than the primary motivator of it. We learn from Tolkien[1] that he considered himself primarily a scientific philologist. His love of writing was more academic and the works he considered most important were his professional publications while his fantastical creations were to him simply a personal hobby. The societies of enthusiasts which came to surround his

---

1: The Letters of J.R.R. Tolkien - H. Carpenter (1981) – #4, #7, #257 fictional work greatly surprised and sometimes alarmed him. Unlike the FiNe, Tolkien's personality was far from dream-like, focused far more on his career and interest in world history and languages. Yet he presents to us a curious case of a TeSi with a healthy sensitivity to his own polar Fi's influence.

2. THE ECCENTRIC NERD

As a Te lead type, the TeSi can also suffer, particularly in their youth, from a difficulty understanding the causalities of their own emotions and those of others. But unlike other types such as the TiNe or SiTe, whose difficulties commonly lead to an introverted and invisible demeanor, the TeSi's proactive energy will place them front and center; in the spotlight of criticism – causing them to be seen as **eccentric nerds**. These types may be the ones who not only engage in geeky activities, but who, whether accidentally or intentionally, publicize them to their peers such as by indiscriminately vocalizing databits as a situation causes them to be recalled. They may do this with little consideration of the social atmosphere or level of receptiveness of the audience. They may have a talkative bent and not understand when other parties are becoming exhausted with their heavy Te or overwhelming information.

These initially awkward types often develop into successful adults after the pressures of grade school have lifted, and they enter into an adult world which gives higher priority and value to their innate traits. At this point they may also develop more capacity for socialization, however, their relationship with co-workers may still manifest challenges. TeSi may be challenging to work with, as their awareness of their own logistical efficiencies, combined with an unawareness of other people's sensitivities, may lead to an inability to grasp the views of others and compromise when collaborating. We see a very convincing portrayal of this subtype in actor Jeff Daniels' role as Will McAvoy in HBO's *The Newsroom* (2012). Throughout this television series we see a realistic drama of the difficulties faced by a TeSi, both emotionally and in the workforce. Often the reactions a TeSi will have to their own emotional difficulties will be very direct – perhaps calloused, blunt and excessive as they combat human fears and vulnerabilities with Te's methodologies. The overwhelming power of human emotions will prompt every type to utilize their entire cognitive arsenal toward resolving emotional difficulties in whatever way they can. For the TeSi, this can involve rearranging the logistics of a situation to make it impossible to face the problem or person in question (by resigning, firing, deleting contacts, by moving away), seeing it as the most direct and efficient way to resolve the immediate discomfort. The refinement of a TeSi's emotional register often happens largely externally, as they receive feedback from reality as to what the dynamics of emotions are. Not having the sensitivity of Fe's emotional tracking, they depend more heavily on empirical experience for this, which will inescapably lead to a period of awkwardness until they learn the necessary nuances of human interaction.

In their friction with life, they will manifest the uneducated heart; the raw emotional clashing between one person and another. They embody, like many Fi types do, an excellent window into the reality of the emotional register. TeSi's, like all Te-Fi types, will have a uniquely created way of managing their own private feelings as well as a very particular Fi emotional palate for things they do and don't like.

3. THE HISTORIAN

As we noted with Tolkien, history and the accumulation of facts or datasets can become an integral part of this type's disposition. The TeSi can often be seen as the student in class with unreal, encyclopedic memory or an ability to remember vast amounts of mainstream trivia. As they go about their life, the TeSi, like the SiTe, will show a keen capacity for archiving isolated tidbits of information for specific use in some future occurrence. But the Si tapestry of the TeSi is also under constant filtration, as their Te manages the inaccuracies of Si. Because of this, Si will be less nostalgic and more functionally oriented. While SiTe types are more prone to grandfather their Si worldview into their personality, often operating through the same thematic premise that they acquired in earlier decades, the TeSi type will not hold itself so rigidly to these veteran ideas.

We will commonly find this subtype in politicians, news reporters and lawyers – domains that engage many of the TeSi's chronological and managerial strengths – but equally so in hobbyists and fans of a certain franchise. Their affinities for taxonomy and history can manifest in a diversity of topics, both professional and recreational. At times this subtype is combined with the eccentric nerd subtype as is the case with TeSi Stephen Colbert; a political satirist, writer and television host.

4. THE LOGISTICAL ETHICIST

If the TeSi grows a special interest for the ethical dimension, then their unique Fi palate will manifest itself directly through their Te's locomotion. While Fe lead types are more predisposed to take a mentoring role in moralistic work, Te types such as the TeSi will utilize their natural ability to organize reality in order to provide practical solutions to social problems which collide with their ethics. Rather than hosting counseling workshops, they may create a charity organization for a certain unfortunate demographic, or donate a great deal of their income toward that cause. TeSi, having polar Fi, may be heavy philanthropists and advocates of minority groups. They may become a political spokesperson of a cause and use their naturally hard energy and articulation to be the stoic representative for these demographics. We see a strong example of this subtype in Rebecca Watson, a famous American blogger, podcast host and avid feminist.

But the ethical convictions of Fi can take vastly different shapes, not all of which are focused on an altruistic motive. At times the ethics of Fi may become subordinate to Te and merge in such a way that a point of alignment is found between both polarities while still retaining Te as the prime directive. We find a fascinating example of one such philosophy in TeSi Ayn Rand. Through her books *Atlas Shrugged* (1957) and *The Fountainhead* (1943), Rand proposes an ethical code formed through an objective rationality and which operates wholly independent of the social/emotional economy (Fe). Altruism is counted as an abhorrent philosophy which praises the destruction and sacrifice of the self. In Rand's *objectivism*, the principle of reciprocity is entirely rejected, and each human is liberated from the ethical burden of others, becoming a single entity responsible for their own happiness and for achieving their own success in all professional and private areas of life. Yet this does not deny the possibility of giving to others freely out of one's own love, however it will never be from the intention of forming an implicit emotional contract with others. Here we see an absolute application of Fi's *individualism* via Te's practical approach towards life. It demonstrates a convergence of Te-Fi psychology and a unique reconciliation of Ji and Je where principle is always applied in practice.

Notice, however, that the convictions of Ayn Rand and others like Rebecca Watson equally stem from the personal resolve of Fi, championing for the self-direction and freedom of individuals, absent of any collectively dependent solution. Despite extremely different opinions across many TeSi, we witness that the Te-Fi oscillation will always adhere to this same method of execution.

For a complete account of this type's vultology, we can look at interviews of the following TeSi public figures:

Name	*Development*
James Cameron	Entrepreneur
Stephen Colbert	Eccentric Nerd
John Carmack	Eccentric Nerd
J.R.R. Tolkien	Entrepreneur/Historian
Fran Lebowitz	Logistical Ethicist
Miley Cyrus	Individualist
Adele Adkins	Individualist
Savannah Guthrie	Executive
Germaine Greer	Individualist/Historian
Ayn Rand	Logistical Ethicist

Figure 49

TeNi

EDAVER

The TeNi type emerges when the Fi-Te oscillation is primary and lead by Te, while supported by the Ni-Se perception oscillation. The combination of this type's empirically-oriented primary process with their Ni's convergent associations creates a psychology that is quick to arrive at conclusions from a situation's apparent causalities. The TeNi will be a real-time evaluator of logistical inevitabilities and the necessities that present themselves. As a result of this functional mindset, which is quite efficient at identifying the most important factors in a situation, we will often encounter TeNi who are rather spartan in their affairs. They may be minimal in their artistry or recreational interests, having only a handful of paths which they will dedicate most of their time toward. Unlike the TeSi, which may wander more often in creative arts, the TeNi will be less disposed to such activities unless artistry itself is their focal occupation.

Like the TeSi, the TeNi will have a firm demeanor, characterized by a sharpness and briefness in their voice and a rigid posture. This type's eyes will often carry what I term a **manic expression**, characterized by sharp and piercing Se eyes amplified by an Ni scowl with slightly raised outer edges. Due to their Te-Fi oscillation pair, their mouth will contract in peculiar, often asymmetrical, ways as they deliver their plentiful articulations. Facial expressions of *disgust* or *distaste* may abound, even when the TeNi feels no particular opposition to the environment.

Together, the TeNi's eyes and mouth may combine to create a rather *intimidating* facial expression. Indeed, TeNi types will often complain about being perceived as angry by others when their inner attitude may be wholly benign. By some coincidence, the functions and the hierarchy of this type combine to form perhaps the most bracing appearance of all sixteen types.

COGNITIVE TYPE

a.

b.

c.

d.

Figure 50

Tension will exist rising up toward their nose and this will often be accompanied by Te's horizontal splitting/indentation of the cheeks. Snippy head shakes, head nods, shoulder shrugs and hand gestures will also accompany this type's naturally stern countenance.

1. THE FERVENT ECCENTRIC

When this type's Te holds an imbalanced relationship to Fi, it will manifest many raw and unrefined emotional motivations through Te's sharp delivery. These expressions will not only be eccentric and unconventional, but firey and unyielding. Unlike the TeSi Eccentric Nerd, whose Ne-Si oscillation embeds an overall more malleable and non-linear demeanor to their bracing Te, the TeNi is entirely linear with this overbearing energy. What results is a headstrong psychology that's predisposed to drown out opposition with an avalanche of rhetoric.

We see a classic example of this subtype in Bill O'Reilly, a U.S. political commentator who has developed a strong reputation for being outspoken, uncompromising, interruptive and dismissive. Another striking example manifests through businessman Donald Trump who, along with the aforementioned traits, quickly becomes personal in the comments he directs at others. As this subtype holds little regard for the refinement of ethics via Fi, it will use Fi's morality only in unseelie ways while cascading forward primarily with Te. Nonetheless, these types may develop strong executive abilities and make significant, practical contributions to society. Even in the fervent eccentric, the influence of Fi may be seen through private contributions made toward causes that touch their particular flavor of ethical consideration. It is not so important to them that they be liked, so much as it is for them to do the sensible thing according to their personal code.

When in a position of authority, the TeNi eccentric may implement decisions which are systemically sound but also somewhat insensitive to the impacts and inconveniences of those involved. For this subtype, logistical methodologies are so causally anticipated that they will not consider their decisions harsh but simply necessary. They may interpret the protest of others as laziness, judging their situations from their own psychological normality and expecting a similar level of systemization to what they would implement themselves. "If you don't like your situation, change it" may be the underlying sentiment, and they will expect others to make their own moves to tilt the game in their favor.

2. THE PHYSICIST

But the TeNi is not always so forward and overbearing. When this type develops a strong relationship with their introverted processes, particularly Fi, this talent for logistical deduction is given an entirely different domain to manifest. As we reviewed in the FiNe chapter, the methodologies of the Je processes are not confined simply to the relationship between elements of the *actual*. The Te process can apply its deduction in any environment or system of parameters, whether it be structured in the abstract realm of mathematics or in a business enterprise. So long as variables are interacting among themselves, Te's comparative thinking will aim to devise methodologies to describe and optimize the interaction of those variables. Likewise, Fe is capable of an identical but inverse operation, able to anticipate or deduce what would be the most adequate translation of emotional energies when given an entirely hypothetical scenario where the relationships between people are conceptually explained. This is because the Je process is fundamentally a mechanism of measuring the causal relationships between the elements in a given informational landscape, regardless of what form or avenue that information arrives in. As such, the TeNi's practical methodology can be applied in highly abstract domains as is the case in complex economics, engineering and even physics – yet it will always be applied systemically and relationally.

Perhaps the most iconic modern example of this subtype is Richard Feynman, who was, like TeSi Tolkien, a highly prolific and articulate lecturer. In a 1981 interview with BBC Horizon, we see Feynman speak about his lack of capacity to appreciate or focus on the arts, humanities or recreational interests in general due to a singleness of focus he held since childhood. He describes the literal, tactile learning style he absorbed from his father in childhood, and which avoided trivia-based knowledge for a better appreciation of realistic and applicable knowledge. We see in this the mark of Ni-Se's psychology, which is also strongly reflected in his eyes, often veering into manic scowling as he accentuates his points. His articulation is snippy, jittery, and uniform in its acceleration, accompanied also by Fi's tension, micro-snarling and a multitude of giddy giggles which are highly concentrated around fond memories of his father. Here we witness direct instances of Fi's internal resonance with the emotional register and strong personal feeling. Feynman's demeanor sporadically transitions from stern and collected to bashful and utterly uncoordinated as he is overtaken by his own emotional radiation, only to return to a stern posture a brief moment later. This demonstrates Feynman's healthy receptivity to his own Fi.

In an example that is far more limited, but from which we may hold sufficient information to speculate a typology, is Isaac Newton. First let us study the psychological dimension. Through his works, and in the many writings that exist about him, we see ample evidence of an eccentric and overbearing, albeit antisocial, character. He is described as unapologetic, concerned with his own unconventional direction of inquiry, bracing, cold and calculative. In a 1995 article for The Fountain Magazine, author J. Qureshi gives an elegant synopsis of Newton's personality in the following:

> "Newton did not marry. He did not, with a single brief exception, form any warm friendships. Though generous enough with his time and money when he had both to spare, he did not give with tenderness – either to relatives or acquaintances. He lived the extraordinarily narrow life of a dedicated auto-didact, hardly ever travelling outside London, Cambridge, Woolsthorpe. He was not given to lightness of manner, nor did he show any capacity for self-irony. When angered, he became unbalanced and, it must be said, vindictive and petty."

Figure 51

Newton had little interest for understanding social dynamics nor for his own societal standing, often neglecting to publicize his groundbreaking works – pursuing them primarily for his own knowledge and satisfaction. We see here perhaps one of the strongest examples of an aloof, dismissive Te psychology as well as a strongly unseelie Fi. We see the ethical function pushed into a crippled state as Te strives to be the singular motivation of the psyche.

Additionally, Newton's contribution to mathematics reveals a pattern of thought that strayed away from the strictly mechanistic philosophy of the times, pioneering many abstract terms such as *forces* and *laws*; overarching patterns of nature. In his later years we begin to see more distinct evidence of this pattern-seeking tendency in his esoteric pursuits of religion and alchemy; a philosophy that supposes all matter is created by the four primary elements of nature and can be transfigured into different substances by varied exposures to these four elements. It is my estimation that these pursuits reveal the operation of Ni in the physicist's mind. However, given the late manifestation of these motivations, we cannot presume that Ni represents his primary function. His overall rigidity of mind and unyielding personality, as well as disinterest in Se's sensational exploration, speaks to a psyche lead by Te with subordinate Ni-Se.

Yet, what is more remarkable still is what we find when we visually examine this renown figure. We see immediately that Newton's precise psychology is represented in his artistic portrayals. If we assume a proper artistic representation of his appearance, both paintings of Isaac Newton by Sir Godfrey Kneller (1689, 1702) demonstrate manic eyes – of the sort only seen in this type – and distinct Fi tension running vertically toward the nose. Lastly we see a *taut square* manifest by both depressor anguli oris muscles holding downward tension in the areas adjacent to the chin, adding a more square geometry to the jawline. These qualities also appear unchanged in Sir James Thornhill's painting of Newton in old age during 1712.

3. THE EXECUTIVE

When the TeNi learns how to better coordinate their social presentation and iron out the impact of their Te, they may excel in a variety of *leadership* positions. Rather than approaching teamwork and institutional success from the heavy perspective of the fervent eccentric, the executive comes to appreciate the need for a convergence of logic with ethics. We see this conversion in TeNi Kristen Hadeed, the founder of the Student Maid service and an advocate of strong women's involvement and leadership. Like the TeSi logistical ethicist, Hadeed utilizes her brand as a testament to the ability of all demographics, but especially those less represented, to be self-sufficient and thrive in their individual pursuits. The late TeNi Tim Russert, a former host and vice president of NBC News, also combined his executive ability with a pointed yet transparent ethical style. In order

COGNITIVE TYPE

to better reveal the views of each guest, Russert interrogated with many morally challenging questions, allowing his guests to put forward their functional solution to each proposed dilemma.

In more traditional positions, we find TeNi Ginni Rometty serving as the current CEO and president of *IBM* and TeNi John J. Legere as the CEO of *T-Mobile*. As one would expect, this subtype can also be found, in high concentrations, both in politics and economics.

For a complete account of this type's vultology, we can look at interviews of the following TeNi public figures:

Name	*Development*
Tom Hanks	Fervent Eccentric
Bill O'Reily	Fervent Eccentric
Richard Feynman	Physicist/Seelie
Selena Gomez	Balanced
Charlie Rose	Balanced
John J. Legere	Executive
Kristen Hadeed	Executive
Tim Russert	Balanced/Executive
Mary Helen Bowers	Sassy
Mila Kunis	Balanced

Figure 52

17

SiFe

MALEIN

The SiFe type emerges when the Si-Ne oscillation is primary and lead by Si, while supported by the Fe-Ti judgment oscillation. This type's eyes will be a prominent feature of their face, carrying a steady, yet *naïve* quality. The very rim of their eyelids will be opened wide, revealing the eyes clearly, while the area around their eyes remains casually settled – giving the eyes a distinctly blank or confused look. The eyebrow will be fixed in a partially corrugated state, with the center of the brow slightly elevated, giving a *concerned* appearance to their countenance.

While this is not the case for every SiFe, in many Si lead types the eyes will be largely concealed by the brow's corrugation and will sit deep within their ocular cavities, creating what I refer to as **Si Indented Sockets**, as seen in Figure 52. This effect, although physiognomic in appearance, is caused by years of muscular reinforcement of the brow due to continual Si Scowling and a deterioration of the obicularis oris muscle's vitality in its unused region immediately around the eyes. Varying degrees of this effect can be observed in all Si types, but it's seen most strongly in high Si types.

The SiFe's gaze will lead the direction of their head and body, drifting in rhythm with their worldview's activity as their eyes disengage to the sides in moments of recollection. Their body will carry a viscous, inertial quality, having a fluid yet heavy posture. But the SiFe will also have occasional breaks from this posture due to Ne's buoyant energy. Especially in moments of humor, they may engage in Ne parodies and temporarily emanate a silly and carefree energy, accompanied by strong eye-toggling. Their Fe will also add to this agreeable undertone by calibrating their interactions and moving the atmosphere toward a desired direction.

COGNITIVE TYPE

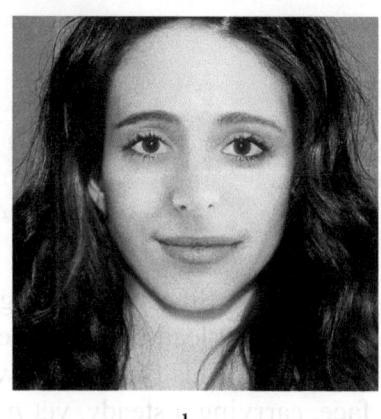

a.

b.

c.

d.

Figure 53

17. SiFe | Malein

Being a reactive type, the SiFe also has a primarily *resistant* attitude toward the world, although this resistance is not decisive or analytically justified to the self; it is viscerally initiated. While they may not view themselves as resistant, the natural flow of their psychology will avoid, whether consciously or unconsciously, that which is unfamiliar to their worldview. For an SiFe, their worldview largely defines their personal psychology and, as with all introverted functions, Si's worldview will be very specifically formed.

The SiFe worldview forms early in life, through the assimilation of Ne's unavoidable perceptions, coalescing into a predictable proxy of reality. Now, it is not the case that the SiFe will be exceptionally vivid or detailed in their perception of the past, as they use Ne's abstract information to construct their sense of reality. As Si itself cannot come outward to perceive, SiFe's depend on Ne for initial information. However, because Si is the lead process, the data collected by Ne undergoes far fewer cycles of abstraction before it consolidates into a dataset/anchor, as seen here in Figure 54. During this brief period of cycling, the data does divorce itself from the literal environment but only enough to take a conceptual form. What is then stored are a series of *static concepts* extracted from the environment. So while Si does not store literal data, as Se provides to Ni's worldview, the concepts it stores have a somewhat similar level of definitiveness as Se's sensory input.

Perhaps the best word we might use to describe Si's specific form of data organization is *trivia*. Let us consider, for example, the act of reading. In literature, we understand that the physical ink that lies on a paper holds no real importance – that is to say, the physical contours and geometry of the letters are not registered strongly in the mind. Instead, the ink brings concepts to mind and those concepts, through imagination, are what register as thought. It is this type of abstracted information, suspended in Ne's imagery, which Si registers. In the case of reading the process is easy to see, but Ne-Si operates similarly in all situations. A scenery or environment is observed much like written letters; objects are recognized as words, abstracted and

COGNITIVE TYPE

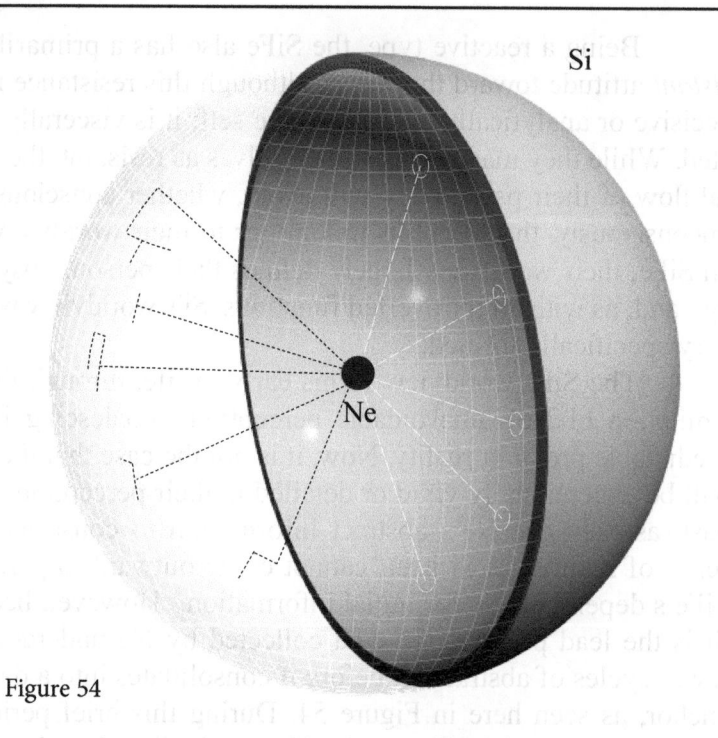

Figure 54

Here we see four black lines (Ne exploration) and four corresponding white lines (their newly formed Si anchors). At the tip of the Ne lines, we see only a 1 or 2 line branching, representing Ne's abstraction. The Ne lines congeal into Si anchors quickly with minimal abstraction compared to Figure 4.b in Chapter 2.

then stored in memory less for their nuanced qualities and more for their overall existence. This is why many Si types such as the TeSi and SiTe may be seen as walking encyclopedias, historians or trivia experts. Si types catalog far more concepts (such as words) than Se types, because Se types focus on the richness of the present and are less eager to compartmentalize the subtle gradients of reality. For Se-Ni types, reading is more commonly a mental simulation of an experience where the expected tactile results of the concepts within writing are what register in mind. What is remembered is the overall evocation and the way it altered or transformed Ni's tapestry by touching it.

17. SiFe | Malein

1. THE TRADITIONALIST

When Si is particularly heavy, this type's worldview will largely define their character, but because life experience can take so many forms and paths, the best way to define this subtype's external manifestation is as a *frozen instance* in time of whatever era they grew up in. The philosophies and normalities gained during those years will define their fundamental flow and this flow will be very slow to evolve. Now, it is not true, as many typologies have depicted, that the SiFe type is any more prone to desire external organization than any other type. Quite the opposite, the SiFe is not a judgment type, and when heavy in Si they will generally fret little over keenly controlling the external world (unless such is their specific storyline). They may only bother with systemization when it resonates personally with some nostalgic habit or personal ritual. Hence, the SiFe traditionalist is more of a **Nostalgic**. Like Ni, Si will simply feel a visceral resistance to erroneous information and a desire to exist as fully as possible with only the information already attained.

To give an example of how differently this can manifest, we might take an SiFe whose youth was spent during the 1960's cultural revolution (the Hippie movement) and another whose youth was spent in the Vietnam war. One may have learned that the key to being ethical and respectful is to value freedom, absence of judgment and acceptance. They may manifest as an entirely carefree soul, choosing much more to live a recreational and unobtrusive existence rather than to fret about the affairs of society or other people. The other may have learned that "life is a challenge", that perseverance is the most important virtue and that one must possess a stable character. Both of these individuals will be SiFe traditionalists and be unmoving in their storylines, although manifesting greatly different views.

This happens because Si's *trivia* based worldview will inescapably form by collecting the memetics of the present as seen by Ne. The tapestry of Si will be more tied to the memetic culture of its time – to the novelties and ideas available – than to extracted overarching patterns as happens for Ni. And when

Si strongly resists new input, what is left is only what already exists in the psyche, causing this past-based reinterpretation of present reality. In general, Si lead types will appear more traditional than Ni lead types although both equally resist new information. This is because Si lead types carry a worldview largely contingent on the more static, situational datasets present during their development. In contrast, in all ages Ni's contours can be quite distinct from its environmental upbringing or era although it may likewise stay ever fixated on its own early-formed views.

2. THE SILLY-SERIOUS

When Ne is especially heavy, the SiFe will be dual in expression, finding themselves in a pickle between the new and the known. They will thirst for fun and novelty but always feel a calling to something more familiar after the fun has been had, making them oscillate between bouts of silliness and seriousness. For the duration of the swing, the SiFe may rival an NeTi in buoyancy and liveliness. Their eyes will light up with Ne's spark, their demeanor will loosen and become more receptive to improvisation, making use of witty references, old puns, and all manner of humor. However, when looked at more closely, the silly-serious will be generating this momentum largely out of themselves rather than through a high level of realtime information absorption. Humor will come more from old gags, rehashing of parodies, and phrases/remarks they found novel in past occasions. Because of this, the SiFe silly-serious may overuse these gags when around familiar people extensively, sometimes beyond their natural expiration date.

At other times their expressions may be more immediately attuned to the moment and allow for more spontaneity. The SiFe will generally feel uneasy about giving Ne such free reign, especially considering the social awareness they receive through their Fe. But occasionally the SiFe will find a special channel, whether through a proxy persona, a prop or tool, which gives the expression a more anticipated, and thus appropriate, context. We see this in the world-renown ventriloquist SiFe Jeff Dunham, who uses his various puppet personalities to express humor which may otherwise be appalling if presented from a direct human voice. Through his various puppets he relays also a diversity of personal voices and perspectives, using his art as his vehicle of self-expression. Dunham, now in his fifties, took up ventriloquism at the age of eight and has dedicated his adult life to this trade – a craft which is neither traditionally practical nor financially meritorious – out of a personal love for the art. He remained largely unnoticed for most of his career until the internet age made his videos go viral. His story demonstrates the SiFe's occasional attachment to (and perpetuation of) early-felt nostalgic past-times independent of factors which might aim to depreciate their sentiment.

Another example of the silly-serious can be found in SiFe James Franco and his TV alias Dave Skylark. Like TeSi Stephen Colbert, Franco plays a secondary personality and through this character he is liberated from his own reputation and allowed to be as idiosyncratic as he'd like. Franco has also performed other parodies of himself through films such as *This is the End* (2013).

3. THE ETERNAL PARENT

The SiFe, when engaging their Fe more actively, will manifest what we might call a *parental* disposition. This disposition exists independent of the SiFe's literal possession of children. It is instead a natural result of Fe being a subordinate process to Si. As the Fe-Ti pair comprises this type's secondary oscillation, pursuits of Fe socialization always occur within the context of their worldview's overarching sense. What results is an Fe that manifests and articulates through a series of lessons and paradigms; the SiFe will counsel others on what has or hasn't worked for them in the past and make this an inherent part of their conversation. They may find themselves parenting not only those younger than them, but also their peers and perhaps even those far older. The tendency to parent is a rather timeless attribute of this type, making them the *eternal parent*.

But when the SiFe engages in this advisory role while having a deeply fixed Si worldview, they will open the door to heavy social friction. They may argue for a certain morality or rationality while not being fairly or equally receptive to the arguments of the other party. Unlike many judgment types, who will debate for the purpose of mutually reorienting their principles, the SiFe may debate only from the inertia of their existing perspective will little desire for a true modification of principles. When debating with this subtype, one might feel that the SiFe is a "broken record", repeating the same position while being wholly closed off to any significant feedback.

For a complete account of this type's vultology, we can look at interviews of the following SiFe public figures:

Name	*Development*
Adam Sandler	Traditionalist
Tom Hiddleton	Silly-Serious
James Franco	Parent/Silly-Serious
Vin Diesel	Eternal Parent
Usher	Standard
Jeff Dunham	Silly-Serious
Orlando Bloom	Silly-Serious
Kurt Schneider	Standard
Brad Pitt	Traditionalist
Kevin Costner	Traditionalist

Figure 55

NiFe

VALEIN

The NiFe type emerges when the Ni-Se oscillation is primary and lead by Ni, while supported by the Fe-Ti judgment oscillation. As with the SiFe, this type's eyes will be a prominent feature of their face, not because of their alertness or size but due to their consistency and subtle dominance. Always relaxed and steady, they will act as the unspoken chauffeur of their person and introduce at once the qualities of their entire demeanor. The upper eyelid will rest lightly over the top part of their eyes, while the area surrounding the eyes will possess a light pull from Se's influence, often elevating the outer edges of the brow. The eyes of the NiFe will carry a hypnotic quality, and this quality will be amplified by Fe's emotional allure and charisma. The warmth and assurance of Fe will find a source of confidence in Ni's steadiness, both psychologically and visually. The result is often a persona that feels parental; possessing great understanding and sense of mentorship. This is an effect I often refer to as *beta charm*, as it exists to varying degrees across all types with the Fe-Ti and Ni-Se oscillations. A natural level of persuasiveness emanates from these types which they can leverage in their interaction with others.

Their head will engage in a *drift-and-jut* rhythm seen in Pi lead types. First the eyes will drift to the sides, causing the neck to relax and the head to roll slightly towards the shoulders, then they will come forward again with a partially accentuated Fe head nod. Another signal comes into focus in this type from the secondary oscillation prioritizing Fe over Ti; the presence of **apple cheeks**. When Ti is prominent in the psyche, the region directly below the eyes flattens considerably due to a complete absence of tension. However, in types who prioritize Fe over Ti, this flat region is far smaller and the tone of the zygomaticus ma-

COGNITIVE TYPE

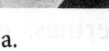

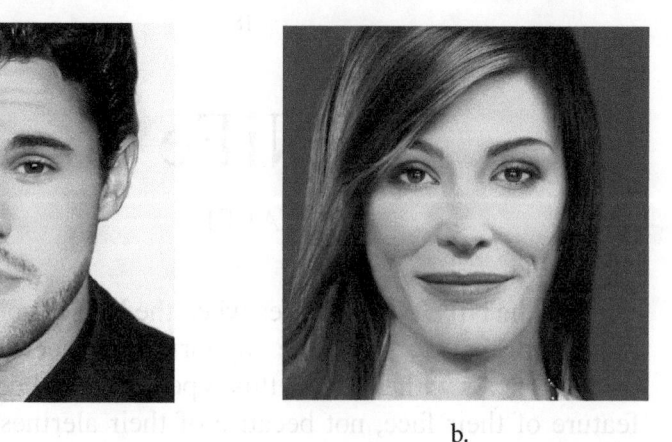

Figure 56

jor increases. As a result, when the NiFe smiles, their Fe smile will often cause a spherical bulge to form on the cheeks as seen in Figure 56.b. Like Te's *taut cheeks*, this signal is not always visible if the user has naturally low cheekbones, but will manifest if the cheekbones are average or strong. This signal is also differs fundamentally from Te's taut cheeks in the way that muscular tension forms the shape of the bulge. For the NiFe the bottom of the bulge is rounder, and this round bulge blends perfectly into the curtain effect of the zygomaticus major where the cheeks are pulled to the sides. In contrast, Te's taut cheeks are typically formed due to the horizontal splitting of the cheeks, giving the bulge a flat bottom edge. In Te types, heavier stretching will also occur, making for an overall less relaxed appearance below the bulge as well as all around the mouth.

1. THE GURU

The worldview of Ni, due to the manner in which it weaves together widescale associations between concepts, offers a paradigm that is rich, full and can in some form account for the causality behind the majority of life's events. This places the NiFe in a position of *teacher*, where the tapestry of Ni can be related to others through Fe's channel. But due to the level of extrapolation embedded within Ni's worldview, the NiFe guru will tend toward a surreal interpretation of reality, often including mystical elements in its delivery. This is different than the mysticism that may be found in a teacher or priest for an existing religion or belief system. In the NiFe guru, mysticism finds its raw origins, creating novel ways of interconnecting all elements of reality, particularly those that relate to life and the ethical principle. We see an example of an NiFe guru in Antero Alli, an astrologer, author of many books on the soul and consciousness, and founder of the ParaTheatrical workshop. In all NiFe's, the polar process Se plays a critical role in feeding experience into Ni in order to maximize its capacity for abstraction and in the case of Antero, paratheatre serves as that channel. Paratheatrical expression is a practice in sensory relaxation that eliminates the rigidity of the body, opening up the self to the visceral, primal and impressionistic through uncoordinated dance.

For Ni lead types, Se is often felt as the **gateway** into a special source of knowledge and a more direct connection to raw sensory experience is often given divine connotation. Here we understand why sensory experience is assigned the role of a *channel* in many esoteric belief systems. To an Ni lead type, novel insights ultimately emerge from Ni, not the sensory world directly, but the sensory becomes a necessary catalyst to their Ni's optimal functioning. What is felt as a gateway into some visceral source of enlightenment is Se's oscillation with the abstraction of their primary function. Yet an Ni lead type might only invite Se's input on its own terms. Sensory connection is not commonly sought through a chaotic influx of stimuli or an overwhelming pace as we find in a physical sport, but in the tranquility of meditation or a guided experience.

For this subtype, Ti is often used to give logical structure to vision; to quantify, often in some linguistic form, what is felt as a core truth. Here, language has the capacity to encapsulate the essence of a pattern felt axiomatically across their entire worldview. What may result is a poetic, proverbial form of Fe articulation that is simultaneously precise as well as general. And if technical metaphors prove insufficient to describe a phenomenon which they sense has more interwoven facets, a lexicon may be devised to define these subtleties. Slowly the NiFe guru may evolve a definition and interpretation of reality where the actual world is replaced entirely by the proxy of their worldview. And when it succeeds in accounting for all facets of life, even itself, the guru may feel as though they are living in a staged or fabricated drama; acting out their part in a larger, now decrypted, puzzle. But they remain, instead, immersed in their own paradigm and deeply disconnected from a very real world.

2. THE CONTENTIOUS VISIONARY

When the Fe function is pronounced in the NiFe, filled with moral concerns and directive agendas, what often results is *contention*. The position of Fe in this hierarchy creates a natural level of friction due to the posession of an impetus which their psychology cannot sufficiently manifest. On one hand, this type is reactive and most at peace in non-action, but on the other hand their ethical process gives them an urgency to leave this inaction to champion the cause of their vision if their vision perceives an injustice or irregularity in the world. Fe, being a far more yang process than Ni, will threaten to overpower Ni and burst out to proclaim the visions of Ni. Always, however, the agenda Fe will pedal will be one emerging from the Ni tapestry.

This frustration is further aggravated by the nearly untranslatable and cryptic element of their Ni. Attempts to convey Ni's vision can often lead to confusion or skepticism when Ni's ideas are felt as having an unquantifiable nature to other people. In extreme cases, the inability to properly communicate the importance of what they envision makes this subtype prone to consider others incompetent; unable to grasp something they feel is so clear. But Ni's tapestry is difficult to perfectly translate to others since it is not only subjectively formed but abstractly congealed. In contrast, the SiFe type does not carry such heavy internal friction between vision and expression. The reasoning for the matters which SiFe types may seek to address are at the very least more easily understood, if not obviously seen, by others. This is because the data which the SiFe type uses to come to a conclusion can be communicated through a series of static anchor points. They can more clearly delineate the necessity for a certain course of action. Add to this the endless levity and buoyancy of their Ne and it becomes far more uncommon for SiFe types to form lasting frictions of this sort. But for the NiFe, the *persistence effect* of the Ni-Se pairing makes ignoring this sort of friction very challenging. They may become the brewing poets or mavericks of society who proclaim the social failures of the establishment to all who will lend their ear.

3. THE GRANDFATHER

Still, not all NiFe are visionaries and gurus. A great deal of them can also be found in commonplace lifestyles. Especially if their Ni does not see a world that their own Fe has very strong ethical investment in fixing, the NiFe will, like many Pi types,

COGNITIVE TYPE

take a more **grandfatherly** role. They may become the soothing voice at the dinner table with many stories to tell or philosophies to discuss. We see examples of this subtype in Morgan Freeman, Garrison Keillor and Leonard Nimoy. There is an unrushed relaxation about them, as with the SiFe, that invites listening and communion. Garrison Keillor, a storyteller and long-time radio personality expressed the sentiment of this subtype in a 1991 UWTV interview, saying:

> "That's one thing that drew me to radio, is that you could take your time. You could talk and talk for a long time, and be invisible (...) without making eye contact. To talk to people without enduring their scrutiny – just to talk – seemed so wonderful; it still does. (...) Half the time it's not that great, but it's sociable. And they forgive you for it. You've done no harm."

The act of storytelling, for the NiFe, is a means by which experience, and thus life, is communicated and shared. And for a type who leads their psyche with their worldview, something fundamentally soulful exists about this form of socialization. To be allowed the opportunity to convey that broad tapestry and have its conveying be a bridge between people satisfies the impetus of Ni, Fe and the human heart. This subtype carries many similarities to the SiFe, who may also share this storyteller tendency. The NiFe may have a rather figurative way of relaying information, making use of graphical descriptions and prose.

4. THE COVERT ADDICT

In all their shades, NiFe will have a noted relationship with their Se, whether it's one of negligence – manifesting as staunch self-denial and conservativeness – or one of private indulgence in some guilty pleasure. In some cases the NiFe may be a highly sensitive person, avoiding strong stimulation for its capacity to interfere with the calm of their primary function, but in others their Se's experiences are happily invited. From the appreciation of landscapes, to the art of photography, people watching, yoga, martial arts and dance, Se will act as a point of relief from the monopolization of their primary process. Other NiFe may feel unable to connect meaningfully with the external or release the grip of their Ni without the need of some stimulant, leading at times to dependency. The NiFe may live a completely sensationally deprived life except for a single vice which they use in excess.

When this rebellious edge is combined with their potential for social charm, the iconic, silent "bad boy" is created. We find this aura in NiFe James Dean, as well as in NiFe Justin Bieber. There is an unhurried, casual air about them which makes them feel *unreachable* yet tantalizing due to their voice's taunting gentleness and warmth. But the vultology of both these men deserves a special note. Dean and Bieber will evidence a brow which rises toward the center, rather than the outer edges of the eyes, as is most typical of the SiFe. But as seen in Figure 56.a, a brow raised above the eyes, whether corrugated at the center or edges, will still confirm Ni if the eyes below retain a lowered eyelid as well as all other qualities belonging to the Ni-Se pairing. As we'll learn in Chapter 30, this is because the actual tension immediately around the eyes is a far more significant indicator of one's perceptive process than the precise shape of the brow, which is more subject to vary. While the SiFe carries a pair of open, naïve eyes embedded in Si's cavity, NiFe like Dean and Bieber will always carry a *sleepy* quality, characterized also by a *faraway* focus, an inertial energy and a strong lack of buoyancy. In both we witness a psychology directed toward a simplicity of interpretation and a visceral experience of events. Topics are explored not through divergence of ideas, but by a rather tentative estimation of how the present may unravel.

In another, somewhat more charismatic example of the addict we find NiFe Leonardo DiCaprio, whose many evasive and scheming acting roles personify a wide range of beta personalities. Although DiCaprio himself is never quite as covert and cunning in person as his cinema roles, the origin of these qualities, which he imbues in his characters, are present in his own distant, sensational and alluring persona.

COGNITIVE TYPE

For a complete account of this type's vultology, we can look at interviews of the following NiFe public figures:

Name	*Development*
Antero Alli	Guru
Ray Kurzweil	Guru
Garrison Keillor	Grandfather
Leonard Nimoy	Grandfather
Leonardo DiCaprio	Balanced
James Dean	Delinquent
Justin Bieber	Delinquent
Morgan Freeman	Grandfather
Larry King	Grandfather
Nicholas Hoult	Balanced

Figure 57

NeTi

MALEER

The NeTi type emerges when the Ne-Si oscillation is primary and lead by Ne, while supported by the Ti-Fe judgment oscillation. Having Pe as their energetic quadrant, the NeTi will have a natural level of excitation that will accompany them at all times. Even when they remain steady or composed, there will be bouyancy and quickness in their movements whenever they do shift their bodily trajectory. Unlike the TiNe, they will not struggle or strain so much to exert an emotional push, but instead accelerate into both gesticulation and fluidity far more seamlessly. Nonetheless, compared to the NeFi, they will still hold more of a technical, glitchy articulation style. The presence of Ti-Fe in this type will cause brief moments of momentum loss right before any judgment is delivered. In contrast, the NeFi will have a completely open channel between Ne and Te, with no stuttering or hesitation. Outside of situations in which meticulous articulation is necessary, the NeTi will have a loose, swaying posture as they're carried about by Ne's energetic undercurrent. Their eyes may carry a sparkle of wonder and appear childish or innocent.

Absent of any damaging life circumstances, the NeTi will express a natural level of optimism and show an ability to speculate roundabout ways of conceptualizing problems which appear to lack any direct solution given all available information. While these roundabout methods don't guarantee a solution each time, the NeTi's mental tenacity will succeed more often than many in resolving unknowns by exhausting even avenues with low probability of success. "Out of 50 guesses, at least 2 or 3 gotta hit the mark" is more or less the unvoiced mentality of this type. This hearkens back to Ne-Si's plurality of perception, as opposed to Ni-Se's linearity of vision. However, in situations

COGNITIVE TYPE

a.

b.

c.

d.

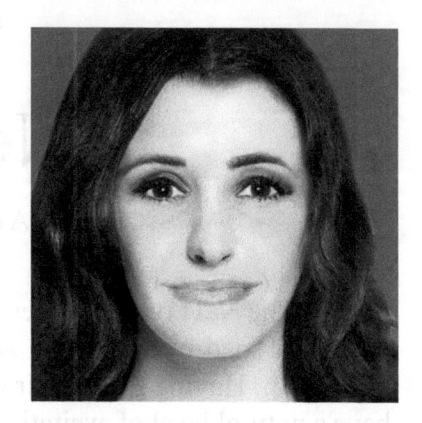

Figure 58

where more data is in fact available, an NeTi may err in relying excessively on the brainstorming process of Ne when a far more direct solution would come from historical study. After such intense energy expenditures, the NeTi may discover that they have reinvented the wheel – although this may be more amusing than upsetting to the NeTi, who deeply enjoys such speculation for its own sake.

Having Ti prioritized above Fe, this type is prone to have an absence of tension in the area immediately below the eyes. Their cheeks will generally remain flat until a smile from Fe struggles to overtake them, only to stop short of a complete consumption, as seen in Figure 58.c. Like the SeTi, the NeTi's use of Fe will be placid and supplementary. Fe is far more commonly used in emulation; as a tool of adaptation and communication. Rarely will an NeTi champion ethical causes with the same vigor as other judgment types. Instead it is Si which plays a more critical role in the NeTi's appearance as well as psychology. The NeTi's eyes will continually oscillate between Si's scowling and Ne's toggling, at times doing both simultaneously when data is created from abstracting or recalled from memory. Like the SiFe, the NeTi may become a trivia bank – a collector of concepts – but the tendency to collect data clusters will not be put to use in the creation of a rigid worldview, but to build a broader range of potential connections.

1. THE COMEDIAN

When their affinity for proxies – the outward dramatization of their Ne's associations and caricatures – overwhelms this type's expression, we come across the NeTi comedian. This subtype is vivid, filled with momentum and has a strong talent for realtime improvisation. Here the term 'comedian' does not refer to a profession, but instead to a personality that, by sheer virtue of its own energy, easily entertains itself and others. Yet, some NeTi do take to comedic performance as a profession, as seen in people like Jim Carrey, Tessa Violet and Tim Minchin. Jim Carrey is an exceptionally clear example of this subtype. Unlike many other actors, Carrey's filmography has been crafted around his own personality and spontaneous energy. Rather than accommodating his acting to a role, more often directors have presented roles to him which they believe fit his character, giving Carrey freedom to add his unscripted material where possible. These types are also usually memetic sponges; they will use the trivia-based caricatures and formations of Ne-Si to expand their scope of references and parodies. A single word, a sound, or scenario may spark a meme into thought and then the meme is immediately enacted, like the singing of the butterfly in *The Last Unicorn* (1982) film by Arthur Rankin Jr.

When seeking to identify this subtype visually, the NeTi shouldn't be identified by their proxies alone but, like all types, through all their facial signals as seen in an interview format. This is because the NeTi comedian will often use articulation itself is as a prop for performance. Facial expressions are also used as tools for comic delivery. This approach is typically different from the NiTe deadpan comedian or other Pi types who speak (rather than emulate) the experience.

2. THE DABBLING THEORIST

Untethered, abstract speculation is a favorite pastime for the NeTi, given the precedent renouncing nature of Ne and Ti's axiomatic rationalizations wich are divorced from the objective situation. Hypotheses, at varying levels of completion, may emerge from this type and continually evolve over time as problems and solutions are reimagined. Yet this subtype isn't without polar functions, which allows this pastime to become a more serious pursuit. We see an example of this subtype in NeTi Adam Savage from the TV series *MythBusters*. Another example we find is NeTi Lawrence Krauss, whose hyoptheses enter a more academic realm. Krauss' articulation style provides us with an excellent example of Ti's glitchiness in the NeTi. In a 2012 interview with Richard Dawkins at ASU, we see Krauss's energetic momentum causing incessant stuttering and repetition as Ne's diversity of thought is bottlenecked by Ti's meticulous speech. Thoughts intercept one another and sentences will veer off into tangents as more related datasets are identified in realtime.

In a fascinating portrayal of this subtype, NeTi Matthew Gray Gubler plays Dr. Spencer Reed in the TV series Criminal Minds. Dr.Reed is a self-kept, socially awkward genius who at first glance reminds us very much of the TiNe. But upon closer examination, despite the efforts of the NeTi actor to convey an introverted personality, Dr.Reed's energetic level still emanates Gubler's psychology in the acceleration of his jittery movements and fast-pace cross-contextualization, hearkening back to the dabbling theorist. Additionally, Dr.Reed is portrayed as being a savant with a capacity to read and perfectly archive any literature work into memory, and this once again speaks more strongly to the trivia-forming quality of Si-Ne. In a reflection of this, throughout the series, his greatest contributions to the criminal investigation unit are in providing relevant information and in brainstorming the probability of certain outcomes. More rarely does he display qualities of decisiveness, judgment and conclusive deliberation.

3. THE INTROVERTED EXTROVERT

In the years since C.G. Jung's initial conceptualization of the word *introversion*, it has come to take an exclusively behavioristic meaning in modern culture, defined by a reluctance to or dislike of social interaction, passivity, shyness, a preference for solitary activities and the like. But these attributes can likewise arise from a person's exposure to life and the many fears, hesitations, avoidance mechanisms and coping strategies that develop in an individual. At times these mechanisms will accompany us for such prolonged periods of life that we may be unable to distinguish them from what would otherwise be our natural selves. All sixteen types have the capacity to be introverts by this modern definition of the word, but cognitive type refers not to any influence of nurture, but to an unchanging aspect of our nature.

In this subtype's title, the word "introverted" refers to our modern behavioristic classification, while "extrovert" refers to a natively proactive psychology. This shade of NeTi will be disconnected from the tangible reality around him, satiating his psychology with purely abstract and conceptual dimensions of inquiry. Nobody he is close to would contend his introverted nature, and indeed, by any existing, semantic description of type, one would be obligated to consider him such. The dilemma we encounter here manifests directly from Ne's innate conflict between engagement with reality (for data absorption) and diversion toward associations. Because of this, both Ne lead types, of all extroverted types, will be most susceptible toward a disengagement from the objective world.

This is not a disengagement in the same manner as we see in introverted types, but rather, the thing which the Ne type is engaging with is simply non-physical; it is in the realm of ideas and fantasies extracted from some initial stimuli. Yet the gravitation toward that 'object' will be as engaging as it is for any extroverted type. This subtype may be described as always having their head in the clouds and as constantly off in their own little world. They may be avid gamers, readers of fantasy literature or fiction writers. But despite a psyche that manifests an introverted behavior, the NeTi will always be keenly engaged with some source of abstract stimulation; a habit which is far easier to sustain in our modern digital age. Restlessness and boredom will quickly set into these types when such avenues of engagement are suddenly unavailable.

Far less enegries will be channeled toward a reconciliation of logical dissonances, or the creation of a consistent and axiomatic philosophy. For the NeTi, experience remains the "propositum vitae", rather than the embodiment of some rational crystallization. The NeTi will instead possess an ever unraveling, ever changing and untethered perspective. We'll also find this difference in their body's energetic momentum. Their fluidity of mind will run parallel with a fluidity of body, a subtly energetic undercurrent, and a spritely curiosity in their eyes.

For a complete account of this type's vultology, we can look at interviews of the following NeTi public figures:

Name	Development
Matthew Gray Gubler	Comedian/Dabbler
Lawrence Krauss	Theorist
Jim Carrey	Comedian
Tessa Violet	Comedian
Tim Minchin	Introverted/Theorist
Adam Savage	Dabbler
Anne Hathaway	Balanced
Jung Eun-ji	Introverted
Elizabeth Olsen	Standard
Chuck "Movieguy" Thomas	Comedian

Figure 59

SeTi

VALEER

The SeTi type emerges when the Se-Ni oscillation is primary and lead by Se, while supported by the Ti-Fe judgment oscillation. As a Pe lead, the SeTi will have a natural level of bodily excitation, but while the energy of the NeTi can be described as *scattered*, the default energy of the SeTi is best described as *amped*. Se's intensity won't manifest as strong jitteriness but as a heightened concentration of *presence*. Their eyes will linger longer on an object, absorbing its subtleties and allowing it a certain level of control over the body. Despite this, the SeTi will still display a fair amount of eye-toggling compared to other Se-Ni types.

Their sharp eyes will steer the direction of their body and cause them to sway loosely, although moments of Ti momentum halting can cause temporary breaks in this fluidity. Due to having Se as a primary proces, the SeTi will seek to explore their environment vividly and realistically. Unlike the NeTi, this exploration will contain a more direct interface with the external world rather than interactions via proxies or constructs. Greater mobility then becomes a far more typical result, leading the SeTi to engage in more kinesthetic learning through fields – such as dance, music, sports or art – which can open up to them a myriad of experiences. The SeTi will not learn meaningfully about life through documentations (through guides or premade protocols) but instead by firsthand exposure and, in many cases, making the necessary mistakes involved for themselves. They will disprove assumptions about the impossibility of certain approaches through creative experimentation. Using their Ti-Fe oscillation, the SeTi will finely calibrate these experiences, often finding methods to optimize output and in the case of Fe, maximize social impact.

COGNITIVE TYPE

a.

b.

c.

d.

Figure 60

1. THE SENSATIONALIST

When Se is strong in this type and other functions suffer from lower development, the magnetic attraction to stimuli will be the overwhelming craving of the psyche. These types will be spirited, sensual and receptive to improvisation for the sake of maximizing their experiences. We see an iconic example of this type in SeTi Chris Tucker who plays James Carter in *The Rush Hour* (1998). As a flirt, partygoer and conversationalist, Carter eases his way into situations by using Fe tactics and charisma in conjunction with his Se energy. A very similar example of this subtype can be found in SeTi George Lopez as seen in the 2002 TV series by the same name. George plays a father and husband who is continually under the moral scrutiny of his wife, playing along with her ethics when convenient but continually disregarding them in secret for an indulgence in his opportunistic habits. This dynamic represents the sensationalist's lack of integration with their judgment pairing; using Fe in purely adaptive modalities rather than from a strongly formed ethical framework. Yet another excellent example of this subtype can be found in SeTi Tyrese Gibson who plays Roman Pearce in *2 Fast 2 Furious* (2003). These three characters share the quality of being strong risk-takers when the output appears highly promising, but quite flighty when a task appears too laborious or dangerous. The sensationalist is not indiscriminately daring; a level of Ni anticipation will always accompany them and inform them of the probability or difficulty of outcomes. For the sensationalist, difficulty is keenly avoided, as is any uncomfortable experience. This is because Se's natural amplification of the present will cause the SeTi to experience discomforts – such as heat, cold, fatigue or pain – as far greater mental distractions.

This subtype is seen most commonly in adolescent SeTi before a proper equilibrium has developed between perception and judgment. Visually, this type will have a highly steady gaze with amped eyes which will continually move in unison with the entire head. Their momentum will be high, verging on restless, and will not be heavily interrupted by Ti halting.

2. THE ANALYTICAL SENSATIONALIST

Over time, the introduction of Ti will refine this type's aesthetic sense and enhance their capacity to adapt to their environment and predict outcomes. The SeTi's heightened awareness of the environment, due to their cascade of nuanced impressions registering in real-time, finds a partial anchor in Ti. And once this nuanced panorama is given definition, it is given systemization through Fe. No longer is the SeTi navigating by a purely visceral sense, but by a premeditated methodology; giving rise to the analytical sensationalist. This subtype is an engineer of experiences, using judgment to help structure events towards an optimal output, rather than drifting between situations by a purely magnetic gravitation to the circumstances which carry the most stimuli. A craft is often assimilated, such as choreography, photography, breakdancing, rap, or standup to name but a few. In more introspective iterations, affinities may develop for sensational poetry/writing and psychoanalysis.

As these experiences are better quantified, we come across the second aspect of the analytical sensationalist: the formation of *stereotypes*. I use the term stereotype here in its constructive form, as a personal and intuitive process of statistical aggregation pertaining to human behavior. Using the worldview of Ni, formed from these numerous Se datasets, the SeTi will gradually develop an anecdotal map which reflects the patterns encountered in various situations and in people-groups. While this happens in all types to different degrees, I have found the SeTi to be among the most aware of these stereotypes and the nuances in persona that differentiate one classification from another. From this knowledge arises also a more keen coordination of emotional energies and understanding of social structures. The SeTi may become a social connoisseur, reading body language and appearance to discern the class, affiliation, habits and interests of people.

This subtype will be less intensely locked onto the environment, possessing a somewhat more casual posture which will alternate between fluid and stop-start articulation styles depending on the subject matter. Their eyes will lead their head but their gaze may disengage downward occasionally when more meticulous distinctions are being drawn between impressions.

3. THE ANTI-SAGE

In certain curious conditions, the SeTi will manifest as a rather anarchical psychological inversion of the NiFe guru; a type of *anti-sage*. This subtype is, like other high Ti users often are, opposed to the coordination of people through collaborative thinking and social protocols. The anti-sage will use an antagonistic Fe to shame the suppression of free expression. Such individuals may become champions of hedonistic philosophy and explore freely into all areas of life without regard for their prohibited status. This activity is far more than mere youthful rebellion, as the anti-sage may develop a sophisticated ideology and interpretation of life's meaning and human purpose which itself stands pivoted against more widely held norms.

The anti-sage sees Fe as directly pivoted against their own Se, and in their pursuit to dissipate this internal tension, their psychic drama seeps outward into their physical life as an opposition to tangible representations of that inner suppression. Unlike the SeFi, FiSe and NeFi, who at times share the sentiment of unbridled emotional and sensational liberty, the SeTi's possession of Fe obliges him to fight social protocols at their own game. We see an example of this subtype in SeTi Marshall Mathers, who played a counter-culture game at a national level through music in the early 2000's. In contrast to counter-culture Fi users such as Madonna, who embed their message self-righteously, while remaining reserved from their social appreciation or demonization, Fe's game is far more forward and rhetorical.

In a twist of irony, through this unconventional path, the anti-sage may resonate with people and gain an audience or following but may largely avoid this newfound responsibility and advocate non-dogmatic personal development. In more esoteric iterations, the anti-sage may more closely resemble the NiFe guru in their advocacy of spirituality, the transcendence of all constraints and the use of Se as a channel into their own Ni.

COGNITIVE TYPE

For a complete account of this type's vultology, we can look at interviews of the following SeTi public figures:

Name	*Development*
Chris Tucker	Sensationalist
George Lopez	Analytical Sensationalist
Tyrese Gibson	Sensationalist
Marshall Mathers	Anti-Sage
Jack Black	Sensationalist
Auburn Williams	Standard
Gabby Douglas	Standard
Ryan Sheckler	Standard
Paul Rodriguez	Standard
Shawn Phan	Analytical Sensationalist

Figure 61

TiNe

ALEMIN

The TiNe type emerges when the Ti-Fe oscillation is primary and lead by Ti, while supported by the Ne-Si perception oscillation. This type will be reserved in posture and deliberate in its motion. Stillness remains the default disposition of the body, while any outward expression is prompted by the temporary waves of Fe and the energy of Ne. Such expressions are quick to fade and return to the neutrality of Ti. Their face will contain an absence of tension in their cheeks, causing them to lie flat, especially in the area below the eyes. This flatness will also have a level of resistance to Fe's warm smile, containing it at times to the bottom half of the face and causing it to spread widely, as seen in Figure 62.d. The TiNe's articulation will be accompanied by a series of glitchy Fe pushes and meticulous puppeteer hands. More than in any other type, the TiNe is subject to heavy momentum halting and moments of technical articulation due to the stop-start nature of Ti-Fe.

For the TiNe, articulation is often a struggle to communicate the structure of a private framework, formed through the precision of Ti, but not always perfectly solidified into language. When the meaning of a sentence is felt to be imprecise, they may self-correct their grammar mid-sentence and stutter to convey the nuance felt within their compass as precisely as they can. As they process this self-correction, their eyes will disengage downward, wander or blink excessively while their body temporarily freezes then releases once the right word choice is found. When not engaged in a strained translation of ideas, the TiNe will be adaptable and receptive. Their eyes may casually scan their environment, drifting along with their thoughts without fixating heavily on objects. As with the NeTi, moments of heavy memory recall will prompt an Si scowl that contracts toward the

COGNITIVE TYPE

a.

b.

c.

d.

Figure 62

center while drooping toward the outer edges of the eyes.

1. THE MINIMALIST

When Ti is pronounced in this type, we come across the minimalist. This individual will be a ghost of a presence, exceedingly sparing in all energy expenditures and mostly quiet. When there is some engagement with the outside world it's through passivity; lukewarm smiles, soft gestures and brief conversations. Given their empty countenance and receding composure, one might believe the TiNe suffers from depression, but a closer inquiry will find them to be quite neutral and easygoing individuals. As is true for any type, existing so heavily in the primary function is deeply satisfying to the primeval psyche, however unbalanced, and this comfort is felt by the TiNe in dispassion. It's common for the minimalist to not take any efforts to compensate for their Ti's momentum halting using Fe animation. Instead, interfacing with the minimalist may lead to slow, semantic conversations that aim to sterilize a concept from a rather philosophical perspective.

More commonly, however, the TiNe minimalist will play the role of listener. They may let the other party fill the conversation with their own musings, while they reactively assess the commentary for internal, conceptual consistency. Their responses may be brief, passive, but selectively pointed at key areas of confusion or ambiguity. Often times if the TiNe doesn't understand the sequential cascade of principles behind a person's ideas, they will inquire meticulously and perhaps uncomfortably to the point of dissipating all flow within the interaction. At times this may flatline the conversation, especially as the TiNe may not offer any compensatory material, solutions or ideas after highlighting the conceptual challenges of the other person's thoughts. In this way the TiNe minimalist functions more as a diagnostic entity for others. As Ti by itself is not a creative process, deconstruction and negation are hallmarks of this subtype. Consequently, a rather absurdist philosophy can easily take hold of this subtype. An *absence of purpose* or truth is quickly felt underlying existence and this perspective will not be met, as in other types, with a proactive process which adds its own motivation.

2. THE ARMCHAIR PHILOSOPHER

When Ne has a moderate level of influence in this type, we find ourselves amidst a mind that enjoys generating and interconnecting ideas by the shape, so to speak, of their mental contours into purely linguistic objects. This subtype is the counterpart to the NeTi dabbling theorist. As with all Ne-Si types, concepts are seen as objects to mentally manipulate, and this subtype of TiNe takes the role of engineer for these concepts; building from them an elegant, crystalline structure – a *castle in the sky*. These theoretical architectures propose an explanation for a certain phenomenon of reality but always with a certain level of idealized detachment from the actual dynamics of the world. They may find an affinity for topics such as philosophy, psychology and linguistics where abstract rules can precisely organize information.

But the scrutiny and deconstruction of the minimalist transfers into this subtype as well, often causing these abstractions to dwindle into only a handful that the TiNe may feel certain about. Although linguistically airtight structures and aphorisms can be found in all Ti types with an introverted bent, the TiNe is not always the most prolific among them, given the heavy filtration of a primary Ti process. While many thoughts may be entertained, if the TiNe should succeed in generating any substantial works, it is only when their worldview has significantly evolved to provide a satisfying foundation of datasets from which to consistently extract the same logical deductions. This is not the case for other Ti users such as the NiFe, whose leading function is a worldview that Ti serves to help structure, while ultimately coming short of systemically archiving each of its impressions and insights. The Ti of the NiFe will serve to provide form to an expansive vision, while the TiNe carries no vision; there is only a relatively faint precedent from which principles might occasionally consolidate. As such, in practice, the TiNe armchair philosopher may live a relatively ordinary lifestyle, often times as a professor or artist with an inkling for fantastical patterns and transparent expressions. They may become the hermit which, although never venturing far into societal affairs, will be mild and generally approachable.

Having a healthy dose of Ne, this subtype will carry a soft but occasionally *quirky* composure. They will enter into tentative bouts of silliness which will parody some niche idea before they softly recede; deflating shyly as their composure returns and their energy neutralizes.

3. THE TECHNICAL SCHOLAR

Whenever heavy Si accompanies this type, forming only after decades of very gradual expansion, we find a TiNe whose understanding of a topic is exhaustive and highly nuanced. Unlike the SiFe, who naturally but incidentally accumulates data clusters, this subtype will be very particular in how each data cluster relates to all else – carrying the imprint of the compass process' individualistic formation. We find an example of this subtype in linguist and philosopher Noam Chomsky, whose view of American and world history is every bit as historical as that of any scholar but strikingly self-interpreted. The meaning of each event and the ethical-logical place each event falls within is under constant analysis by a dispassionate calibration scale.

We see in Chomsky's many works the imprint of Si-Ne's compartmentalized worldview, stitched together from a mountain of static events and sequences. This heavy use of Si is likewise reflected in Chomsky's appearance. His soft, naïve eyes toggle gently in his sockets, blinking excessively underneath the weight of Si's contracted scowl. Yet Chomsky's body is anything but fluid; carrying all the rigidity and deliberation of a judgment type, as well as the instantaneously receding energy of an introvert. In youth as well as old age, his articulation is clear and intentional but low in volume and quick to neutralize, indicating a heavy use of Ti. Psychologically, we find indications of Ti in his every analysis, which divorces the topic at hand from himself or anyone else and weighs the situation by logical principles, not by any function or utility. We see further evidence of Ti in his formation of grammatical "deep structures", which are a type of abstract scaffoldings for organizing linguistic information.

Chomsky not only presents to us an example of the TiNe scholar, but one with a classic relationship to his own Fe polarity. As is true with any polarity, Ti's relationship to Fe will be one of rivaling priorities where each is keenly aware of the other, but assertive of its own principles. Chomsky shows a dislike for emphasis in articulation, rhetoric or persuasion – as is well captured in the following quotes:

> "I know I'm always put off by people who are called good speakers, by those who can rouse an audience. That's just what you do not want. If you have the capacity to do it, you should suppress it."[1]

> "Rhetoric is the art, or science (whatever you call it) of persuading people by appealing to their emotions; undermining their capacity for independent thought and inquiry, for challenge, for invention, for creation. It's exactly the opposite of what it ought to be."[2]

For Chomsky, the alteration of another's opinions should arise from the encouragement of independent investigation, not through persuasion. To that end, rhetoric is altogether a hindrance which inflates the viability of otherwise less substantiated arguments by the charisma or authority that lies behind them.

But despite this common internal conviction, for the TiNe the question of Fe's expression is a challenging one. Should they decide not to partake in the social spectacle, they will run the risk of being overlooked or underestimated by their community. Having Fe as their primary means of execution and locomotion (Je), the absence of social engagement may lead to multiple life inhibitions and loss of opportunities. Consequently, many TiNe's may decide to utilize a placid form of Fe when necessary to help navigate their life, but their use of Fe may be felt

1: The Science of Language, pg.115, Noam Chomsky – 2012
2: Interview with Lawrence Krauss at ASU – March, 2015

as artificial; filled with pleasantries and overdone in positivity. Here, what is known about social protocols is enacted in its most iconic form and functions as a thin mask which the TiNe uses to interface faintly with others.

4. THE PSYCHOANALYST

The fourth and most well-rounded subtype comes into play when the TiNe properly exercises and develops his Fe polarity. The TiNe becomes a diagnostic entity in the realm of social dynamics, human nature and ethics. In this sense, the TiNe psychologist is the counterpart to the FiNe scientist. Rather than taking an affinity for the dynamics of Te, the TiNe takes an interest in the dynamics of their polar Fe process. For him, the social world does not become a direct channel for vibrant interaction and engagement, but a place of study through the emotional tracking that their Fe offers them as they remain detached in a speculative place. TiNe Alanis Morissette explores this dimension of humanity in her music, with all the vibrance and drama which is native to its expression. But outside the recording studio, Alanis evidences a philosophy of the heart that is dispassionately interpreted; spoken of from an abstracted, third person perspective even when the matter is about herself. To her, this emotional dimension is a gateway into another terrain - a needed release - but not somewhere that represents her native psychological resting place.

From a more academic angle, we again find a perfect example of this subtype in TiNe linguist Noam Chomsky who has authored many works analyzing human psychology, language, power structures and global politics. Among these works we find *The Responsibilities of Intellectuals* (1967), *Problems of Knowledge and Freedom* (1971) and *Language and Mind* (1968). A certain silent directivity accompanies this subtype, as ethical principles are stated with conviction and precision – albeit low volume. It remains the case that the TiNe will not champion causes as energetically as the FeNi visionary but instead act as a refined societal compass within their culture.

COGNITIVE TYPE

For a complete account of this type's vultology, we can look at interviews of the following TiNe public figures:

Name	Development
Amy Cuddy	Psychoanalyst
Alanis Morissette	Psychoanalyst
Noam Chomsky	Scholar/Psychoanalyst
Lynn Hoag	Scholar
Hayao Miyazaki	Psychoanalyst
Arin Cumley	Standard
Mark Kessell	Armchair/Artist
Michael DiMartino	Armchair/Artist
Damon Waynes Jr.	Standard
Ashley Olsen	Psychoanalyst

Figure 63

TiSe

ALEVIN

The TiSe type emerges when the Ti-Fe oscillation is primary and lead by Ti, while supported by the Se-Ni perception oscillation. This type will have a reserved and sparing presence, often receptive in form, but gently resolute. As a compass type, the TiSe will be technical and meticulous in speech, often leading to a pause in their body as they search for the most accurate phrasing of their thoughts. During these moments their face will neutralize all emotional energy as their eyes disengage downward for the duration of their search. Their hands may also stiffen, taking a spidery and delicate shape before releasing a small push of emotion with each point of emphasis.

Yet, despite these many pauses, the TiSe will remain well coordinated and timed to the social situation. The additional time invested in forming articulation will not insinuate that the TiSe is wholly at a loss for words. By contrast, the TiNe's speech, which is embedded with Ne's divergent energy and thought, will more often appear uncertain and hesitant when Ti's pauses are notable. Having Se as a supportive process, the TiSe's pursuit of clarity follows a more causal and implied trajectory. Especially when Ni is involved, Ti's deductive ability is given a general vector which it can use as a starting point and arrive at pointed logical conclusions using all known parameters and axioms.

The TiSe will aim to create precision in definitions and to understand the *quality* of things. While the SeTi may focus more on the experience and use Ti to identify and optimize that experience, the TiSe will identify the qualities of a thing by evaluating its overall conceptual reality. Differentiating traits will remain the primary focus of deduction, but conclusions will be arrived at by the use of Se's tangible information. In this way, the TiSe differs from the TiNe which will dabble with Ne's linguis-

COGNITIVE TYPE

a.

b.

c.

d.

Figure 64

tic objects and arrive at more semantically concise but detached conclusions. Here a more tangible quantification will replace the TiNe's habit of fantastical philosophizing.

1. THE TECHNICAL SPECIALIST

When the TiSe aims this precision toward a somatic practice, they may strive for *perfection* both in reception and overall sensation, often becoming highly invested in a field. Domains which contain sufficient interlocking variables to necessitate a special methodology and path to mastery will be especially attractive. Precision in technique will be applied where it can – whether it's in sketching, music composition, dance, martial arts or any other art form. As a result, a unique sense of aesthetic quickly develops in this type, due in part to Ti's tendency to search for logical alignment within existing data. Themes of symmetry and contrast may be noted in their work as subjective, logical differentiations and crystallizations are manifested in visual metaphor. Unlike the SiTe dabbler, who is also known for his interest in crafts, the "look and feel" of a thing will more sensitively guide the TiSe's process of creation. It will become more of an aesthetic and ergonomic creation than a nostalgic or novel piece.

If their Ti's focus is aimed instead at conceptual distinctions between the elements comprising an object, then they will become analysts and critics. TiSe Marques Brownlee, an online personality whose made a career by reviewing emerging technologies, aptly embodies the composition of this subtype. Marques will carefully evaluate the sensational experience of each product, focusing not only on its specs, visual presentation, fit, comfort, ease of use but also its overall feeling. He will analyze technology from the perspective of an expert as well as the expected end-user. There is always an understanding of the general population's tastes and concerns (Fe), making the TiSe's aesthetic partially shaped by, or at least sensitive to, a more societal resonance. This is in contrast to the aesthetic of the FiSe, which more often follows its own path of refinement. To the Ti+Se duality, the pinnacle of mastery becomes the point

COGNITIVE TYPE

at which the experience of a piece or product is honest, precise, simple and universal. There will be a general aspiration toward *elegant simplicity*; the convergence between functionality and minimalistic form. From a visual standpoint, we will see a moderate level of Se influencing this subtype. The eyes may remain steady and locked for long stretches of time, yet the body's energy will stay rigid, methodical and internally oriented.

2. THE ACE ATHLETE

In some TiSe, Se is more vividly and directly explored. However, being a judgment type, a level of premeditation will permeate their explorative process. If receptiveness toward exploration is decided, then it is pursued with keen intention. Consequently, the TiSe will often seek to *concentrate* their experience, aiming at times for sensory overwhelm or for its furthest pursuit. More than a few TiSe have taken to drag racing, extreme sports and combat sports. The daring, world-renown TiSe Tony Hawk fits appropriately into this category, but also the more methodical TiSe Tiger Woods. The TiSe's reserved composure might give the impression of a person unprepared for high stakes, but at other times they may unexpectedly outshine more established athletes with their execution. Yet despite these and other special cases, the ace athlete will not represent a major demographic in these physical activities and may just as quickly shrink out of the limelight and take to more sedentary interests.

Still, like all other high Pe types, the TiSe does have its own spontaneous and playful side which manifests when no specific agenda is in sight. Their sense of humor will be jesting, if a bit daring and rowdy. Some may use their special artistry in flashy ways to complement their social interactions and rapport. As with other Se types, their recreational exploration can become edgy, primal and visceral. And in some cases, if the TiSe's lead function is overshadowed by this recreation, their visceral indulgence can evolve into a habit.

3. THE POISED ACTOR

The TiSe, although not wholly tactless in social settings,

is rarely charismatic, warm or especially inviting. But when a deeper passion for human nature emerges, Fe and its dynamics begin to take a central interest. Humanity is understood primarily from the outer; from typical social responses and the sensitivities of their culture. As the question is eventually turned to their own place among the collective, the TiSe will gradually participate in the crafting of a social persona. And as with the persona-sensitive FeNi, the self will be used as the raw material to mold a character reflective of the agenda of their primary judgment oscillation. Still, for the TiSe, this persona will never remain a permanent fixture, but something which requires constant adjustment and emotional upkeep. It will remain instead an instrument that revolves around their specific values and ethics, aimed to give them agency in the outer world. The Fe-using TiSe, like the TiNe, plays the role of an *actor* in many social settings.

Christian Hudson, an emotional engineer and creator of "The Social Man" program, gives us a window into one TiSe's persona construction. Hudson delineates his methodology from the most subtle head tilt to the timing of eye contact, being as meticulous with his engineering of tactics and gestures as the TiSe is with any other interest. Ti's deductive scalpel is applied here to the subject of human dynamics, leveraging emotions and general instincts toward his personal goals. At other times a persona is crafted not with the intention of manipulating others but for presenting a poised appearance. We see this cool-headed character in many Japanese or Korean celebrities and also in the general East Asian demographic. The male idol group *SHINee*, which is comprised entirely of TiSe individuals and other compass types, exemplifies this emulation. A female group from Japan named *Perfume* holds a similar composition, defined by a rigid, respectful, polished yet classy character shared among all group members both on and off stage. While the SeTi and FeNi will proactively engage others with their charisma, the TiSe will play the "cool geek" persona and respond to the approaches of others with this poised presentation.

COGNITIVE TYPE

For a complete account of this type's vultology, we can look at interviews of the following TiSe public figures:

Name	*Development*
Christian Hudson	Poised Actor
Marques Brownlee	Technical Specialist
Norman Chan	Technical Specialist
Elon Musk	Technical Specialist
Tony Hawk	Ace Athlete
Yan S. Huang	Technical Specialist
Jason Reitman	Balanced
Choi Min-ho	Poised Actor
Kim Jong-hyun	Poised Actor
Topher Grace	Standard

Figure 65

23

FeSi

ALEMER

The FeSi type emerges when the Fe-Ti oscillation is primary and lead by Fe, while supported by the Si-Ne perception oscillation. As a Je type, the FeSi will demonstrate a natural aptitude for bodily coordination. Their gesticulation will be well delivered, on-beat and embedded with an emotional undercurrent that aims to extend their sentiment onto others. From an early age the FeSi will be keenly aware of the dynamics and economics by which the world of people operates. This awareness, in combination with their proactive disposition and engagement, brings into mind the question of how to manage oneself in the world and to the FeSi this becomes the central question of their psychology. They will exist in a constant relationship with the world of people – forming and orienting their own presentation, ethics and motivations toward a desired symbiosis with the environment or an alteration of it.

Being a judgment type, perception is not pursued for its own sake. What is gleaned from perception is primarily utilized toward a better understanding of interpersonal dynamics and the optimization of harmony. To that end, the FeSi uses the hypothetical speculations of their Ne and the static datasets from Si to form a concept of social arrangement that emerges from the present cultural context, but which also contains a degree of spontaneity and allowance for diversity. While the FeNi visionary may seek to uproot or reinvent a societal structure with an imagined Ni projection, the FeSi is rarely so inclined. They will seek instead to amend a culture by working with the existing structure and addressing particular areas of dysfunction or injustice. The FeSi will also be more receptive toward conflicting mindsets in people, often developing a habit of mentally simulating the experiences of others and running this proxy through

COGNITIVE TYPE

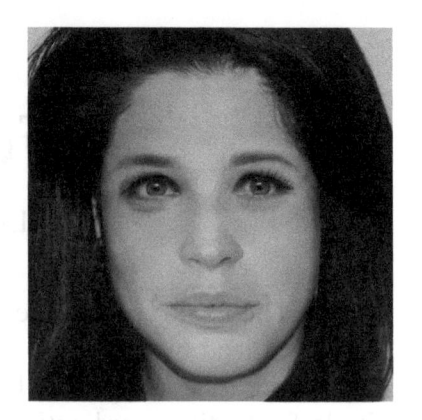

a.

b.

c.

d.

Figure 66

230

Fe to anticipate responses, affinities or sensitivities. This gives them a more democratic character overall, which they may use to act as a mediator between people.

1. THE MATRIARCH

If the FeSi is directive, which is a more typical manifestation for this type, they will act as a moral anchoring point; at once a fellow participant and chauffeur through the many trials and escapades of life. Unlike many low Fe users, who are more content with using Fe as a tool only for tactful social accommodation, the FeSi may decide to establish needed changes in the social protocol, overriding aspects of it with their own proposed structure. They often land in positions of authority, whether to a small family group or a large community, and become a mentor to those with more ambivalent views. The matriarch will, like the SiFe eternal parent, be inclined to utilize the paradigm of Si as a blueprint for real-world navigation and teaching. Especially when life experience has allowed for Si to flourish, the matriarch may take the position of *life coach*, using their many anecdotes to highlight realities about human nature and how to most effectively orient oneself to these realities. Many times the FeSi will rely on proverbs and truisms to explain their framework and social methodology. An inclination will exist in this type to consolidate experiences into simple and elegant precepts. This stems from the subordinate use of Ti, aimed at the organization of Fe and Si's expeditions into logically consistent factoids.

However, due to this shade's heavy reliance on personal narratives and the consolidation of limited experiences into wider principles, their understanding of people and society will risk being more memetic than realistic, and rely disproportionally on the customs of their home culture. In some cases the ego will not properly differentiate itself from the general cultural wisdom that surrounds them – and through Fe's conviction to align with others, these ideas will be set as a rather permanent life philosophy. In such cases the matriarch can appear dogmatic, echoing the environment around them while being unaware of the degree to which collective convictions have shaped their consciousness.

COGNITIVE TYPE

This subtype will also be prone to overextend the circumference of their ego onto those whom they nurture. In such cases, the matriarch may begin to manage the emotions of others, intruding into their life affairs and pressuring their perspectives and positions to align with their own. Attempts may be made to dictate to others what feelings they ought to possess. Here, the FeSi develops a *heavy* personality which on the one hand appears cordial and friendly, but on the other will continually transition from friend to director. But this endless oscillation between adaptive and directive Fe will, in time, erode away any meaningful connections. The FeSi must learn a level of disassociation from the external environment in order to regain a proper sense of self and to interact with others with an appreciation for their unique and different perspectives.

2. THE CHARISMATIC CHARMER

But a post as a mentor or director is not the only hand this type will play. In different manifestations, they may care little for the advisor role, focusing instead on recreation, liveliness and interaction. They will aim to be likeable, charming and malleable; using their energy to project a fun-loving and charismatic persona. Ne begins to play a more prominent role, adding its curiosity and childish momentum into the mix. This brings a quirky sense of humor to the FeSi's personality, and the charismatic charmer becomes a juxtaposition between an authority figure and a child. They will always retain an air of respect and control in their social situation, but simultaneously allow themselves to be spontaneous and silly to such an extent that any other person might loose social favor by it. We see this mixture in a variety of FeSi males who combine a polished and heavily masculine persona with a comical presentation. FeSi actor Terry Crews is one such composed, confident and sociable man who doubles as a humorist known for his many self-parodies; a duality that can also be found in his personal character. Here, Ne's humor is utilized as the bridge between personalities, while Fe works to tactfully convert Ne's initiative into a lighthearted social atmosphere. We see this again in FeSi Michael Strahan, a

23. FeSi | Alemer

former football athlete, current NFL analyst and co-host of *Live! With Kelly and Michael*. Strahan is no stranger to humor, often adding his own dose of parodies and goofy enactments to his broadcasts while tending to the emotional energies of the crowd and guests.

At times, however, the charmer's methodologies may be far too general. By relying so strongly on the antics of Ne and aiming to maximize their Fe's reach, they may appeal to the lowest common denominator in terms of human reactions and repartee. Like the SiFe silly-serious, the charmer runs the risk of overusing or oversimplifying certain concepts and presenting a cliché performance. This subtype will have the composure of a Je type, but their Fe pushes will have a somewhat gentler execution. Despite a reduced Je assertiveness, we will not see these Fe pushes glitch or strain in the same way as in the NeTi or TiNe, nor will there be a pronounced presence of Ti's momentum halting. The combination of Fe and Ne will create a rather easy flow in body and rhythm.

3. THE MARTYR

If the FeSi is an adaptive sort, doctrinal assertions will be rare and a relativistic philosophy may be adapted where everyone's life perspective is seen as right in its own way. An inviting aura is emitted where judgment and criticism are generally waived while diplomacy and collaboration become more pressing motivations. This FeSi will "meet people where they are" and once at this place, they will aim to use their judgment primarily to help troubleshoot potential discomforts and conflicts. This tendency exists in all Fe users but is most pronounced in the FeSi and SiFe types.

The adaptive FeSi may become so talented at this integration that insufficient focus is given to the self. If the emotional economy does not properly factor in their own necessary reciprocity, the needs of others will be a consuming obligation. All power is yielded to the objective realm of people while the subjective faculties are ignored, earning this subtype the title of **martyr**. The martyr will know the importance of all courtesies specific to their society and abide by them ritualistically without the creation of their own renditions. They will be the listening ear which never shies away from a troubled guest or request. Here the ego is invested in the approval of others and Fe's sense of competence becomes dependent on an external definition of success. If the FeSi is not careful, they may come to feel that their identity has been lost to the collective and grow resentful of the world they so wished to help foster. Paradoxically, this resentment may be felt even if it was the FeSi that was most keenly holding herself up to such an obligation. Such a psychology will certainly be haunted by an imminent actualization process, whereby the darker, directive and self-focused parts of their nature are to be integrated. The FeSi cannot sustain such an altruistic self-perception without suppressed content which will threaten to errupt in fits of anger due to a fragmented psyche.

4. THE PHILOSOPHICAL MORALIST

When this type's Ti is well developed, it will act as a *centering* apparatus; an avenue for arriving at a conceptual refinement of the reasoning behind their ethics. The dispassionate truths sensed about reality through Ti are used as a perspective from which Fe's motives become even more relevant and important. The following are just some examples of what these philosophies might look like:

> "All that we are will soon vanish, but the mark you leave behind will endure beyond your life. You will be remembered not for what you thought of yourself, but what others thought of you – for what you gave back to the world."

> "Life has no meaning; we give meaning to life. Our purpose is to create our own destiny."

> "We know from studies that a healthy baby, deprived of human touch and affection, will die. We are undoubtedly a social species. We depend on one another to survive."

Although there are no doubt many types which can manifest the same conclusions, the above statements demonstrate an orientation toward life, ethics and human nature which draws upon the dispassionate; from the inevitability of death, the arbitrariness of meaning or the scientifically verified. When such quotes arise from the FeSi, logic is used as a subordinate process while Fe's ethical paradigm is the ultimate beneficiary of these deductions.

The philosophical moralist will retain a greater level of cerebral detachment from the environment when compared to the FeNi academic. The mind will be turned to the theoretical and a greater tolerance will exist for contextually void speculation. As with the TiNe, more philosophical paths are navigated which invite a bird's eye view of a society's psychology. Still the aim of the FeSi's many musings will be oriented toward some eventual manifestation or practical change in lifestyle. The presence of Ti cannot fully abate the naturally forward and *invested* psychology of this type.

For a complete account of this type's vultology, we can look at interviews of the following FeSi public figures:

Name	*Development*
Harry Lennix	Patriarch
Jill Biden	Patriarch/Martyr
Terry Crews	Charismatic Charmer
Dwayne Johnson	Charismatic Charmer
Tom Cruise	Patriarch
Rachel McAdams	Balanced
Emma Watson	Balanced/Martyr
Michael Strahan	Charismatic Charmer
Eddie Murphy	Comedian
Jackie Chan	Comedian

Figure 67

24

FeNi

ALEVER

The FeNi type emerges when the Fe-Ti oscillation is primary and lead by Fe, while supported by the Ni-Se perception oscillation. The FeNi, perhaps more than any other type, will appear comfortable in their body. Their presence will elicit from their entire posture and they will wield their body as an extension of their psychology – projecting with it their emotion, attitude, deliberation and rhythm. For the FeNi, perhaps more than in the FeSi, this bodily familiarity will carry a weight and inertia. Their movements will be firm, accentuated, but not particularly spritely. Spontaneity is not common in this type, although never absent altogether. As an Fe lead type, their gestures will be well coordinated, exacting and embedded with an emotional undercurrent which can both apply social pressure as well as accommodate to it. More commonly, however, the FeNi will be directive. They will be the creator of their own ethical values and resulting protocols, often playing the role of social engineer; crafting themselves and the situation they're amidst to align with the communal order they see as rational.

The eyes of the FeNi will have a less eye-centric focus than those of the NiFe, but still be relatively steady when contrasted against the FeSi. In the NiFe, the eyes are heavily zoned out; the muscles around the eyes are peeled back in unison with few other resistances or internal muscular conflicts. For the FeNi, Ni manifests not in an absolutely hypnotic gaze, but typically in an Ni scowl formed by the collaboration, and the clashing, of all facial muscles surrounding the eyes, as seen in Figure 68.a. In this sense, the eyes of the FeNi are more reminiscent of the manic eyes of the TeNi, but the FeNi's eyes will tend toward a more heavily lowered eyelid as opposed to the TeNi which has more Se intensity in the mix.

COGNITIVE TYPE

a.

b.

c.

d.

Figure 68

In Figure "a" we see an FeNi with an Ni Scowl. Notice how the brow is raised off the eyes while, in some cases, the eyelids droop toward the outer edges. It's important to note that this is not indicative of Si; what constitutes Si's visual signature is a pair of wide eyes being weighed down by a heavy brow. It is the slanting of the brow over the eyes, not the eyelids, that defines Si's signal.

1. THE ALPHA VISIONARY

When the FeNi develops a particularly forward attitude, leading their social circle with charisma and energetic exchanges, we encounter an alpha male or female personality. This type will certainly use directive Fe, establishing a culture and atmosphere that will emanate unbroken across the group's circumference. Unlike the more diplomatic FeSi, this type will join their group together using linearity of *vision*. This linearity will result in less adaptability or receptiveness to feedback from those under their wing, as the FeNi may feel that the group's efforts must be carried out in a very specific way. As such, often this cultural atmosphere may weigh heavy on those involved in the form of pressure, obligation and guilt. We see this social dynamic accurately portrayed in just about every Hollywood role played by FeNi Denzel Washington, such as through John Quincy Archibald, Frank Lucas, Tobin Frost and Alonzo Harris. Denzel's roles, in which he always gifts his own FeNi nature, range from loving and fatherly to cunning and manipulative. In each role he is either holding unanimous social control or is striving to regain it while faced with many ethical decisions, as is often the case for the FeNi alpha visionary. One famous example of this personality can be found in the late FeNi Steve Jobs, who struggled to sensitively manage his coworkers, often asserting a stressful level of emotional control over them and prioritizing his vision above collective ethical principles. While this represents an extreme example of the alpha FeNi's shortcomings, it does not speak for every case of this subtype. The FeNi alpha visionary can equally represent balance, fairness, respect for human life, and necessary societal change as we see in FeNi Martin Luther King Jr.

The second facet that constitutes the FeNi alpha visionary is the marked influence of mysticism and esoteric views within their philosophies. In many ways, the alpha visionary is the aspiration and realization of the NiFe contentious visionary. We certainly see these influences in Jobs, who spent much time in Japan and under the teaching of Zen Buddhism, but perhaps more heavily in FeNi Bruce Lee. Lee presents us with a personality that is every bit as self-regulating as Jobs' (the FeNi holds themself first and foremost to the protocol which they outline for others), setting very high standards of efficiency, willpower and personal mastery. The self-regulation of Fe merges with the somatic focus of Se, giving rise to a *mind-over-body* approach. In this philosophy, the mental and physical converge both in the personal and cosmic sense. A purpose lies behind each action and these acts are woven together in their trajectory by Ni's concept of life's overall destiny. The alpha visionary uses their supportive Ni to cohesively intertwine ethical principles and navigate life through a consistent paradigm.

2. THE ORACLE

When the FeNi holds a more adaptive, yet still parental, Fe we come to see more emphasis given to emotional concerns. Vision becomes less important than considering the specific needs of those before them and the FeNi takes a more personal interest in people rather than following an overarching worldview which excludes such fine, anecdotal detail. Oprah Winfrey is perhaps the most iconic case of this FeNi in America, having spent her career working through and detangling the emotional challenges of many individuals and demographics. For over thirty years Oprah fulfilled, in a sense, the role of *oracle* for the entire nation. We see this subtype again in Iyanla Vanzant, whose style of counseling focuses on family challenges. In the oracle, the emotional register, its causalities and resolutions always take a front and center role, and in time the FeNi becomes well adept at understanding and managing the human condition.

A somewhat different variety of the oracle can be seen in advisors such as FeNi Drew Canole: a health coach and motivational speaker who touches on topics of self-esteem, positive thinking and the law of attraction. This variation of the oracle, much like the shaman of many ancient cultures, comes equipped with some special trade or practice and their spiritual counsel is interconnected with, and emerges from, their practice. There is often an emphasis on the connection between the psyche and physical wellbeing, allowing for alteration of one's attitude to catalyze bodily healing and vice versa.

3. THE PERSONA-SENSITIVE SENSATIONALIST

Like the SeTi sensationalist, the FeNi can also develop a strong affinity for gaming social interactions with the stride and swagger which defines a beta type's signature charm. As was mentioned of the alpha visionary, self-discipline can become a heightened concern for the FeNi and this concern extends to self-presentation; *persona*. Although all types will craft their persona to interface with the external, the most intense crafting is often done by types with a strong influence of Fe. The persona-sensitive FeNi is one such example that engineers a presence which can, according to the present culture, convey a desired affiliation or style. Unlike the indie artist FiSe, who crafts a persona from the internal resonance of Fi, it is important to the FeNi that their persona be understood by the general populace – obliging them to find creative yet contemporary means of building this personality. In this sense, the presona-sensitive FeNi's creation is engineered in part by them and in part by the inescapable stereotypes and associations available in their environment. There's a subtle air of conceit to this subtype as well as a sensual undertone. We encounter this subtype in the film *Hitch* (2005) where FeNi Will Smith plays Alex Hitchens, a date advisor who specializes in the art of engineering personas for other men. In this sense Hitchens is comparable to a more charismatic form of TiSe Christian Hudson. The social game is decrypted and one's presentation is controlled through a series of tactics. Indeed, this subtype is more similar to the TiSe analytical sensationalist than to the SeTi sensationalist. While the SeTi sensationalist is preoccupied with maximizing his visceral experience, the FeNi sensationalist is more concerned with sensitively maintaining their persona, making sure not to overdo it or risk being too forward or off-putting.

4. THE ACADEMIC ADVOCATE

It's not always the case that an FeNi decides to craft a

community around themselves or a persona to explore sensation. At times an academic direction is prioritized and knowledge is sought for its capacity to better inform them on the nature of man. We see this subtype in political commentators like Cenk Uygur who take an interest in psychology, political structures and the way they build and collapse world powers. In this sense, the FeNi academic's pursuits are not without an underlying ethical agenda. We find this to be the case even in more dispassionate fields of study such as math and physics, where our understanding of the natural world is related back to the human element. Astrophysicist Neil DeGrasse Tyson is perhaps the most iconic modern example of this subtype of FeNi. As a science communicator, he relays a strong appreciation for nature and highlights the capacity for a prioritiy on education to enrich our society. Derek Muller likewise exemplifies this iteration of FeNi – broadening public awareness of science by presenting counter-intuitive ideas to mainstream audiences in a personable fashion. These types will hold their ethical-logical pair in equilibrium, understanding the duality of the primary oscillation.

For a complete account of this type's vultology, we can look at interviews of the following FeNi public figures:

Name	*Development*
Kazimierz Dąbrowski	Mystic/Oracle/Academic
Mandy Patinkin	Mystic/Academic
Denzel Washington	Alpha Visionary
Neil DeGrasse Tyson	Academic
Oprah Winfrey	Oracle
Patrick Stewart	Academic
Drew Canole	Oracle
Derek Muller	Academic
Cenk Uygur	Academic
Iyanla Vanzant	Oracle

Figure 69

25

SiTe

MEDAIN

The SiTe type emerges when the Si-Ne oscillation is primary and lead by Si, while supported by the Te-Fi judgment oscillation. This type, like the SiFe, will possess a prominent set of eyes which retain a steady, if somewhat confused, appearance. Their eyes will stay open wide while the area surrounding them is relaxed. The brow will be slightly elevated above the center of the eyes while the outer edges remain slightly lowered. The bottom half of the SiTe's face will be largely disconnected from the eyes, containing their Fi's many expressions and snarls below the nose in most situations.

The SiTe's body will flow rather casually, not straining too terribly toward any specific presentation or accentuation. Their posture will be inertial, yet not altogether heavy or dense. Of all the types, the SiTe's general composure will come closest to a middle ground or average. Their animation is not especially distinguished or dramatic, nor is it so reserved that it calls attention by virtue of its withdrawal. This will also be true of the SiTe's psychology, which takes a *moderate* orientation to life. As events and situations are encountered, the SiTe will piece together a steady understanding of the world in all of its shades of grey. Rather than aiming to find fixed truths in this array of data, the SiTe will understand that the constitution of life is a conglomeration of many variables and datasets. They will seek to always have at least a little bit of know-how about each scenario, while ultimately understanding their worldview is incomplete.

Unlike the TeSi, the SiTe will not wield Te so brashly, having instead a more introverted and heady execution. And while the TeSi and NeFi's eccentric tendencies often lead to social misunderstanding, the SiTe's nerdiness is of a quieter flavor.

COGNITIVE TYPE

a.

b.

c.

d.

Figure 70

They may playfully immerse themselves within certain domains of knowledge, preferring those with rich, conceptual or fantastical libraries to gather from. Yet they will always appear capable of returning to a more grounded physical world. The prioritization of Si over Ne gives the SiTe's data a more static, albeit memetic form.

1. THE ENCYCLOPEDIA

This memetic tendency translates to an aptitude for passive data assimilation. While any type can nurture a large archive of information, the SiTe will assimilate life events, both trivial and important, more organically than most. An iconic example of this quality is found in SiTe Ken Jennings, who holds the record for the longest winning streak on the U.S.'s *Jeopardy!* game show. Ken describes his capacity for enormous memory recall as an automatic process, one which populates seamlessly from his every day exposures. In a 2012 interview with Adam Curry, Ken said about his ability:

> There is something a little bit freakish about it. Y'know, I was at the age of like 6 or 7 years old; I read world atlases for pleasure, instead of reading Hardy Boys or whatever a normal kid would be reading. I just had always loved maps, something maybe hardwired in me from birth.

Hardwired indeed. Ken has also published a book titled *Maphead: Charting the Wide, Weird World of Geography Wonks* (2011) which gives us a brilliant narrative into the mind of this off-beat subtype. From his enormous stack of childhood boxes stored at his parent's house, to his attachment to familiar places and his eccentric love of geography, Ken paints a picture of a carefree and curious Si-Ne duality, as lead by Si but also quite affected by Ne's exploration. The interests of this subtype can vary greatly from person to person, but in each field of interest, datasets are easily stored and recalled when the occasion presents itself. Naturally, this leads many SiTe's into the habit of *documentation*, as they quickly become archives with much to say about fields that have not been properly quantified.

2. THE LAWYER-POLITICIAN

The SiTe's trivia/language oriented approach to perception and recollection, when supported by Te's mechanistic relation to the outer world creates a psychology quick to grasp the nuances of existing bureaucracies and their legal interrelations. Given their appreciation for layered contexts, the mechanics of these policies are seen more clearly to the SiTe lawyer than many types. The creative navigation of such policies, in order to create business enterprises, then becomes a common pursuit. Not surprisingly, we see a strong representation of SiTe in law, politics and political media. In the United States, we discover this iteration in George W. Bush, Scott Walker, Mitt Romney, Sean Hannity and in a wide variety of other high profile positions. However, when the SiTe takes to such a public position, they will confront the problem of properly conducting an outward persona. The SiTe is not exceptionally equiped for this task, often resulting in a *falseness* accompanying their composure. They may smile widely from ear to ear and give cordial signals through voluntary effort, but their articulation will continue to demonstrate micro-snarling, asymmetrical expressions and a rhetoric lacking any cohesive emotional persuasion.

When in less public positions, we might find this SiTe subtype in real estate, clerical jobs or any variety of occupations which require the management of policies. They are rarely wholly unsuccessful at world affairs, although the world of human relationships may remain a more elusive domain. As with other Te users, when Fi is not properly calibrated into the psyche, the SiTe may lack a sensitive means of emotional implementation, often leading to roundabout, quirky or abrupt displays of affection. The young SiTe may, in the absence of a polished means of delivery, dress their affection in a nonchalant form. At other times they'll demonstrate their regard for others in tangible ways by quietly crafting their environment and routine around them. But if their unique form of expressivity is understood by those they care for, the SiTe can create and nurture lifetime friendships.

25. SiTe | Medain

3. THE PRACTICAL DABBLER

The SiTe is not without a quirky side which emerges from their polar Ne and dictates what subjects they choose to tinker with. This type will take a somewhat more practical approach to dabbling than the NeFi, who can at times confine their musings to the realm of imaginations. The practical dabbler's explorations more commonly manifest through the careful hand of craftsmanship. I've often discovered this subtype happily immersed in some nostalgic art; the hand sculpting of figurines from a favorite franchise, the collection of certain rare artifacts or the renovation of older vehicles. But at other times they may take to more scientific tinkering through chemistry or physics. We see an example of this subtype in SiTe Jamie Hyneman who, along with the more spontaneous NeTi Adam Savage, co-hosted the TV series *MythBusters* since 2003. In the show's online portal *Tested* we are introduced to their workshop where Hyneman and Savage hand craft many stage props as well as personal artifacts. Hyneman's creations range from high-pressure air guns and mechanical racing spiders to several home improvement projects. Receptiveness will exist in this type for novel compounding of existing components or technologies.

Another example of the dabbler is SiTe Scott Adams, the cartoonist behind the *Dilbert* comics and author of *How to Fail at Almost Everything and Still Win Big* (2013). In his book, Adams makes note of over 30 business enterprises he's tried and failed at, ranging from grocery home delivery services and web applications to restaurants and a variety of unfeasible inventions. Adams' philosophy, however, is one that believes every success is a failure in progress, and that achievement is better looked at as an evolution rather than an end goal. As each failure leaves behind some general knowledge or skill of its respective trade, one emerges from the failure more enriched and with a wider skillset to tackle future projects. Here we see an attitude where Si values the trajectories of Ne for their eventual contributions to a broader Si worldview. Adams relies on his Si's ever growing arsenal of experiences to achieve success, using Ne's prolific optimism as the fuel. Ne's improbable escapades are not considered a waste of energy but a learning experience. This is a great perspective to have toward one's Si-Ne oscillation pair. In a talk at the 2015 NSDA Symposium, Adams said of himself:

> You have to know my personality a little bit. When I reach a concrete wall, if I need to get on the other side of the wall.. I just start chewing. I don't care how long it takes, right? If I need to get on the other side of the wall, I'm gonna chew through...

This is often echoed in Si's more patient approach to the inventions of Ne. The SiTe may share all the same interests and aspirations as the NeFi but have the sense of pacing to give them some more cohesive manifestation. An aged and time-tested sense of limits will be used to tone the edge off of Ne's ideas and a more conservative methodology, often favoring simplicity, will be selected as the vehicle.

4. THE WITTY JESTER

But Ne doesn't just manifest through personal projects. The SiTe will also use Ne for self-expression and parodies in a similar way to the SiFe, but their expressions will be much more sly, indirect and understated. Rather than going straight for the punch line or aiming for a mutual laugh, their witticisms may be more dry and highbrow. This is due to the way Te's humor capitalizes more on the absurdity of certain situations or potentialities, while stating these conclusions in a factual manner. We find one such SiTe in Craig Kilborn, a comedian and former host of *The Daily Show*. As with Kilborn, the jester may combine their logistical parodying with cultural references to create unexpected juxtapositions; the erroneous combination of concrete elements or qualities.

We quickly discover a much more active and engaging personality in this shade. As one would expect, due to this type's private emotional world which is governed by Fi, they will often seek to connect with people primarily through their Ne-Te duality. Friendships may often revolve around banter and a never ending game of clever association. But despite this amplification of Ne, when we encounter this SiTe visually, Ne will not overpower the body with momentum, giving very little of its spontaneity and alertness. The SiTe's posture will instead remain every bit as casual and grounded, but their psychology will all the same go adrift in multiple directions.

For a complete account of this type's vultology, we can look at interviews of the following SiTe public figures:

Name	*Development*
Craig Kilborn	Jester
Ken Jennings	Encyclopedia
Scott Adams	Practical Dabbler
Mitt Romney	Lawyer/Politician
George W. Bush	Lawyer/Politician
Scott Walker	Lawyer/Politician
Jamie Hyneman	Practical Dabbler
Matthew Lewis	Standard
Steve Carell	Jester
Mary Landrieu	Lawyer/Politician

Figure 71

NiTe

VEDAIN

The NiTe type emerges when the Ni-Se oscillation is primary and lead by Ni, while supported by the Te-Fi judgment oscillation. NiTe have among the most consistent appearances, varying little in their animation or emotional expressions. Their steady, Ni eyes will retain a permanent position on their face, not being interrupted by their Fi's snarling smiles. We will see a dynamic division in the face between the area above the nose and below it, with the area below conveying expressions in a contained perimeter as seen in Figure 72.d. While the eyes of the NiFe have a more hypnotic and alluring quality, the eyes of the NiTe carry a more unapproachable and often intimidating gaze, earning this signal its fame as the NiTe *death stare*.

Moreso than the TeNi, this type will tend toward a nasal and monotone voice, due to a lack of gesticulation and rhetoric, which more heavily accompany the TeNi. The NiTe, by contrast, will often speak in a matter-of-fact voice without any adamant investment; conveying instead a personal opinion, experience or logistical observation of the present. When Fi is involved, these personal opinions can be shared with pointedness reminiscent of the FiSe. But due to the NiTe's nature as a perception type who is not heavily motivated toward fixed and crystalline conclusions, these subordinate Fi judgments are not always seen through to the end. They may seep out occasionally but not be given enough time or thought to congeal into arguments. As such the NiTe may dismiss their own stirrings after the moment has passed, causing them to appear passive aggressive to others.

Despite this sometimes aloof composure, the NiTe is no more ill-willed than any other type. They are often quick to channel their energies into causes they believe in, and can be quite effective in executing on those beliefs. These beliefs will,

COGNITIVE TYPE

a.

b.

c.

d.

Figure 72

26. NiTe | Vedain

as in the FiSe, have a selectivity to them and not shy away from the unconventional if it can better represent their alignment in matters of life-principles.

1. THE DEADPAN

In cases where Ni and Te are heavily favored, and a disconnect exists between function polarities, a stoic character will accompany the NiTe. In this subtype, holding the Te process under the wing of the worldview process causes, to some degree, a casual dismissal of new information. Things which don't appear to align with their existing sense of predictability automatically fall on the wrong side of Te's judgment blade. An aura of suspicion surrounds this subtype, as the privacy of Ni guides their perspective along very particular trajectories. They may earn a reputation as naysayers and pessimists; channeling very little energy toward the pursuit of experimental directions which they view as unpromising.

When personally engaging with this subtype (especially when the other party possesses Fe) social signals may be ignored by the NiTe; they will often yield surprisingly direct and honest responses. Indeed, the deadpan can relay information about themselves or their experiences which may be shock-worthy, but with an incredibly calm composure. The extent of this honest and unfiltered dialogue will, of course, be subject to the level of trust that exists between the two parties. Unlike the TiNe minimalist, who also does not participate in the dance of social protocols, the NiTe won't flatten conversations so easily; being able to respond quickly and flow uninterrupted from one topic to the next. Their voice may be low-key but cascade as a series of brief comments. This speech will be accompanied by small, snippy head shakes, shoulder shrugs as well as light body swaying. Actress and comedian Aubrey Plaza is one such example of the NiTe deadpan who has formed a career in large part due to this iconic stoicism and sarcasm. Her many roles, while certainly exaggerating this facet of personality, provide some window into the reactions and attitudes which accompany this subtype. A similar deadpan sarcasm is depicted in the fictional characer

Daria from the 1997 TV series by the same name, who enacts a simplified representation of the deadpan. In actuality, the deadpan's character is rich with private emotion, unique quirks and atypical perspectives, even though their stoicism may occupy the largest role in their persona.

2. THE POLITICAL CRITIC

The thick skin of the deadpan subtype does not lend itself to the sensitivity of Fi, remaining largely unfazed by disturbances or stressors, but when Fi is developed in the NiTe, new concerns arise from the desire for fairness and justice. These concerns often remain hidden behind Te's stern composure and can exist unnoticed until the NiTe suddenly responds to a comment in a way that reveals a pointed internal opinion. But when a more active consideration for Fi is engaged, the NiTe may go out of their way to articulate these injustices, taking to politics or other public platforms. We see this pattern manifest in NiTe Zinnia Jones; an outspoken vlogger who addresses the misconceptions and prejudices existing toward atheism, feminism and transgenderism. Being herself a transgender, she speaks frankly about the religious condemnation, social discrimination and phobias often directed against the LGBT community. These comments are given from an unapologetic composure as her face remains ever in line with her steady, unchanging gaze. The young NiTe Hillary Clinton, before decades in demanding political roles had prompted excessive Je reliance, demonstrated this subtype in a less confrontational tone. In Hillary's case, women's rights and women's equality have been the prevailing themes of her activism. In recent years, she has taken on a more *managerial* shade quite reminiscent of the TeNi executive. Her gesticulation is exceptionally polished, yet despite this level of modulation, her eyes and the facial division they instigate remains steadfast.

3. THE SARCASTIC JESTER

A lighter and more casual composure appears when Se is well favored and the NiTe enjoys more loose and friendly conversation. Like many other high Te users, the NiTe's flavor of friendly interaction will be indirect; showing affinity without losing their individualistic composure or resorting to seelie Fi energy. They may be playful but sarcastically so, interacting with teasing and joking; dishing out snarky comments and shrugging off the same. They will combine Te humor with Se real-time observation, giving their commentary a immediately-oriented tone. Often their remarks will relate to the quality of things around them and they will judge them offhandedly by their level of utility, convenience or inconvenience. For this type, the stimulation and amusement of Se may also derive from probing sensitivities, riling people up and being argumentative. In some the thrill of Se can go as far as to give the NiTe a daring, sensationalist edge.

This subtype's body will carry more momentum, body swaying and energy than other shades. Their articulation will be witty and brief, delivering individual packets of speech in rapid succession. Indeed, the NiTe sarcastic can be quite talkative and involved in the scene. However, the sarcastic will not inherit any of Se's amplitude or intensity. While their commentary becomes more immediately focused, they will not experience an augmentation of *presence* or feel heavily pulled to connect to the environment. Their eyes will retain all the qualities of Ni, although they will toggle more freely and frequently.

3. THE PRACTICAL MYSTIC

As we discovered from the works of Isaac Newton, the combination of Ni and Te lends itself at times to the pursuit of a connection between the mystical and the empirical. Compared to the NiFe guru, the NiTe mystic will be somewhat less prone to turn his attention toward the experiential and subjective (via meditation and introspection) and will seek more thoroughly to relate elements of reality in some physically significant way. The alchemy of Newton is matched, in this sense, by the numerology of NiTe Wolfgang Pauli. An acclaimed physicist and colleague to Neils Bohr and Werner Heisenberg, Pauli also appreciated the more archaic origins of his field. He pursued internal suspicions

---

1: Deciphering the Cosmic Number, Arthur I. Miller – 2009

about the significance of whole numbers such as three and four – a topic in which he and NiFe Carl Jung collaborated – and sought to find confirmation for his belief that the number 137 held deep cosmic relevance[1]. Nevertheless Pauli remained the more steely and critical of the two, as their relationship traveled through quantum physics, the I Ching, ESP, astrology, alchemy, synchronicity, dream interpretation, archetypal psychology and many such topics. We see in their relationship an elegant example of Ni at work – of the journey towards the quantification of its impressions by both judgment oscillations. It is not uncommon to see this subtype of NiTe preoccupied with the unknowable or at times holding superstitions – perhaps even unbeknown to themselves – about how the world functions which carry some logistical grounding but reveal themselves to be rather farfetched. This abstract detachment from the more concretely causal is different from the abstractions we see in the NeTi or NeFi, whose viewpoints arise more from an active pursuit of alternative explanations than from unsolicited feelings of inevitability. It is, to the NiTe mystic, a sense felt as a necessity.

For a complete account of this type's vultology, we can look at interviews of the following NiTe public figures:

Name	*Development*
Clark Duke	Standard
Juan Manuel Rivero	Political Critic
Joseph Marquez	Sarcasic Jester
Stella Duffy	Developed Te
Zinnia Jones	Political Critic
Wolfgang Pauli	Practical Mystic
Aubrey Plaza	Deadpan/Jester
Brian Clough	Standard
Hillary Clinton	Political Critic/Executive
Luke Russert	Balanced

Figure 73

27

NeFi

MEDAER

The NeFi type emerges when the Ne-Si oscillation is primary and lead by Ne, while supported by the Fi-Te judgment oscillation. Due to this type's prioritization of both Ne and Fi, giving birth to a duo of off-beat processes that seek their own unconventional interpretations of meanings and reality – the NeFi can manifest a very diverse range of interests, specialties and lifepaths. There's no position that other types occupy where an NeFi cannot also be found. Indeed, the search for one's occupation may be a vexing dilemma for this type, often involving several shifts in career trajectory before a stable balance is achieved. The NeFi, chiefly among Ne types, faces the challenge of giving structure to an unsorted array of imaginations. Having Fi rather than Ti as a supportive process, the monitoring and calibration of Ne is accomplished through a strong empathic resonance in values, rather than the purely logical dissipation of extraneous or contradictory data. Thus, the momentum halting effect of Ti gives the NeTi a stronger neutralization of Ne's energy, while Fi's invested sensitivity can work to fuel Ne's buoyancy. It is only when Te has been properly integrated into the psyche of the NeFi that Ne encounters an objective negation to its many hypothetical suspicions and interpretations; the tangible world acting as the sole measure of their feasibility.

As with many proactive types, the energy of the primary process can at times be felt overwhelmingly. Especially during their youth, the NeFi may find herself unable to quell or direct this mental energy, eventuating all too commonly in a medical diagnosis of ADHD. But as we are coming to understand, such a condition has been improperly conceived of as a disorder or illness in the past when it is instead far better described as a developmental challenge. This perspective shift has gained pub-

COGNITIVE TYPE

a.

b.

c.

d.

Figure 74

lic support in recent years through Lara Honos-Webb Ph.D., the author of *The Gift of ADHD* (2013) and other professionals who have analyzed the long-term developmental differences between children diagnosed with ADHD and regular children. Research has demonstrated that throughout the years and into adulthood, there remain few notable differences or anomalies in brain scans between the two groups.[1]

But to highlight yet another dimension of social misunderstanding directed toward this type, the NeFi, when in possession of strong Fi, will also be prone to a mild diagnosis within the autistic spectrum. In youth, this type may start out unable to understand the social landscape around them and will manifest Fi very rawly in its most uncoordinated form, as discussed in previous chapters. The result of these ill-assigned definitions is the overall portrayal of some iterations of NeFi as the rather ditzy, odd and socially inept genius. A duality will exist between the NeFi's perceived lack of intelligence in matters of people and practicality, and a talent for generating novel solutions and interconnections between problems. We see an expression of this in NeFi Albert Einstein who, along with having very noticeable Ne eyes, Fi giddy giggling[2] and Fi snarling smiles, is believed to have had a form of autism.

The NeFi will display an animated pair of naïve eyes which gently brushstroke their environment, carrying with them the head and body in a syncopated rhythm. Their eyes will oscillate between this casual toggling and occasional moments of Si concentration. Their buoyancy will be sprite-like, somewhat effeminate and unbridled. These traits are mirrored in their voice, giving them an invitingly playful and sing-song tone. If Te has been sufficiently developed, their articulation will be speedy, rivaling that of the TeSi. Ne and Te will collaborate in this type to produce an avalanche of visualizations, ideas and methods; an

1: Philip Shaw, Ph.D – 2007
2: Abraham Pais, a colleage of Einstein noted in the PBS documentary *How I see the World* – 1991: "The thing I wish most is that I would have a record in which I could capture Einstein's laughter when he heard a good Jewish joke. His laughter sounded something like the bark of a contented seal. It was a very strange sound."

off-the-cusp articulation. This may cause them to stutter and trip over their speech when they try to avalanche forward before having the words properly synthesized. In contrast, the NeTi more commonly struggles with hesitation *before* articulation due to its preemptive Fe-Ti filtration.

1. THE SCATTERED ENTREPRENEUR

The directive of Te is initially opposed to the agenda of Ne, which seeks endless exploration where Te desires closure and operationalization. But when properly integrated, the combination of Ne's momentum and Te's logistical coordination creates a type with a high level of creative output. The scattered entrepreneur will have a thirst for experimentation and dabbling which is more functional than theoretical. We see this entrepreneurship in NeFi Eesha Khare, who at the age of seventeen invented a new method of charging batteries using supercapacitors by growing nanotubes in the lab. In an different case, biologist NeFi Richard Lenski is pioneering a 25+ year experiment examining the natural mutations of an E. coli bacteria strain toward the acquisition of new traits. But such innovations are not confined to science, spanning instead a wide area from gadget-building to cartoon animation and even comedy. Their education is often diverse, rather than specific, and may leap between many seemingly disconnected disciplines. This multidisciplinary tendency has been noted by TEDx guest NeFi Emily Wapnick, who encourages the polymath lifestyle for its interconnective potential. When at their best, the entrepreneur will weave together their varied occupations to come up with novel and complex real-world solutions. When at their worst, the NeFi may suffer from a lack of focus, a tendency to tackle too much at a time and not give any interest enough resources to bring it to mastery.

2. THE FAUX-FE SEELIE

As with all high Fi users, the NeFi can manifest in an emphemeral and emotionally sensitive form when Fi is nurtured. These types often take to more artistic pursuits such as music, theater and dance. Florence Welch and Lindsey Stirling are two such examples of the seelie NeFi. Stirling also demonstrates the aforementioned multidisciplinary tendency by effectively combining a violinist, dancer and dubstep remixer into her person. But these types will possess another peculiar quality. The NeFi may gain sufficient mastery of the logistics of people and their sensitivities to execute a crafted presentation in a similar way to Fe. The NeFi manages these social dynamics through Ne's ability to simulate situations in real-time, anticipating reactions based on association and responding via emulation. Their presentation and delivery will use Te gesticulations embedded with Ne's levity and Fi's seelie energy, resulting in a warm and actively inviting aura. We see this approachable presentation in NeFi talk show hosts Ellen DeGeneres, Craig Ferguson and Jonathan Ross who possess an amiable and playful personality capable of managing intereactions with a diversity of guests.

We can, however, discern the subtle differences between this impact and the impact of Fe. The delivery of the faux-Fe is caring, good-willed and affable but lacks an element of social interdependency. For an Fe user, every interaction is an unspoken contract; a dance in which a dynamic is anticipated and its satisfaction or dismissal alters the energies of both parties. For the faux-Fe, their emotions do not become entangled in quite the same manner; allowing them to retain their Fi's independence. As a result, they will not dance in parallel to the flow of emotional energy; keeping their disposition, however generous, uniform or changing it only as they decide to from their own Fi.

3. THE INTROVERTED EXTROVERT

This type, like the NeTi, can also manifest in quite withdrawn and externally unavailable forms. A disconnect may develop between this type and the tangible reality around them as the impetus of their Ne is addressed with purely abstract and conceptual dimensions of inquiry. This occurs due to Ne's unique ability to divert its attention from the literal environment, despite being a proactive perception process. As a Pe process, Ne will still be deeply engaged with some element of reality, but this engagement is turned to an object or element that is non-physical. They may be avid consumers of literature, fantasy, digital media, video games and all forms of sedentary interests. Indeed, the NeFi who has not nurtured an understanding of human logistics and customs may turn to interests that do not center around human interaction; making them appear highly *introverted* in the common sense of the word.

Yet this attitude is quite different than what exists in the FiNe. The NeFi's psychology will express a heavier indecisiveness in many topics, a greater tolerance for stimuli (of an abstract sort), and a markedly less conclusive Fi palate. The FiNe will carry a far more definitive crystallization in their framework, which the NeFi might find suffocating and restrictive. It is the NeFi's very receptivity to new information (as a Pe lead type) that causes a constant evolution of values as well as a feeling of restriction when pivoted against a definitive paradigm. The NeFi introvert may find herself searching for her own deepest essence (Fi), but struggle with personal skepticism in deciding who they are as they re-imagine themselves often. The NeFi introvert may dabble in many mystical or psychological systems of categorization, finding and keeping the tidbits that resonate with them and making from this a collage of an identity or philosophy.

For a complete account of this type's vultology, we can look at interviews of the following NeFi public figures:

Name	*Development*
Jonathan Ross	Faux-Fe
Craig Ferguson	Faux-Fe
Kristen Schaal	Seelie/Faux-Fe
Emily Wapnick	Seelie/Scattered
Robin Williams	Comedian
Lindsey Stirling	Seelie/Scattered
Amy Lee	Standard
Vanessa Woods	Te-Heavy
Florence Welch	Introverted Extrovert
Jason Zimmerman	Aspie/Introverted

Figure 75

SeFi

VEDAER

The SeFi type emerges when the Se-Ni oscillation is primary and lead by Se, while supported by the Fi-Te judgment oscillation. The SeFi's countenance is among the most distinct. There's an open dialogue between the eyes and mouth, with both seeping into each other and sometimes competing for facial space. Their Fi tension will often rise high, breaking through their cheeks and elevating the skin under the eyes. But unlike the NeFi, whose relaxed eyes yield to the intrusion of this upward tension, the SeFi's eyes remain uncompromising in their sharpness. This causes a clash to occur, giving rise to a *manic* look as seen in Figure 76.d. Considerably more accidental expressions of disgust, shock and upset result from this clashing than what we see in other Fi-Te types. Yet SeFi's are among the more amiable of people, harboring a natural curiosity and receptiveness toward new encounters and personalities.

As an Se lead type, the SeFi will aim to absorb data as it appears to them – allowing the experience itself to auto-populate the richness and subtlety of their reality – rather than diverge their imagination toward a tangential associative process of data absorption, as is more typical of the NeFi. The SeFi will, like the SeTi, feel a heightened sensitivity to both the pleasure and discomfort of touch, sound, sight, smell or temperature; allowing this stimuli to be at times deeply compelling as well as deeply disquieting. But although they are connected to the world in an immediate way, the SeFi will have an altogether different subjective experience of these sensations. An additional layer of affectivity will accompany them which is absent in the SeTi; the placement and judgment of these sensations along a private (although initially ambiguous) ethical palate. The sentiment of a thing will register itself as important, and the SeFi will gravitate

COGNITIVE TYPE

a.

b.

c.

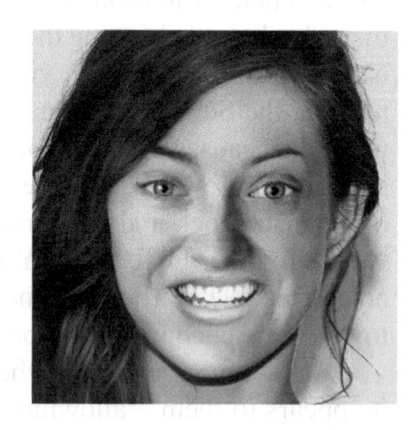

d.

Figure 76

to things not just for the stimulation they provide but for their capacity to uplift the life-principles they hold. As the SeFi goes about life, their exploration will lead naturally to that which has certain energetic qualities and they will learn more about their own Fi's values through this experimentation. They will develop a relationship with their own Fi by encountering many situations and people who prompt an occasion for its palate to be unearthed and refined.

The SeFi will carry a loose body posture that is receptive and alert to environmental inputs. A fair amount of toggling will accompany their eyes, although for the most part they will stay locked on to one element of the environment at a time, absorbing its many nuanced qualities. As with many perception types, their head may swivel easily toward the shoulders as they talk, with their eyes directing a series of swaying motions. They may have very identifiable laughter which reverbs freely at an unusual volume and rises high on their face. Their articulation will involve many asymmetrical snarls and contain a voice that is either nasally pinched or breathy and sprite-like.

1. THE SEELIE SOCIALITE

When Fi is open, sensitive and receptive in this type, the SeFi will be highly motivated toward seeking out experiences which amplify a sense of vitality, transparency and interconnection. Just as each explorer type pursues that which satiates their thirst for novelty, the SeFi socialite will aim to enrich the moment through the exploration of others and the many interactions they bring. Yet, unlike the FeSi and FeNi, who more often coordinate such interactions in order to facilitate a mutual and established atmosphere, the SeFi seelie will be far more unscripted and allow for their own unique expression to ripple across that of others and collide with them as it will. Artistic avenues of exploration may be entertained, often taking the form of real life performance and improvisation. Perhaps more than any other type, the seelie socialite embodies a very tangible appreciation of life, diversity, the human heart and the body. In this sense, the SeFi echoes the sentiment of many SeTi who seek to partake in the complete availability of experience. But opposite of the SeTi sensationalist, whose lust might only be tempered by their Ti's evaluation of risks and their Fe's level of concern for social repercussions, the SeFi seelie may be more reluctant to abandon a concern for their body, choosing many times to avoid exploration that is life-harming in principle. This may also extend to the nature of the selected setting. They may decline a friendly outing to the zoo for a desire not to enjoy the caging of animals or will avoid restaurants that engage in animal cruelty.

However, notwithstanding these ethical precautions, the seelie socialite may be so turned toward the amplification of experience that insufficient precautions are applied to the effects which those experiences might bring. Just as the NeFi's consequence for uncoordinated Ne energy is a fragmented sense of direction or identity, the SeFi socialite may find herself in logistical disarray, drifting between jobs or romances with no firm anchoring. But if Te is properly integrated into the psyche, it brings with it an indispensable structure and focus through which their exploration can be directed.

2. THE MANAGER

The collaboration of Se and Te naturally produces far fewer discrepancies in priorities than what we witness between Ne and Te, due to Se's literal and linear comprehension of reality. The operation of Te can leverage this 1:1 relationship to generate a more streamlined methodology, giving the SeFi a more steady psychic assembly from the initial input source to an eventual, functional output. As such the SeFi's capacity as a coordinator and administrator, once matured within their Te, is substantial. At work they may demonstrate an acute awareness of systemic necessities, a strong and proactive energy, and a quick response time to changes; steadily growing into leadership positions. As a proactive *gamma* type, the SeFi manager is the sister subtype to the TeNi executive. For symbolic purposes I assign the title of executive to the TeNi and manger to the SeFi, due to their relative level of Te prioritization, although both types are easily found in either occupation. Generally, however, the SeFi will prefer a po-

28. SeFi | Vedaer

sition that is more interpersonal and level with their peers than one which stands detached and high above them. They may be the human resources clerk, the head nurse or veterinary director which doubles as the catalyst of responsible fun and laughter at the facility.

3. THE FEISTY UNSEELIE

When the SeFi is unseelie, holding an Fi aesthetic that is closed or particularly selective in its receptivity, any physical discomfort that also registers as being against their life-principle will prompt a very malcontent reaction; a twofold distaste from their leading processes. An inclination toward volatility and social friction will persist as their Fi's palate oscillates between resonance and dissonance among the many situations they encounter. Unlike the FiSe, whose dissatisfaction with situations may brew a sullen inner distaste, the SeFi may extrovert these displeasures at the very point of their emergence. The immediate moment is rejected and their unyielding Fi will defend its stance through nasal Te articulation and snippy, sassy gestures. Here, Fi has not yet been properly tempered, causing these flare-ups to be raw and often not properly matched to the degree or severity of the situation. They may be rashly vindictive and impatient when confronted with a sensation or behavior from a person that they disagree ethically with. We see an example of this subtype in the young Ella Yelich-O'Connor (better known as "Lorde") who has promptly developed a reputation for her passive-aggressive social media commentary directed at the actions and lifestyles of dozens of other music artists. Where others might be more prudent not to needlessly burn bridges between one's peers and potential collaborators, Lorde allows her Fi palate to inform her on the character of people and this personal evaluation is made audible. For the SeFi feisty unseelie, no qualms are felt from the loss of an opportunity to collaborate with those already deemed incompatible.

But as is true of any ethical type, this antagonism is often expressed in defense of a cherished ethical stance. These quarrels may arise from the SeFi's strong advocacy of certain rights

COGNITIVE TYPE

and the insensitivity of others to those positions.

4. THE GYPSY

In a few rare instances, when Ni is highly favored by the psyche and strong credence is given to its impressions and interpretations of events, we come across the SeFi gypsy. I select this term for its capacity to bring into our imagination a traveling magician, performer or practitioner of obscure and often discredited arts/crafts – not by any ties it may have to the Romani people of Europe. As we have previously discussed, the polar process is most commonly channeled for the agenda of the primary, and in the SeFi these far-reaching interconnections are pursued for their capacity to relate together and explain the events of the present. As such, interconnections are intuited to exist beneath the immediate and sentimental and in some cases this stimuli can bring forth the larger *pattern* that lies underneath. For example, the SeFi may feel that an energetic network exists which touches and travels between the hearts and minds of individuals. A blending may occur where the inner radiation and spirit of Fi is given a physical definition; the SeFi may dabble in the reading of auras, the channeling of chakra or Ki energy. They may seek for the significance behind palmistry, tarot reading, taoism, kamasutra, and all manner of extrasensory arts. When the archetype is fully embodied, the SeFi may adorn herself in eclectic and colorful attire, reminiscent of the indie FiSe, and establish themselves as an artisan of their particular interest.

For the SeFi, this practice is born from an aspiration to fully assimilate and synthesize their polarity, yet a proactive novelty will propel this curiosity forward with all the energy of a Pe lead type. Unlike the NiTe and NiFe, the gypsy will more rarely be the originator of doctrines and will more commonly explore the pathways made available by those before them. They may lie under the wing of an NiFe guru or FeNi alpha visionary and learn from them what they can before traveling along another path.

For a complete account of this type's vultology, we can look at interviews of the following SeFi public figures:

Name	*Development*
Elle Fanning	Seelie Socialite
Sia Furler	Gypsy
Cillian Murphy	Standard
Robert Pattinson	Standard
Natalie Portman	Manager
Dakota Fanning	Seelie Socialite
Chris Martin	Artist/Performer
Bam Margera	Sensationalist
Keira Knightley	Artist/Performer
Cameron Diaz	Seelie Socialite

FUNCTION QUADRANTS

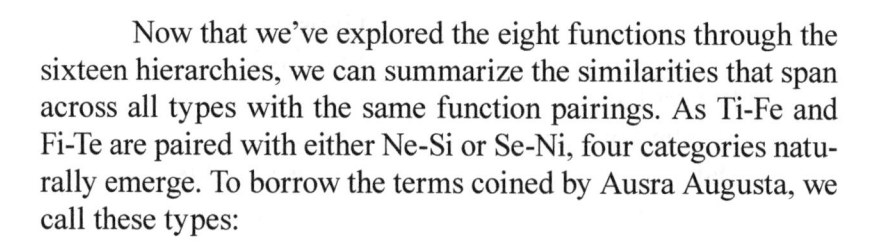

Now that we've explored the eight functions through the sixteen hierarchies, we can summarize the similarities that span across all types with the same function pairings. As Ti-Fe and Fi-Te are paired with either Ne-Si or Se-Ni, four categories naturally emerge. To borrow the terms coined by Ausra Augusta, we call these types:

	Je	**Pi**	**Pe**	**Ji**
Alpha:	FeSi	SiFe	NeTi	TiNe
Beta:	FeNi	NiFe	SeTi	TiSe
Gamma:	TeNi	NiTe	SeFi	FiSe
Delta:	TeSi	SiTe	NeFi	FiNe

Many times the most visually apparent aspect of a person will be their function quadrant, while we may not understand immediately which energetic quadrant they belong to. At times the reverse is true, but always when both are known, we understand what type a person is – as there is but one Je-Alpha, or Pe-Gamma and so on. The four types within each function quadrant will share crossover with each other; many times the qualities of one's subtype manifest in another type of the same quadrant. This is because the subtypes are first and foremost *modes* of expressing the same functions, arranged in these sixteen chapters by what modes are most common in a type. To that end, let us surmise the qualities that run across all four types within each of these quadrants.

Alpha

In the four alpha types we find a special sense of humor which invites social participation and calls upon culturally known (and "safe") memes. And since humor relies heavily on the unexpected, the more Si-heavy alpha types can manifest as being cliché and unoriginal in their socialization style. But if Ne is engaged creatively they may be great hosts and entertainers, surprising guests with their off-the-wall commentary. The alpha types will try hard to create harmony and will be quick to see solutions for social arrangements. They will be optimistic about avenues for connection, diplomacy and peace.

On the flip side, these continued efforts to gain and maintain a positive social opinion may be overdone, raising suspicions of neediness and lack of personal identity. They may become social *doormats*, keeping their hands full with the troubles of others and the obligations they put themselves into. Their receptiveness to alternate ideas may backfire and cause them to listen too eagerly to information, especially if it comes from sources predetermined to be accurate.

But this quadrant does have a special countermeasure to these shortcomings in their philosophical edge. In their best form, the alpha quadrant's ideas will be constructed from axiomatic logic as it pertains to human nature; specifically coordinated at an improved societal architecture. They may be the idealist which reminds the rest of society that malleable collective opinions create the limitations we perceive as so unmovable.

Beta

Next we have the beta types, which often develop as smoothtalkers and persuaders. From the articulate and empathic FeNi, to the hypnotic NiFe, to the affable SeTi and the cool geek TiSe, we are drawn to their tailored presentation and confident aura. In their best form, their cultural know-how can lead to the creation of social cohesion, community, stability and equality. Like with alpha types, a strong sense of brotherhood/sisterhood may flourish and invite involvement between people of all demographics. But this acceptance won't always come free. There may be peace and order but only in the confines of a certain paradigm which may carry superfluous restrictions and misconceptions about human nature. A type of sectism can quickly develop and an *us-vs-them* mentality stretches its roots. When this hostility is at its worst, we will find opportunistic social and emotional exploitation, shaming, oppresive social hierarchies, bullying and misleading visions from oracle figures. But this stubbornness can find a source of relief in a feeling of cosmic embrace. When Ti and Ni collaborate to create an *all-inclusive* principle, sensitive to the empathy shared by all conscious beings, then the beta quadrant recovers its generosity and leniency.

A sense of aesthetic will permeate the quadrant which aims for simple elegance and function. These types will often make an art of sensation, creating luxurious displays and channels for stimulation. An insatiable gravitation toward richness of experience will ebb across all four of these types and sometimes clash with the moderation suggested by their ethical code.

Gamma

The four gamma types share an opposite orientation toward society and culture. While the alpha and beta types advocate a culture with a decent degree of uniformity, the gamma quadrant aims to meet the outer world with an objective approach and the inner world with a subjective approach. Logistics manage the necessities of life while individuality is cherished and preserved – even though they may not always agree among themselves.

Themes of philanthropy span across this quadrant and their absence of social protocols and obligations is answered with a heartfelt concern for incapable or less fortunate people. Especially in high Fi types, there will be a strong agency for the underdog. While the beta quadrant is susceptible to throwing some under the bus of social condemnation, the gamma quadrant will be passionate about reducing this type of inequality. On the other hand, gamma types will generally expect for people to remain self-sufficient once they can stand on their two feet and will have little sympathy for those who cannot make a success of their life after being given a fair start.

In its worst form, the gamma quadrant can develop a highly utilitarian mindset which feels self-justified in its success and indifferent toward the weak. They may become materialistic and vain, exalting beauty and individualistic perfection.

Delta

We have seen that among all delta types run themes of quirkiness and nerdiness. Whether it's in the form of the eccentric nerd, the walking encyclopedia, the unsocial yet sensitive seelie, the tinkering collector, or the fantastical entrepreneur – all share the qualities of independence and off-beat spontaneity. They are imaginative but not always to any conventional means. They are efficient and productive but also quite scattered and roundabout; expending energies in novel directions with signs of promise or resonance with deep personal conviction.

Like the alpha types, deltas will have a higher level of leniency toward human failure and weakness. They will aspire to create an arrangement that allows for privacy, freedom and functional support. At their best, delta types will be keenly sensitive to the most ethically sound position, however obscure or unconventional, and find novel ways to organize their life to suit that ethical sense. They may also pioneer a new field of study, trailblazing into uncharted territory with the empiricism and mentality of a researcher and the heart of a child.

In their worst form, their nerdiness can manifest a rather autistic persona and mechanically-minded detachment from people. A father may be an expert at tennis, with halls of trophies in his house and a CEO position, but have an aloofness toward his children; a lacking parental touch. The emotionally oblivious delta type can remedy this by turning their attention within. A connection with their own private world is necessary for this quadrant to avoid the desensitizing steel of capitalism and allow for a convergence of life and work.

ON VULTOLOGY

This chapter is dedicated to a detailed explanation of proper vultological practices, according to my own current understanding of this newly rising topic. I must begin by reiterating that type is a vastly more complex matter than what these first principles of visual reading could account for by themselves. One would be at high risk of err by exclusively using an objective avenue of measure (such as vultology offers) to determine the properties of a subjective matter: the psyche of an individual. Psychological avenues of analysis *must* be used in conjunction with this methodology for the achievement of a refined understanding of the psyche which it is attempting to identify. And there is no other substitute for accurate psychological insights than what time and firsthand experience can birth.

In this light, vultology presents but a small and partial window into the happenings of the psyche, yet I find it so deeply fortunate that we should receive even such a window into our humanity. We must never forget, however, that the information elicited by the psyche always holds priority over the signals presented by the body. Should there be a contradiction between the psychology anticipated by visual signals and the actual psychology of the person, the signals must be given less authority. Never must the nature of the actual person be ignored for the preservation of a signal's consistency. Vultology seeks to approximate the psyche based on reading the secondary effects that emerge from the psyche itself. As such, vultology can only ever be a useful tool if it can properly manage to predict psychology; it cannot define it.

With that said we must always remain willing to question and revisit our understanding of a person's psychology, and measure whether or not such visual signals can better inform us on the cognitive dynamics of the person.

Differentiating Between the Three Expression Types

But before we are ready to read type, we must first tease apart the signals which indicate cognitive processing from all other signals that comprise the spectrum of human animation. To help simplify the matter, we can divide this spectrum into three distinct categories, as per Figure 77. Each of these categories is a rich and complex field of study, and for which many books have been written. Not all signals elicited by the body indicate type, and when we are first confronted with another human, all at once we receive the entirety of their presentation; their essential nature, their persona, cultivated through years of adaptation and culture, and their emotional state at that moment.

Emotions – Is the most direct of these categories. We witness emotions expressed through the face, and by them we understand the state of the person's feelings. We can see anger, sadness, surprise, disgust, fear and many other universal signals that visually communicate with us. This is the subject of books such as *The Expression of the Emotions in Man and Animals* by Charles Darwin, *Telling Lies* by Paul Ekman and *Liespotting* by Pamela Meyer. They reveal to us the functional use of emotional expressions from an evolutionary standpoint: they are the means by which we convey our own internal state to others. However, as Ekman well understood, a study of emotional expressions requires a differentiation from what he called "symbolic" expressions; gestures that are cultural in nature and not universal to humanity.

Persona – Is that which Ekman avoided, and it's that which contains all cultural symbology, social dynamics and rituals. It is the contemporary realm, where body language reveals to us things such as a person's social affiliation, financial standing, their probable life path and receptiveness or avoidance toward certain ideas. Leaning one's back against the wall, with arms crossed, speaks to us about a person's attitude. A woman who dresses modestly and whose back is always vertically strung may reveal to us something else. Another person may

COGNITIVE TYPE

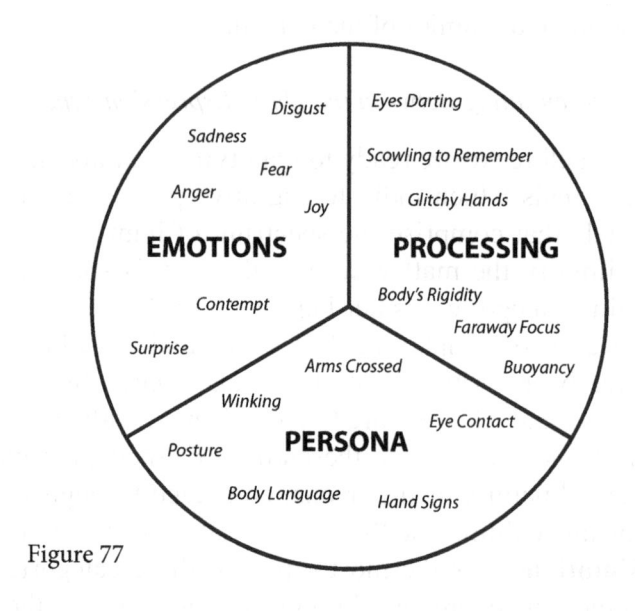

```
           Disgust    Eyes Darting
      Sadness
            Fear      Scowling to Remember
      Anger
                Joy   Glitchy Hands
       EMOTIONS       PROCESSING

           Contempt   Body's Rigidity
                      Faraway Focus
    Surprise
                Arms Crossed   Buoyancy
            Winking
                      Eye Contact
         Posture  PERSONA
            Body Language  Hand Signs
```

Figure 77

never make eye contact while speaking, or behave far more respectfully around certain demographics. This dimension of expression is the subject of books like *The Art of Speed Reading People* by Paul D. Tieger, *What Every Body Is Saying* by Joe Navarro, as well as the cold reading methods of psychics. It accounts for, and makes a discipline of, all societal factors that affect a person's presentation, as well as certain complexes that may be at play within a person.

Processing – Yet there is a third category which also comprises part of what humans manifest in their expressions, and that is processing. Independent of emotions and persona, humans also do peculiar things with their body that may otherwise not seem to hold any purpose; things that are neither emotions nor acts of cultural symbolism. For example, we may look up when we are imagining a hypothetical scenario. We may look at the ground and scowl intently when we are trying to remember something. When talking, we may find ourselves struggling to find a certain word and unconsciously form claws with our hands as we try to mentally grasp it. This is the subject of some aspects of Neuro Linguistic Programming (NLP) such as "eye accessing", as described by Richard Bandler. These signals arise incidentally and autonomously, not through cultural adaptation, and are more analogous to Ekman's universal emotions than to persona, but represent an altogether different phenomenon. Regardless of what emotional state a person finds themselves in, these signals of cognitive processing will remain consistent, as they reveal one's manner of formulating thoughts, not the status of the heart.

***

While cognitive type concerns itself solely with *processing*, when reading cognition, we must be keenly aware of these two extra dimensions and the way in which they may influence our identification of processing. To that end, I would not advise the learner to ignore these dimensions altogether, since an ignorance to their workings would leave us susceptible to err in cases where their animations overlap the expression of type. As we go about our interactions with others, knowledge of all three expression types becomes ever available to us. It's the task of the vultologist to differentiate one from the other by understanding the origin of each signal while not discarding any available knowledge.

The Expansion of our Personal Database

As we start to enter the topic of vultology, we each begin with a limited database of body types to call from. We remember the mannerisms of our parents, family members or close friends, and we depend on those patterns to inform us on the subtleties of their respective types. Indeed, I would not discourage this initial anecdotal over-association, as many of the subtleties that are to be learned from the sixteen types come from the coutless bits of data we extract from interaction with real individuals. Were one to approach the matter seeking to identify only the signals outlined in this book, one would fail far more often in capturing the true psychology of a person. The signals found in this book – which are only the least disputable – can bring one's attention toward the right individuals, but those individuals themselves carry the richness, nuance and demeanor that defines their own type, and which my sincerest efforts utterly fail to quantify fully.

To build a comprehensive personal database of the types we must honor subtlety, but be prepared always to examine more individuals and remove contradiction whenever it appears. Tentatively retain your behavioral associations to a certain function or type, silly as they may be, until contradictory observations are seen. Exposure itself will oblige you to discard what does not remain axiomatically true for all those of a type or function in question, while still leaving you with the richness and subtlety that corresponds to them. Vultology as a practice becomes highly accurate only after the practitioner's scope has significantly broadened to account for the majority of body types in their environment and the psychologies underneath them. Learning vultology is a growth process, which both releases our prejudice towards others, showing us that all types have the potential for great or small feats, and leads us to a deeper understanding of our overall place within humanity.

Identifying Functions

Firstly, we must always strive to identify the eight functions based on precedent, not deduction; by cues we legitimately see, not by the absence of cues. If you are reading a person and trying to identify what their judging functions are, and you don't see the cues for Fe/Ti whatsoever, it would be wrong to assume they have Te/Fi. You should only conclude they have Te/Fi if they demonstrate the signals of Te/Fi. Otherwise, remain always undecided on the matter. Avoid impulsive typing and the desire to have complete certainty in your views. We can never be too careful when asserting a reality about another's psyche.

Secondly, the identification of a function is not done in parts but in whole. If all of the signals of a function are not seen, then remain skeptical. If only one or two signals are present, keep observing. Ask yourself why a certain signal of a cluster may be missing and what it may imply about their psychology. At times we may find that the omission of a certain signal is

30. ON VULTOLOGY

due to another function overshadowing it (such as very heavy Pi steadiness disallowing the expected amount of Ji eyes-down disengagement when Ji is a lead process). Should this be the case, then the psychology of the person will reflect this and we can place this hypothesis to the test. A Ji lead type heavy in Pi will have a twofold *gravitas of thought* and a soft (low Je) manner of speaking that is strongly divorced from the world, but attempting to convey a very conceptual, surreal framework. If we witness that their psychology does match this expected outcome, then we understand why the discrepancy in cues was first seen; we will come to realize that the absence of a specific signal is not itself indicative of the absence of the function, but of the presence of a specific interplay between Ji and Pi. We can then correctly confirm their type, having used their psychology to cross-examine the signals seen, better understanding both in the process. In such cases, although not all signals were revealed, the function itself was rightly identified through a holistic analysis. Indeed, even in cases where all signals of a function are seen, we can never confirm a function's presence without first checking their psychology for a match.

Identifying Energetic Quadrants

The four energetic quadrants necessitate a more relative means of quantification than the cognitive functions. While a function pairing either exists in an individual or doesn't, energetic levels and the manner in which they are used in people can vary. Even within the same person, at different periods of their life, their energetic qualities can change. This is because the *expressivity* of our functions will align to the requirements of our environment. For instance, a Ji type whose lifepath necessitated public speaking and demanded high competence in practical matters, will display heavier use of their Je process than their other Ji counterparts. Yet the level of variation that can occur in an energetic quadrant is still limited.

To understand these limits, we can begin by evaluating a person's use of the four energetic quadrants by a matter of degrees. We can tally the number of Je/Ji/Pi/Pe gestures they

COGNITIVE TYPE

	SUBJECT A			SUBJECT B	
Je	70	57%	Je	46	46%
Pe	04	03%	Pe	36	36%
Ji	09 (10)	12%	Ji	14 (15)	15%
Pi	34 (37)	30%	Pi	03 (03)	03%

	SUBJECT C			SUBJECT D	
Je	42	25%	Je	12	26%
Pe	41	24%	Pe	09	19%
Ji	40 (44)	26%	Ji	11 (12)	26%
Pi	38 (41)	24%	Pi	12 (13)	28%

Figure 78

perform per minute to give us our first rough estimations. When tallying this way, it is important to remember that the proactive processes will naturally be more generous in the display of signals than Ji and Pi, so we must account for this in our approximations by giving slightly more weight to each of the reactive signals we observe. At this point we might have tallies that look like those in Figure 78. As you can see I've added some 10% more weight to the introverted processes in the calculation of ratios. Let's try to evaluate these four scenarios to see what they may reveal to us.

    In Subject A we see a typical breakdown of the ratios in the signals of a type. We see that the Je process accounts for 57% of their overall signals, followed by Pi with 30%, Ji with 12% and Pe with only 3%. Considering the overwhelming representation of the Je process, we can safely expect this individual to lead their psyche with Je. The second most represented process (Pi) shows us that this type is also heavy in the Je-Pi axes, while weak in their bottom two functions. The slightly higher representation of Ji over Pe is also to be expected due to the primary oscillation pairing being Judgment. From this initial observation, we can expect Subject A to be goal-oriented, assertive in their agenda, and less interested in exploring new ideas than applying their existing information to a paradigm which they have constructed over several years. This disconnect from the two polar functions will also manifest in less refinement of the primary and supportive functions, due to the lack of a strong calibrator. Quite ironically, those with the strongest reliance on their primary functions will be less masterful in their use of those processes than those who properly develop their polar functions. Hence, if they are an Fe type, they will lack logical analysis and refinement of ethics via Ti and if they are a Te type, they will lack the ethical sensitivities of Fi and any intelligent strategies for managing situations that involve people.

In Subject B we see immediately that the Je and Pe processes are high, while the Ji and Pi processes are both low. Considering the size of the gap between the two, we can safely expect this individual to be an extraverted type. However, this does not give us sufficient indication as to whether Je or Pe is the primary process. A ratio difference of 10% (between Je-46% and Pe-36%) can easily be overwritten with more information. And since this represents only the first minute of analysis, we would continue our investigation to see whether this gap increases with more exposure. However, there are other clues we can gather from this initial ratio breakdown. The Ji process, although weak, is better represented than the Pi process. This shifts the total weight of the J-P dichotomy toward Judgment being the primary oscillation pairing. In total, the two perception processes account for 39% of the signals while the two judgment processes account for 61% of the signals.

Another clue we find is in the low representation of Pi. If we assume that this person may lead with Je, then Pi's low representation is peculiar. If we look at the data from the Je-Pi/Ji-Pe axes, we see that the Je-Pi functions represent only 49% of the signals while Ji-Pe accounts for 51%. In other words, this breakdown equally supports Je or Ji being the lead process, if we assume Judgment is leading the psyche, ultimately adding Ji as a less likely, yet possible candidate for the lead process. Nonetheless, from this information alone, Subject B is most likely an extroverted type leading with Je with a proficient and balanced use of their compass process. We can expect Subject B to have a passion for analyzing and debating matters of both logic and ethics, while being receptive to new observations and using that new information to arrive at new deductions in realtime.

Lastly, we have Subjects C and D. Both of these examples have no exceptional representation in any of the quadrants. This implies that the individual has a high level of balance in their processes. They will evidence a fair level of receptiveness to new information, as well as an ability to keenly call from previous experiences that are relevant to the situation. They will also weigh this information's implications both ethically and logically, and hold a private internal framework while executing one outward that is in alignment with the internal. I have found such cases to be rare and representative of an antinomous type – one which holds the dualities inherent to their psychology in a constant state of calibration. Such individuals could very well fit multiple type descriptions at once. An FiSe, so balanced, may scarcely differ from a similarly balanced TeNi, or to any other judgment type. As proactivity, reactivity, logos, ethos, abstract and concrete perceptions all converge, all sixteen types find a common point of relation to one another. In such cases, their cognitive type may be of little relevance to their personal life. However, no human begins at this place of balance – and such a balance is a response to personal and environmental pressures. To understand such a person, we must rely more heavily on psychology and inquire into their earlier years of life. There, we will often find the visual and psychological imprint of their native type, which will still underpin their psychology; influencing it in a million subtle ways.

If no film or media can be found from their earlier years of life, we can still identify certain visual signals to better understand such a person. In our example we see that while Subjects C and D are balanced in their ratios, they have a very different number of signals. Subject C averages 40 signals per quadrant while Subject D only averages 10 signals per quadrant. This indicates that Subject C operates at a higher general psychic frequency than Subject D, implying that Subject C is a balanced

30. ON VULTOLOGY

extroverted type while Subject D is a balanced introverted type. Other signals can be gathered from the cognitive functions themselves, such as the quality of their articulation, which can help identify which function in an oscillation is taking priority.

Clarifying the Subtleties of the Eight Functions

The following is a list of several important notes to keep in mind when reading a person's type. They cover common misconceptions as well as ways to remove extraneous elements such as native bone structure, race and age from the reading process.

a. A Smile's Wideness and Tension

Fe's smile is not necessarily wider than Fi's smile. Previously I've mentioned how Fe has a diagonal, rather than vertical, elevation of the cheek muscles. This naturally causes Fe's smile to travel more horizontally than Fi, given all other variables are equal. But the wideness of a person's smile is affected by many other factors. To give an example, we see artist Janet Jackson is

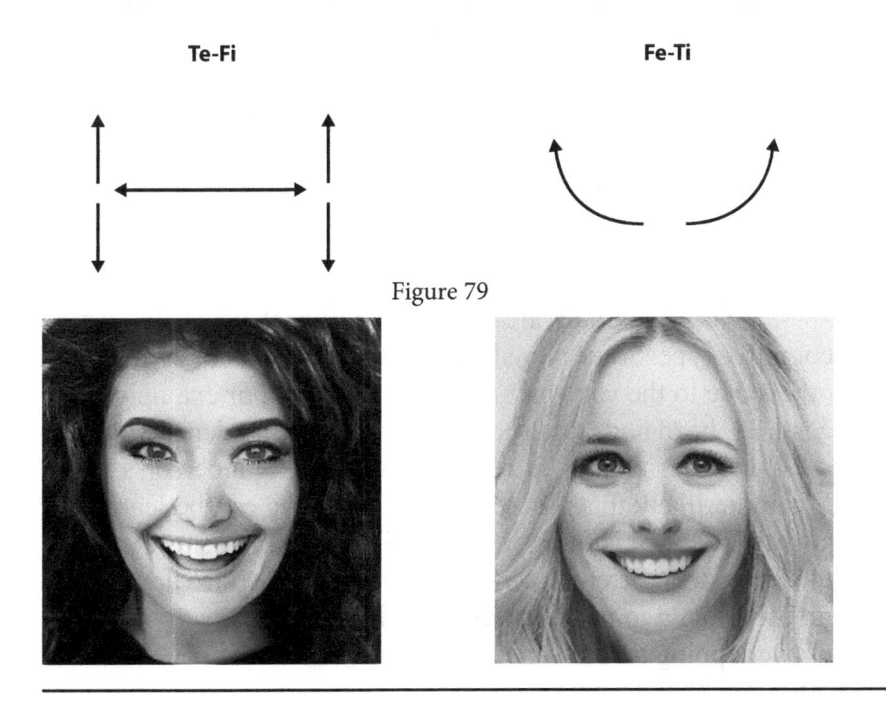

Te-Fi　　　　　　　　**Fe-Ti**

Figure 79

an FiSe with a very wide smile. Yet, if we look closely we notice that at the corner of her lips the tension of Fi is distinctly present, elevating directly upward and clashing with her cheeks. The smile first stretches horizontally and then completely vertically. In Figure 79 we see a comparative example between an FiSe (to the left) and an SiFe (to the right) whose smiles are equally wide but different in quality. First we notice the taut square effect visible in the FiSe, as well as a horizontal splitting of the cheeks. The SiFe lacks both of these qualities, and also has an element of relaxation to her cheeks, with the skin defining the smile not stretched so tightly.

Despite this clarification, it's important to keep in mind that skeletal structure and muscle tone has the ability, in rare cases, to make an Fe type's smile appear like that of Fi and vice versa. The static presence or absence of upward tension alone cannot perfectly differentiate these two functions. If a person's mouth appears to move with very conscious intention, having no accidental snarls and possessing a yang emotional delivery, then regardless of the quality of their tension, this individual is certainly an Fe type. Likewise, a mouth that is relaxed with plenty of slack in their cheeks, but which demonstrates many accidental snarls and asymmetries when speaking, and which lacks a coordinated impact, most certainly reveals an Fi-Te psychology. Fi tension cannot be the only signal that is examined in order to determine a person's ethical process.

b. Hand Gestures

Not all signals are equally significant when discerning cognitive type. Some signals have a stronger level of fidelity than others due to the very nature of their origins. For example, hand gestures, head nods and shoulder shrugs are less dependable signals for discerning Fe vs Te than the quality of a person's smile. It is more likely that a certain gesturing style can be learned or adopted, while it is far more difficult to train one's smile muscles to elevate in a different way. The muscles of the face are autonomously linked to neural activity while gestures are at some risk of overlapping across functions due to their level of deliberation.

30. ON VULTOLOGY

If we observe, for instance, an NeFi type whose hand gestures follow an Fe-esque pattern, but whose facial tension, smile, articulation and psychology directly parallel with the Fi-Te oscillation pair, then we understand that their gesturing may have developed into its present form through external influences. We would then inquire further to understand what the origin of their gesturing pattern may be. A former position as a public speaker, actor, performer or the influence of an Fe lead parent are some examples of what may condition an Fi-Te type to have such expressions where an Fe-Ti type would hold those qualities without any outside influence.

c. Flatness of Cheeks

The size of a person's cheekbones is unrelated to type. Low cheekbones don't automatically indicate Ti and what may initially appear to be *Ti flat cheeks* may instead be tension resting upon very low cheekbones. Because of this it's important to see the contractions of the person's mouth muscles to confirm whether or not they follow the Fi-Te or Ti-Fe pattern of contraction. Inversely, higher cheekbones might predispose us to judge someone as an Fe type and we must be wary of this tendency as well. While round, lush cheeks do better indicate Fe than Ti, this is only accurate after factoring out skeletal structure.

Having said that, the same dichotomy is not true for Fi-Te types. The tendency for high Fi type's cheeks to be lush and round is just about equivalent to that of high Te types. There is instead a slightly higher tendency for high Te types to have bulging cheeks due to the way their Fi's tension is confined in a smaller region around the nose, rather than spread up to the eyes. This would make Fe and Te types slightly more predisposed to having round cheeks than both Fi and Ti, with Ti being the least likely.

d. Slanted Eyelids and Slanted Brows

Sometimes we'll encounter a pair of sharp eyes (Se) with eyelids that droop toward the outer edges of the eyes, as seen

Figure 80

occasionally in NiTe Brian Clough or NiFe Leonard Nimoy. We must remember, however, that it's the slanting of the *eyebrow*, not eyelids, over the edges of the eyes that defines the signal of Si. In Si the eyes remain open rather than sleepy or partially obscured by the top eyelid. From this we can see that any heaviness of the eyelids is more indicative of Ni than Si, regardless of the shape of the eyelids.

In other interesting cases, we find individuals with lowered eyelids but who demonstrate a brow that curves in the Si manner (up toward the center). These individuals will most likely possess Ni since the tension immediately around the eye, which remains hypnotic, is the prime indicator of perceptual *focus*. Usually, however, even when an Ni type has a center-raised brow, the brow will remain elevated above the eyes, as we see in NiFe Justin Bieber. We discover the Si-Ne pairing when the brow is not just center-raised but weights down on the eyes, while the eyes remain wide but unfocused.

e. Explorer with Strong Articulation

As stated earlier, it's unreliable to determine the dominant function based on the ratios of the four energetic quadrants when two quadrants are tied or very close in their ratio of expressivity. But what may be more surprising to some is that certain shades of Explorer types demonstrate far higher rates of Je expressivity than Je types themselves. This is a direct result of *momentum*.

30. ON VULTOLOGY

An Explorer type may have so much momentum that the rate at which their body moves will escalate, causing their mannerisms and gesticulations to also speed up. They will therefore elicit far more Je signals per minute than a Je type would. Yet, each of these gesticulations will have less solidity and impact than those of a Je type; they will be loose and lack rigidity, both in body and thought. A Je type's gesticulations will not be born out of the overflow of excited energy – they will be deliberate, emerging from intentionality rather than acceleration. It is more common to see Je types have medium levels of energy than to see them with high levels of it.

Hierarchical Order

When seeking to identify the hierarchy of a person's functions it is better to look for signals that specifically isolate hierarchical order. Signals such as a rigid versus fluid body and a face-centric versus eye-centric head should be given more weight in determining function order than the energetic levels of the quadrants. In most cases, however, these two will complement each other. At times every aspect of a hierarchy cannot be discerned from a single encounter or video. We might be uncertain of whether someone is FiSe or NiTe and it's perfectly alright to leave our evaluation pending. It has become my habit to suggest an alternate typing whenever evaluating people solely through video unless their type is unambiguously clear. However, it would be erroneous to be conflicted between two types such as the FiSe and SiFe since the two share no common functions and the similarities they might express would be relatively superficial.

Uncertainty, Twin Shades and Beyond

Inevitably, the vultologist will come across individuals who are altogether challenging to decipher from the partial list of signals outlined in this book. In such cases, I would strongly recommend honoring that uncertainty and cultivating the capacity to measure one's level of sureness on a given matter. Keep a personal, written log of those who you have typed and reference these samples when seeking to discern the psychology of a new person. If you are debating between two types, review footage of those who you've previously identified to belong to those psychologies in question.

But more importantly, both for the refinement of this model and for the pursuit of its full understanding, do keep a personal log of those who you have not been able to quantify – a sort of *shadow database* of those people who suggest inconsistent or contradictory qualities. It is my belief that, even for those with little proficiency and experience in visual reading, this shadow database should not overwhelm the actual database which they will come to nurture. That is to say, far more often we will arrive at an understanding of an individual that is clear, even if it does not initially narrow down to just one of the 16 types. We may, for instance, confirm a person only to be an Explorer type, and still their psychology will perfectly match the signals outlined, or a person may be a Judgment type with Ne-Si as their supportive oscillation. We can, even from these partial confirmations, learn volumes about the people around us while nurturing a more organic appreciation of human variation. And in keeping this secondary database in sight, often the advent of a new sample will crystallize into consciousness a connection which required an adjacent, but hitherto missing point of data. As continued exposure catalyzes an evolution of perspective, more such points come into awareness and allow us to gain a broader and more accurate paradigm of the many variations of types. When our sample of readings has expanded to encompass all varieties within humanity, we quickly discover that there are more than enough shades in humanity to give rise to dozens of very common expressions of each type. Differences in age, race, facial structure and culture will make the mastery of vultology a rich and exhaustive journey.

But as we traverse this labyrinth, we have an indispensable tool of agency, what I sometimes call the phenomenon of *twin shades*. At times, when nurture has been significantly similar between two people of the same type, despite differences in race or facial structure, their visual signatures will echo strongly and unambiguously, alerting us to a definitive link. We may be struck by the feeling that these two individuals are different incarnations of the same fundamental essence. Twin shades will echo in this manner despite certain demographic or cultural differences, allowing us to expand our social awareness by confirming for us what this type looks like in cultures and races we hadn't yet encountered. It is generally unadvisable to analyze a demographic too far divorced from one's own, especially of a different language, without first developing a sensible awareness of the culture's mannerisms and normalities to properly contextualize the signals. However, at times these twin shades can offer us a direct channel into a new culture due to type being a far more prevailing factor than the net capacity of their heritage to obscure the reading. This initial parallel can then open the door to discovering the mannerisms of similar types and from there, potentially, the rest of the culture.

31
DEMOGRAPHICS OF TYPE

It's been my observation that although all sixteen types can be seen in every culture and population, heavier concentrations of some functions exist in different demographics. I have no satisfying answer as to why this is, and the question of whether a child's type is selected wholly at random or influenced in some way by direct inheritance from their parents, is a question that still remains. Yet I find it important to mention what I have gleaned from this topic, in the hopes that it can help further conversation and research.

European Culture

The influence of Te-Fi is heavily represented in Anglo-Saxon appearance, psychology, as well as mythology. We first see the influence of Fi in its centuries of folklore and in the very nature of their magical creatures. Scotland, Great Britain and surrounding cultures together comprise a vast encyclopedia of enchanted creatures, typically small in size, secretive and selective in their interaction with humans. Katharine Briggs catalogs many of these creatures in her book *An Encyclopedia of Fairies* (1976), in which she extends the definition of *fairy* to include all of these magical beings such as hobgoblins, bogies, boggarts and brownies. We can see that the iconic, flower-dwelling, insect-winged fairy belongs to a wider definition of fairy that spans through all of Anglo-Saxon imagination.

Fairies are often feisty, always emotionally radiant, very independent and private. They rarely group together unless there is some common goal involved. Each species of fairy will have a favorite area of habitation and carry a different emotional disposition. Some fairies are fiendish and foul, others may be tender and protective of one place in nature, others are gluttonous and greedy, while others are rarely anything but gripey. Some are friendly to humans, like the brownie, and may tidy up the owner's house unseen at nights, but require a daily glass of the best milk or cake. In all of these creatures we encounter the same underlying theme – they are each an anthropomorphizing of a raw instinct of humanity. No fairy is without some sensational or sentimental signature – a calling toward an unconscious bliss or indulgence – but each is selective in what it desires.

A second theme we find across all fair folk is morality. If the owner forgets to leave cake out one night, or in some way transgresses a pact, a fairy is quick to repay the transgression to whatever proportion they find fair. Indeed, their standard of fairness is often less than fair to humans, as even benevolent fairies have no hesitation for appropriating anything they please through fairy-thefts or fairy-borrowings. There is a strikingly independent form of righteousness among fairies; one which humans must accustom themselves to if they are to deal well with them. Fairies also don't take well to mortal dishonesty and, in the words of Briggs, it would be "very unwise to try to cheat them in a bargain"[1]. But if one deals well with them, they will repay in kind through acts. As fairies are not gregarious or affable, they will convey affinities for certain humans through small acts or labors and will be perfectly unfailing in this. In many stories, a fairy will restock a farmer's grain each morning or secretly refill their flour vase so it never runs low. It would seem that a fairy's identity is inseparable from their specific morality, however benevolent or malicious it may be. And it's beyond me to write a very exhaustive account of all these creatures and their many peculiarities, but I would refer the reader to the contemporary works of Susanna Clarke[2], Tony DiTerLizzi[3] or again the extensive archive of Katharine Briggs for a more thorough account.

We see in these creatures all the elements of a psychic entity: immortality, supernatural ability, elusiveness, vagueness,

1: An Encyclopedia of Fairies, Katherine Briggs, pg.353 – 1978
2: Jonathan Strange & Mr.Norrell, Susanna Clarke – 2004
3: The Spiderwick Chronicles, Tony DiTerLizzi – 2009

facets of light and dark, and an instinctual drive. For those versed in analytical psychology, it is clear that the fairy, through its thematic portrayal across many generations, is not only a figure of the Anglo-Saxon imagination, but a deep reflection of their own psychic experience. By them the English conveyed their symbolisms, expressed their affinities, their troubles and all manner of common-day feelings. But unlike a complex theology, fairies have an altogether more personal and individual expression. They are not the means by which the great questions of purpose, existence and God are addressed, but instead the subject of soulful, day-to-day experiences.

In this we understand that the subject matter of fairies deals less with the collective unconscious and more with the personal unconscious. They are the embodiment of a psychic absolute – a raw and unfiltered sensation which is none other than the introverted ethical function – reimagined from each folk author's personal experience. We see in fairies all the qualities of Fi amplified and represented in forms liberated from realistic constraints. Just as we have seen in previous chapters that types heaviest in Fi are prone to be touchy and unyielding in a feeling, and very selective in their emotional palate, so too the fairies – but to an even greater extent. Being given a supernatural medium, Fi's individualistic, flighty sense of emotional aesthetic finds new embodiments. Fi is deeply connected to the emotional register, and so can feel very sharply each impulse and desire. These creatures become vessels for our impulses as experienced from the psychology of Fi-Te. Additionally, the logistical execution of feeling (Te) is also represented in the fair folk's dealings which are altogether action-oriented.

Naturally, as Fi is represented in Anglo-Saxon psychology, so is Te. The presence of Te is remarkably evident in Western philosophy and thought, and perhaps the epitome of this influence is seen in the United States of America. The States, as a relatively young and ambitious country, has persevered forward while abandoning much of the soulfulness of their parent nation; retaining little mythology or a cultural grounding point of its own. The industrialization of the States in the last two hun-

31. DEMOGRAPHICS OF TYPE

dred and seventy years has been largely due to a culture-wide domination of proactive logic (Te), progressing largely with an ignorance to their own ethical dimension. In the zeal and optimism of the West's capitalistic philosophy, Fi has fallen into the *unconscious* of the culture; the heart of the West has fallen into long abandoned myth and folklore. As Jung described in his *Liber Novus*[3], elements of the human collective transition continually from myth to actuality and back to myth, according to the passing of ages.

The word "fairytale" itself now bears witness to how Fi and its talents are repurposed toward a purely fictional dimension. It is pushed into the realm of childhood fantasy, Disney movies, and plays no important role in adult life and spirituality. If there is any representation, it is from a romanticism fixated too strongly on the light aspects of the heart without a proper respect for the more frightening and dark elements of humanity. This is not the case in many other cultures, where the mythologies of society are given more legitimacy and practiced outside of childhood – such as in Switzerland's Fasnacht[4] – adding with them a wisdom of the human heart. The often distant, calculative, and corporate aura we witness in the States is one result of this culture-wide cognitive imbalance. Other European nations such as Scotland, Ireland, Great Britain and France still lie embedded within centuries of art, music, history and the humanity that accompanies such a past. By comparison, their cultures carry a deeper respect for the introverted, the ethical, sentimental and nostalgic while still being heavy in the Te-Fi oscillation.

Individuals of Anglo-Saxon origin are somewhat more likely to carry the Te-Fi oscillation pairing, which is very visible also on their face. It would appear, in fact, that the visibility of Te-Fi on their face does not stop at facial expressions alone but also carries over into the physical structure of the face. Physically, the Anglo-Saxon countenance more commonly displays a small area between the mouth and nose, a type of tension running between the two, as well as an upturned, or *pixie,* nose. Be-

3: The Red Book: Liber Novus, pg.229, C.G. Jung – 2009
4: A carnival of masks that takes place in Basel in February or March.

cause of this, we must be exceptionally careful not to over-type these individuals as Te-Fi, since many Ti-Fe individuals will exist intermixed in this population but with physiological qualities that allude to Te-Fi.

African-American Cultures

A significant demographic bias toward Fe-Ti, both visually and psychologically, can be observed in African American individuals. Beginning from a single family unit and scaling up to a neighborhood, a city and the nation itself, the African American culture manages its societal structure using emotionally directive methodologies. Establishing placement, reverence and authority is largely done through emotional economy; by relationships and affiliations. Yet this culture's existence, during the past two hundred years, under the wing of America's utilitarian philosophy, has not gone without its effects. There is, in many African Americans, a deep conflict between a financially oriented philosophy of social acceptance – one which believes that to be economically successful is the solution to gaining social respect – and a more tender approach which accomplishes respect from carefully tended relationships. The former, due to its intermixing of Te priorities within an Fe framework, is far more susceptible to executing directive and confrontational emotional methodologies.

When a function pairing adopts the priorities of an opposing function pairing, heavy amounts of stress fall upon the individual. They may develop a functionally incompatible view of what it means to achieve success, struggling to use an ill-suited tool toward an ill-conceived solution. Even more troubling, such prioritizations will not yield the anticipated satisfaction upon the solution's realization. Logistical success cannot give the Fe lead type the gratification they might have had as an ethical pillar and matriarch in a less endowed but more soulfully enriched neighborhood. Yet, the soul of the African American community still travels through the veins of the United States, giving it a desperately needed vitality and sensitivity. We find this emotion and charisma in the chapel, the kitchen, the studio and in many radio and talk programs. If only it was allowed to exist in a less cold and calculative economy, a fuller appreciation of this demographic's gifts may be seen.

East Asian Cultures

The cultures we see in many East Asian nations, such as in Japan, South Korea and Thailand, are also heavy in Fe-Ti, but demonstrate a predominance of Ti over Fe. The reverse is true for African American culture which expresses more of Fe's tendencies and philosophies. In Japan we find a culture that has refined a system of emotional economy over centuries and in which respect, self-regulation of emotions and communal thinking are commonplace. We see an overall less proactive disposition, a heightened precision in the arts and recessiveness in philosophy. These all speak to a predominance of introversion in the culture, but more specifically of Ti's refinement in the topic of emotional interplays. Etiquette plays a large role in Japanese society (Fe), and their philosophy is rich in logical, axiomatic principles (Ti) and proverbs. From *"mono no aware"* to *"wabi-sabi"*, *"kanso"*, *"seijaku"* and *"zen"* – a deep solemnity exists underpinning this culture's aesthetic which carries several of Ti's attributes: dispassionate analysis, detachment, transparency, acknowledgement of life's imperfections and a tranquil attitude toward the happenings or troubles of life. No culture presents such a striking contrast against the capitalistic striving of the States.

In appearance also, Japan will demonstrate a far greater concentration of Fe-Ti than Te-Fi. Fe exists not in its charismatic and forthcoming form, but in a more placid and accommodating iteration. The TiSe type is especially represented in this culture, with many other Ji types following suit.

PART IV

TYPOLOGIES

ON MYERS-BRIGGS & KEIRSEY

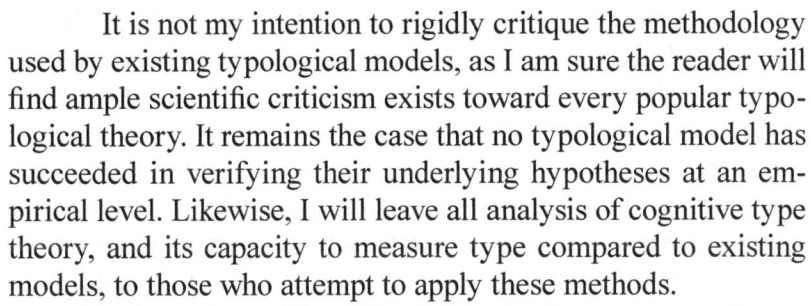

It is not my intention to rigidly critique the methodology used by existing typological models, as I am sure the reader will find ample scientific criticism exists toward every popular typological theory. It remains the case that no typological model has succeeded in verifying their underlying hypotheses at an empirical level. Likewise, I will leave all analysis of cognitive type theory, and its capacity to measure type compared to existing models, to those who attempt to apply these methods.

What I do wish to offer the reader is my perspective on typology's struggles and progress within the past decades to approximate, from different angles, the phenomenon of types. Typology has long existed divided between two general methodologies. These two methodologies are what we might call behaviorism and psychoanalysis. The behaviorist approach is of the opinion that what is most discernible, quantifiable, useful, and relevant, is a description of the manner in which a person's lifestyle can be determined by longstanding patterns of behavior. The psychoanalytical approach is of the opinion that the psyche should be understood as the primary source of insight into a person's nature, while behaviors are treated as end effects of internal psychology and not themselves indicative of type. The temperament system of David Keirsey presents an example of this pure behaviorism, as surmised by a statement on his website:

> Keirsey is not concerned with "what's in mind", but what people do. He is interested in what are the long-term behavior patterns: temperament. (...) If one tries to "talk about" what is "in the mind," one can start talking nonsense because we can't observe "mind" [1]

1: http://www.keirsey.com/difference.aspx

Indeed, it is entirely reasonable to depend on what information we are legitimately able to notice, rather than hypothesizing blindly about the dynamics of a system outside of observation. Were there no accessible avenue of exploration into the human mind – if it truly was wholly outside of observation – then I would be of the same opinion as Dr.Keirsey. However, it is possible, although by no means easy, to learn about the operations of the mind in both concrete and conceptual ways. But such knowledge cannot be understood through broad generalities. The nature of our psyche will utterly escape any attempts to simplify the topic at hand. We can expect nothing less than a complex and nuanced answer to such a complex question as the nature of consciousness. We must therefore come prepared to be immersed into the confusing and paradoxical if we are to make any headway in psychology. Yet such efforts are not fruitless, as the alternative position – a typology such as Keirsey's, however convenient and straightforward – could never properly inform us about the deeper reasons for our motivations, expressions, or our experience of reality. It can tell us *what*, but never *why*.

On the opposite side of the specturm we encounter typologies such as that of Carl Jung, which are strongly analytical and psychological. Jung's typology is a system of causality that explains the progression of our natural impulses into eventual behaviors, even at times from deeply unconscious motivations. Yet this too may be frustrating to a learner, as we are often left with no means to anchor such abstract explanations to our observable reality. Any attempt to rationalize perceived behaviors through a model such as Jung's may quickly lead to unintended confirmation biases. As all people display the individual qualities of introversion, extroversion, logical/ethical judgment, and abstract/concrete perception, it becomes increasingly challenging to discern which of these expressions is emerging from a single cognitive function or simultaneously manifesting through a combination of severeal alternate processes. In using a psychological approach, differentiated from specific behaviors, we are restricted to language and the use of semantic differentiations between what transpires in the minds of people. And when we consider how many people can fit the same semantic definition, as language is inescapably stretched and fitted by different audiences to suit alternate meanings, we understand that psychological definitions, however perfectly crafted by the author, are always fallacious due to their inability to universally communicate information. This complication has rendered Jungian typology largely unreliable and less popular than other models which offer a consensual means of quantification.

Myers-Briggs Typology

The typology created by Katharine Briggs and Isabel Briggs Myers (the Myers-Briggs Type Indicator) takes an intermediate approach to this problem; utilizing aspects of Jung's theoretical foundation and giving them tangible, behavioral definitions. This combination offered a partial solution to the challenges Jung's model faced by presenting a more standardized means of quantification – yet it encountered problems of its own.

a. Conflicting Paradigms

The MBTI, while most commonly viewed as a single system, does not address both its quantification and its theoretical foundation through a single system. Instead, it operates as a combination of two systems of measure; a four letter code (for example: INFP), and four associated functions (such as Fi-Ne-Si-Te) which define each of the sixteen types. The former is a behavioristic instrument which categorizes people based on the predominance of one attribute over the other. The latter is a cognitive system that describes people by their underlying psychology. We might be tempted to say that the first is the face of MBTI while the latter is what's at heart, but even this is also disputed among practitioners. The role that each of these systems plays in MBTI is contested, with some practitioners giving priority to the four letter code, making it more similar in ways to Keirsey's model, while others prioritize the Jungian functions.

Furthermore, these two systems carry fundamental differences such as in their definition of the J/P dichotomy. The four letter code does not match the functions 1:1 and this quickly becomes evident when we attempt to extrapolate behavior from the functions (or vice versa) to find a stark mismatch. Often a person will be typed as ENTP through the four letter code's methodology, then go on to read their description and be told they possess Ne and Ti. This process of *reverse deduction* is rather fallacious, as we can no more infer that possessing Ne-Ti results in ENTP behavior than we can infer that ENTP behavior implies the functions Ne and Ti are prioritized in the psyche. Theoretically speaking, these two systems of measurement should be kept separate. However, their union has persevered due to a moderate level of statistical correlation between the two measures. As we read in earlier chapters, a cognitive type can manifest the behaviors expected by their four-letter-code designation when their development is infantile. But because of this, the correlation between these two systems can only accurately type those with **one-sided** development. The MBTI, by its simplification of the functions to behavioral polarities can only differentiate people whose development is so outwardly unambiguous that the sheer overreliance on certain processes makes the type evident.

In seeking to give Jungian functions a tangible form, Myers & Briggs formulated a behavioristic system that moderately approximates itself to the functions, accepting some of the discrepancies that come as a result. Such is the philosophy of the Je process, which is far more content with some form of imperfect application than a theoretically sterile but inapplicable system.

b. Yielding the Analysis to the Test-Taker

Yet another fundamentally incorrect, yet functionally appealing decision made by Myers-Briggs was to structure the instrument as a *self-analysis*. For valid reasons, it is generally considered poor practice to have the test taker, in any topic of study, score his own results. Originally, Carl Jung evaluated his patients personally over many sessions and used decades of experience to make a determination about their psychological type. Type, when being gauged purely from the psychological angle,

32. ON MYERS-BRIGGS & KEIRSEY

is far too nuanced to be measured by a set of binary questions. Nonetheless the questionaire approach proved useful in the wake of World War II, where the test was administered for the purpose of finding best-fit positions for labor tasks to the influx of people being drafted to war. Given the circumstances, it would have been impractical to offer each person a lengthy psychological evaluation. Yet this approach persisted after the war, causing MBTI evaluations to become a *matter of opinion*, where no consensual or authoritative body or standard existed to definitively confirm a person's type. Instead, authority was yielded to the test taker, who must himself decide the reality of his type from the type descriptions outlined. We can find this approach explained on Myers-Brigg's own website in the following:

> "You, the person receiving the results, are the expert. By this stage, you should know the basics about type theory and the preferences. Ultimately, you are the only one who can decide your type. The practitioner needs to use open-ended questions and listen, listen, and listen some more."[2]

This is a profoundly dangerous approach to take, as it opens the door to cognitive biases and a variety of fallacies such as the well known *Forer Effect*. As Jung covers extensively in his concept of the archetypes, we are by no means experts of our own psyches. Countless influences from the unconscious guide a man's behavior and self-perception in ways unbeknown to him. Many times our rationalizations of life, our sense of ego and sense of placement in our environment are formed principally for their capacity to offer us utilities that meet challenges of our specific life-path. Our views of ourselves are in part crafted by the inner and the outer; by not just what our nature is, but by what the physical world demands that we believe of ourselves. If indeed type has a legitimate physiological or genetic basis, then we cannot decide on our type any more than we could decide on our own blood type. A method must be devised to properly

2: http://www.myersbriggs.org/my-mbti-personality-type/my-mbti-results/your-mbti-best-fit-type.htm gauge the reality of this phenomenon without a dependency on the person's own self evaluation.

Notwithstanding these and other complications, which become ever more apparent after increased exposure to the indicator, the MBTI's explanatory power at the onset of exposure to the public has shown itself strong enough to give it considerable momentum and popularity, leading to the several million users of the instrument to date. It is my opinion that this popularity is a direct result of the practicality inserted into it by Myers and Briggs, not due to any stronger empirical or theoretical foundation than alternative theories. However, over the past decades, the MBTI, through it's sheer popularity, has perpetuated the search for further clarity into Jung's functions, as the dissatisfaction in MBTI's shortcomings soon sets into serious learners who delve deeper into its origins. From this searching, many refinements have arisen in the topic of Jungian typology. The recent works by Naomi L. Quenk, Dr. A.J. Drenth and Michael Pierce present promising paradigm shifts to the Myers-Briggs community.

Myers-Briggs in Global Culture

Typology, as a subject, is fundamentally captivating to the human psyche due to its promise to offer insight into our self, tailored guidance relevant to our individual life circumstances, and a sense of belonging, camaraderie and kinship. Independent of typology, these are all important and relevant needs of humanity, which are necessary for the proper growth and development of our psyche. In all ages of human history, sources for insights into the self and answers to our psyche's ever-present question of "what or who am I", have risen anew. In our modern culture, the Myers-Briggs plays a heavy part in fulfilling this role. For better or worse, the structure of the MBTI allows it to address many of the needs of the human soul with sufficient experiential power to be perpetuated even if only for these purposes.

Due to this, the question of MBTI's success begins to overlap somewhat with the domain of the achetypes; innate themes of human experience and drama. While our cognitive type describes the functional mechanism with which we intake

32. ON MYERS-BRIGGS & KEIRSEY

and process our reality, the archetypes represent deeper impulses of the psyche that may direct a person's life-path toward the fulfillment of a certain psychic complex. The sixteen types, as often described in MBTI literature, will play a twofold role, being simultaneously expressions of cognitive psychology as well as archetypal complexes. Type will be described in conjunction with the difficulties and dramas faced by certain attitudes, idealisms and coping mechanisms. Questions of openness to others, avoidances and frustrations are embedded within the definition of a type. And while more Jungian approaches to this typological model depreciate these behavioristic addendums, they remain a significant influence in the overall community. Below is a short analysis of some of the major archetypal myths which the MBTI infuses within its type descriptions. Now these descriptions will have some relevance to the person in question as they will better inform them about their psychic complex, it's overall operation and the challenges it births for them. Although indirectly, a phenomenon is indeed being explained, along with the many characteristics that accompany such an attitude/mechanism. These characteristics may even seem typological because a set of consequential attributes can be expected from a particular orientation or attitude, but that attitude is not itself cognitive type. The Myers-Briggs wrongfully describes these attitudes as naturally emerging from certain cognitive functions when they arise instead from an unconscious place.

a. The INxx Types & Self-Reflective Attitudes

Those who have invested considerable time within Myers-Briggs communities know that the four INxx types in particular are given qualities of exceptionality, rareness, talent and innate wisdom. We see in these profiles many descriptors such as "deep thinking", "self-reflective", "intuitive", "creative", "insightful" and "intelligent". Many times the most innovative people are assigned to these four types. The challenges these four types are said to face in daily life are the struggles of existing in a world that misunderstands one's innate gifts. At times this misunderstanding is described as being due to the high level of psychological complexity these types hold in relation to others.

However, the qualities of being exceptionally self-reflective, removed from the general population and pursuing, perhaps melancholically, a personal direction of conceptual inquiry are not a sign of type. The impetus for the contemplation of larger questions of life, philosophy and existence occurs in all types, although certainly not in all people. Difficulties in youth and unaddressed matters of the heart, for example, will prompt the individuation process by which a person faces these and many other personally meaningful questions. The TiNe, FiNe, NiTe and NiFe types themselves are not synonymous with deep thinking nor do they always manifest the highest complexity of internal world. Any type who enters a sobering period in life, which removes or isolates them from the social and physical world, will better acquaint themselves with their inner thoughts and will manifest greater levels of creativity and internal refinement.

What is being described by the Myers-Briggs when it speaks of "deep insights, intelligence, and wisdom" is what psychologist Thomas Moore terms the **Gifts of Drepression** in his book *Care of the Soul* (1994). Moore describes this attitude as a Saturnian process after the Roman god Saturn, the veiled, old god of time. The Saturnian process is the natural initiation of the aging/maturation of the soul, the loss of the carefree innocence of youth, the vanishing of enthusiasm and the call of emptiness. Those who are in such a process are likely to type as INxx in Myers-Brigg's typology, finding affiliation and refuge with the INxx descriptions due to the way it speaks to the melancholy path of their life and the excommunication from the world which results.

b. The xNFx Types and Romantic Idealism

Another deeply intimate concept which the MBTI treads upon is that of the heart's idealism. The NF preference, due to its combination of ethical concerns (F) with abstract conceptualizations (N) is conceived as a type of pure romanticism, divorced from the tactile world and living within the idea of romance itself. The NF preference is therefore iconized as the embodiment

32. ON MYERS-BRIGGS & KEIRSEY

of the ethical process' creative manifestation and intelligence. This is an understandable misconception, considering abstract perception does indeed conceive conceptually, and if a person holds an imbalance in their psyche from an overuse of their abstract process, then they may indeed remain in a conceptual relationship to ethos. However, the MBTI fails to acknowledge that "N" types are not without their sensory function. Due to the way the MBTI conceives its letter preference dichotomies, polarizing Sensation from Intuition rather than understanding that the primary difference between perceptions in people lies between the orientations of extroversion and introversion (between the Ni-Se pair or the Ne-Si pair), "sensory" persons are described as severely lacking a proper capacity for abstraction. But it is not the case that "S" types can't strongly appreciate the pure conceptualization of a matter just as it's not true that "N" types are unable to become attuned to details.

Particularly when we speak of any archetypal and thematic topic, such as the heart's nature and function, its preoccupation within the minds of people is fairly well distributed within the sixteen types with only slight statistical leans toward certain types. These slight leanings can by no means be a justification for their inclusion within a type's description or their use as criteria by which to exclude an alternate typing. All those who value untethered ethical and humanistic concepts will resonate deeply with the NF descriptions. But as we explored in the type descriptions, even concrete types such as FiSe's Björk and Enya elegantly capture the abstract romanticism of the human condition. As the NF description greatly appeals to a certain dimension of human nature, we will more commonly find, within NF type communities, humans of all types whose psychic preoccupation is presently involved in this topic's *searching* and expression.

c. The xNTx Types and Affinity for Rationality

The inverse idealization problem is suffered within the NT type descriptions. The stark separation of 'sensation' from 'intuition' in the MBTI yields all creative and conceptual properties of logic to the NT preferences. But the ability to appreciate logic divorced from context or situation is a function of logic itself, void of any association to either 'sensation' or 'intuition'. This again forces self-typings to gravitate heavier toward the N preference due to its association with attributes that better apply to all people. Then, as an inverse reaction, the 'sensory' preference is highly depreciated by the way it is described as having a lack of many basic capacities of human imagination, creativity and ingenuity. Few people wish to think of themselves as lacking in such basic abilities, and because the MBTI possesses the fatal flaw of relying on self-evaluation and self-testing, this personal bias becomes all too relevant in the model's widespread adaptation and use. The amount of people misrepresenting their own psychology multiplies exponentially into a drowning, collective voice that functionally transforms the MBTI's overall message. The MBTI opens up the channels of typology to an affiliation with the preferences of the *ego* and *persona*.

From another perspective, it is easy to understand why people with ethical types may find an affiliation with the attributes described under the NT description. An affinity for truth, clarity, calculation and the unemotional can as much be due to natural instinct as it can be due to a desire for the security, stability and refuge it offers from the convoluted human heart. It is often the case that ethical types come to understand the ambiguity, hardships and turmoil their own innate disposition births, and from a desire to control or escape such confusion, a fetish evolves toward the sterile and logical, and the ego begins to associate itself with these far more stable elements. Such people will find that their own perceived preferences will align with the NT descriptions as defined in MBTI literature.

***

The MBTI offers no satisfying source of differentiation for such cases as these, other than placing the difficult task of teasing apart these underlying motivations wholly on the individual themselves. In doing so, the successes of those who manage to discover their own type – despite the heavy misdirection given by MBTI – cannot be attributed to the MBTI but to the individuation process of the person herself. And while encouraging the process of personal discovery is certainly something I profoundly advocate, it does the learner no service to clutter their path to that self-realization with confusing generalities.

ON SOCIONICS

Function Quadrants

Of the theories that have spun off from Jung's original work *Psychological Types* (1921), I've found Socionics to come the closest to properly describing the phenomenon of types. The grouping of the sixteen types via four function-based quadrants – *Alpha, Beta, Delta, Gamma* – is a far more legitimate divide than the grouping of types by behavioral manifestations as we see in the temperaments of Keirsey or the letter groupings of Myers-Briggs' Model. The Myers-Briggs model separates type groupings by their primary and secondary functions. The NP and SJ types are considered separate groupings, and as we'd expect, we find in them profile descriptions that only describe people of one-sided development. That is to say, any person with a proper, healthy balance between their functions is either mistyped or does not fit the type profiles altogether. They will see aspects of themselves across multiple contradictory profiles and have no theoretical avenue to reconcile these traits. We cannot correctly group the sixteen types based only on what function is theorized to possess more strength according to a staircase model of hierarchical order. As any practitioner of vultology soon realizes, types can weild their two polar processes quite effectively, even if they do so sparingly due to the energetic toll involved. The traits they exhibit when wielding these polar processes are likewise important aspects of the type's definition.

Such a complication is not present in Socionics, as it acknowledges the significance of the polar processes in producing the overall psychology of the sixteen types. The descriptions for the Alpha, Beta, Delta and Gamma quadrants each attribute the qualities of all four functions to all four corresponding types.

33. ON SOCIONICS

J-Lead and P-Lead

Socionics' position that a type is either Judging or Perceiving depending on the nature of the primary function is also correct, contrary to the J/P dichotomy mixing we see in Myers-Briggs' model. The TiNe type is considered a Perceiver in Myers-Briggs model although its primary function is Ti (reactive logical judgment). Inversely, in Socionics the TiNe type is rightly considered a Judger, and the type's description reflects this characteristic by placing higher emphasis on their tendency toward decisive clarity, albeit abstract and conceptual in nature.

Here once again we see MBTI's stamp of behaviorism in its theoretical foundation. It would reason that a more useful dichotomy to measure is how a person approaches reality, suggesting that one's approach to life is best gauged by what function (J or P) is first oriented outward. However, the primary oscillation pairing (Ti-Fe in the case of our TiNe) is far more significant in telling us what aspects of life heavily preoccupy a type's psychology, than which function comes up extroverted first.

Consequently, due to its method of identifying the J-P dichotomy through expressed manifestations, the MBTI has a fundamentally flawed view of Judgment and Perception. The attributes of Judgment are restricted almost entirely to what is produced by Je and Perception is restricted to the attributes produced by Pe. A Perception type is considered open-ended and adaptable, while we know that Pi lead types (or Worldview types) may also be quite opposed to change or openness. But since a Pi lead type would be considered a J-type by MBTI, this reluctance to change is justified and attributed to Judgment. This in turn affects the way Je is seen in all sixteen types. In like manner, other attributes are crisscrossed throughout the type descriptions due to the swapping of the J-P dichotomy in half of the types.

Unfortunately, a few of the misconceptions observed in the MBTI through the quantification of J and P via extroverted attributes are also seen in Socionics. While the TiNe type may be rightly considered J-type in Socionics, qualities involving external coordination such as planning, organizing and applying rules will be part of the type's description. Yet, the judgment of

TiNe types, or any of the four Ji types, is more keenly expressed through sharpness in conceptual differentiation and a clearly defined personal disposition toward certain topics and ideas. These internal differentiations might even be passive and unobtrusive, not having any significant bearing on the structure of the external world.

Model A

While Socionics presents many useful concepts of type, some aspects of its theory are based on an improper intermixing of psychic apparatuses, seen most prominently in Aushra Augusta's *Model A*. It has been my experience that an individual's cognitive type is positioned amidst all other surrounding psychic processes, yet it retains its own functional independence while being inescapably influenced by all other internal and external forces. The relationship cognitive type holds towards internal elements such as the ego, the shadow and the unconscious is strongly dependent on the content within those elements. The attitude an individual has toward their own functions is dependent on the person's level of recognition and acceptance of their own human dimensionality. It is not always the case that the primary function is well praised and associated to the self, while the polar function is underdeveloped and sensitive to criticism. Weakness, shame for weakness and other dispositions and orientations are a separate psychological matter untethered from cognitive type. In this, I find Model A's merging of type with these psychic elements to be unwarranted, and a source of heavy restriction. If the identification of type is dependent on what psychic attitude an individual is perceived to have toward their own internal world, then type can only be accurately assessed when a person holds the expected attitude toward their own functions. But the reverse is the case, as attitudes evolve over time as the archetypes and myths a person faces through their life also change.

Additionally, the arrangement of the eight functions into a mathematical structure of assigned psychic roles places Socionics on very dangerous theoretical ground. To assign specific qualities to that which is sparsely, if ever, observed (namely the four *unconscious/shadow functions*) quickly creates a rather unfalsifiable situation, and one which is far too dependent on theoretical math for its validity. Such rationality opens the way to confirmation bias, where otherwise extraneous and contradictory information is easily fitted into the existing model by the addendum of an annex for exceptions. Before we venture to profess what is out of our eyesight, we must clearly see what lies before us. Only after we have found an accurate way to identify and quantify the conscious apparatus are we prepared to understand the orientations which the unconscious functions hold in our psyche. We risk incorrectly quantifying the unconscious functions if we have improperly typed the conscious functions first. For this reason, I have little to say regarding the four unavailable functions of a person's psyche, since much research and effort is still needed toward the simple initial identification of the four conscious functions in a person.

Visual Identification

Perhaps the most curious aspect of Socionics' theory is its visual identification (V.I.) model. Socionics is in a peculiar position in regards to visual identification. While there has been considerable and continual criticism towards facial reading even within Socionics' own community, it has nonetheless persisted within the model as a type of black sheep. For a model that seeks to provide such a theoretically airtight approach to typology, it is initially baffling to consider that the insertion of this physical, yet largely unexplained, quantifier would exist. However, the answer lies in Socionics' own success at possessing a relatively accurate psychological conceptualization of the eight functions. Many times we witness Socionics theorists and practitioners, such as Ekaterina Filatova, who strictly practice Socionics using psychological means of quantification, puzzling over visual similarities in their patients which they could not entirely explain. In her book *Understanding the People around You* (2010), Filatova describes this unexpected correlation with a series of photographs of her patients and what she termed "twin" types. The "twin" people Ekaterina Filatova saw were due to a legitimate typing approach. That is to say, she was typing people correctly enough through purely psychological means that visual correlations began to emerge and which she could not wholly ignore. This has been the central dilemma of Socionics, and why it has been lukewarm in its assertion of visual identification as being something at all relevant. It is no surprise that Socionics, having a mostly accurate comprehension of psychological type, should be baffled by the apparent similarities in appearance that are naturally elicited. If only the question of similarities in appearance had been more thoroughly explored, the production of this book may not have been necessary.

The failure of Socionics to fully capture the phenomenon of visual reading is due to an almost complete lack of a systemic progression of signals. The V.I. system of Socionics is far more static, lacking a dynamic flow of causality between all the signals of the sixteen types. What results instead is a type of *physiognomy* where practitioners have little to use for typing aside from the structural correlations between the faces of their patients. Typings by V.I. are most commonly performed by comparing the subject to static photographs, or to an aggregation of many faces belonging to people of that type. This has made V.I. notoriously unreliable, as the static structure of a person's face is not itself relevant to cognitive type, and type must be visually measured by the manner in which a person's facial muscles dynamically contract or rest in tension.

ON EXPERIMENTATION

While the material in this book is an explanation of my own initial observations, controlled experimentations can be devised in which these observations are examined more closely. Vultology makes itself directly available for scientific review, criticism and falsifiability. But as my own profession lies in the arts, not in the sciences, I must depend on the efforts of those in the sciences to evaluate the conclusions found in this book. I would, however, like to offer my humble opinion as to how these experimentations might be carried out to offer a definitive result.

Experimental Control

When I first imagined gauging the accuracy of vultology by comparing the typings it produces to some other measurement point that acts as a control, I quickly realized there is a problem. No standardized method of quantifying the types currently exists. Measuring the capacity of vultology to identify type cannot be done if type itself, the *primary control*, has not been properly defined. Conclusions vary greatly among practitioners as to what constitutes type, and there is even more variation in the execution of those frameworks into actual typings. Therefore, it would not be appropriate to measure the accuracy of vultology against the typings of any one practitioner. Such results would only reveal that two equally unverified systems of measurement are either in accordance or in opposition to each other.

Instead, if progress is to be made in typology, we must first and foremost address the fundamental question of cognitive type's existence. To do so, the reliability of vultology must be measured against an existing technology with a greater level of experimental control than what psychology currently offers.

Neurology

Two such technologies are functional MRI (fMRI) and the electroencephalogram (EEG). An experiment can be conducted in which the subject is visually recorded in a conversational setting while wearing an EEG cap. Questions may be asked that evoke the real-time formation of deductions, memory recall, active cross-contextualization, and expressions. Afterwards a vultologist (one learned in the methodology of vultology) can time-decode the video, giving a second-by-second analysis of the visual signals elicited and a report on what vultology would reveal about their psychology and type.

The recorded brain activity of the subject can then be compared to the vultological analysis given, to see what brain activity was occurring during the expression of each visual signal. This process would be repeated until a sufficient amount of subjects are cataloged for each of the sixteen types, as defined by the signals of vultology. At this point we can also compare the brain activity of individuals typed as the same type using vultology, and determine whether or not a significant neurological parallel exists between these persons.

I hypothesize that a correlation would arise not only in the aggregated brain activity of those of the same type, but also in the use of specific functions. The visual signals that are clustered together under a certain oscillation pairing would demonstrate their own neural signature. This signature would carry over across all types possessing that oscillation – largely at the exclusion of their opposing oscillation's signals. If this proved to be the case, then we would understand type as not only a series of neurological correlations between people, but as a *system* of neural activity that produces the sixteen types inevitably as a result of its own operation.

Cognitive Type Vultology Code

Another important concern I faced was finding a method to standardize vultology, so as to make it non-dependent on the

34. ON EXPERIMENTATION

practitioner's subjective perception of the signals. Now I must reiterate that I consider the subjective factor deeply important for our understanding of ourselves and the people around us, and I would encourage the keen refinement of one's personal worldview, both in the topic of vultology as well as in all aspects of life.

The matter I seek to address here is instead one of open scientific communication; the ability to speak about the basic signals of vultology in a way that can be initially understood by any researcher. For this I have isolated 110 signals, which I believe to be the least ambiguous, and given each signal 10 photographic examples to demonstrating their appearance. When language fails to convey the precision of a concept, imagery may do a far better job at offering us clarity. These 110 signals are divided as follows:

5	*Signals for*	J
5	*Signals for*	P
5	*Signals for*	Ji
5	*Signals for*	Je
5	*Signals for*	Pi
5	*Signals for*	Pe
10	*Signals for*	Ti
10	*Signals for*	Fi
10	*Signals for*	Ne
10	*Signals for*	Se
10	*Signals for*	Ni
10	*Signals for*	Si
10	*Signals for*	Te
10	*Signals for*	Fe

A full list of these signals can be found in Chapter 37, and examples of these signals in action are visible on the web at: **http://cognitivetype.com/ctvc/**. Using such an archive, we are able to give this typology *predictability* and *repeatability*. We can, for example, observe 2 or 3 signals belong to Fi and make a prediction about the inevitable observation of the remaining Fi signals as well as the anticipated presence of Te's signals at the exclusion of most signals belonging to Fe and Ti within a reasonable margin of error. In this way we can measure whether or not these signals are indeed significantly statistically linked to one another and not to other signals. It's my hope that this codex can offer a starting point for any prospective practitioner to learn to type, as well as offer a *baseline* from which the topic of vultology can be empirically evaluated by a broader community.

The Current Accuracy of Vultology

Vultology, as with any instrument of measure, carries in it limitations which must be accounted for and respected to retain a proper understanding of the object of its observation. It's my opinion that the present iteration of this vultological model accounts for, and allows for, the proper discernment of type in the vast majority of people – with only a small degree of outliers who do not adhere to the patterns described. Indeed, these principles and patterns have not accounted for every single human sample I have encountered; a handful of individuals carry a visual signature that intermixes opposing signals or a psychology that does not match their muscular contractions. While it's difficult to give an exact figure, approximately 5% of the people I've encountered cannot be described with this methodology. Yet it remains by far the most accurate means of gauging type that I have encountered and presents a level of correlation that cannot be wholly ignored.

It is unclear to me whether this ~5% margin of error is due to the inefficiency of my own observation, the limitations of what can be determined by the signals elicited, the net influence nurture can have in obscuring nature, or some other factor. But it is my hope that in the eventual future, a method of identifying type can be discovered (perhaps in genetics or neurology) that can confirm type with complete certainty. However, it is also my hope that vultology, perhaps as a bridge to that eventual aim, can provide a *close-enough* gauge for the legitimacy of type and prompt further investigation towards its reality as may be discovered through many more avenues.

ORIGINS & CREDITS

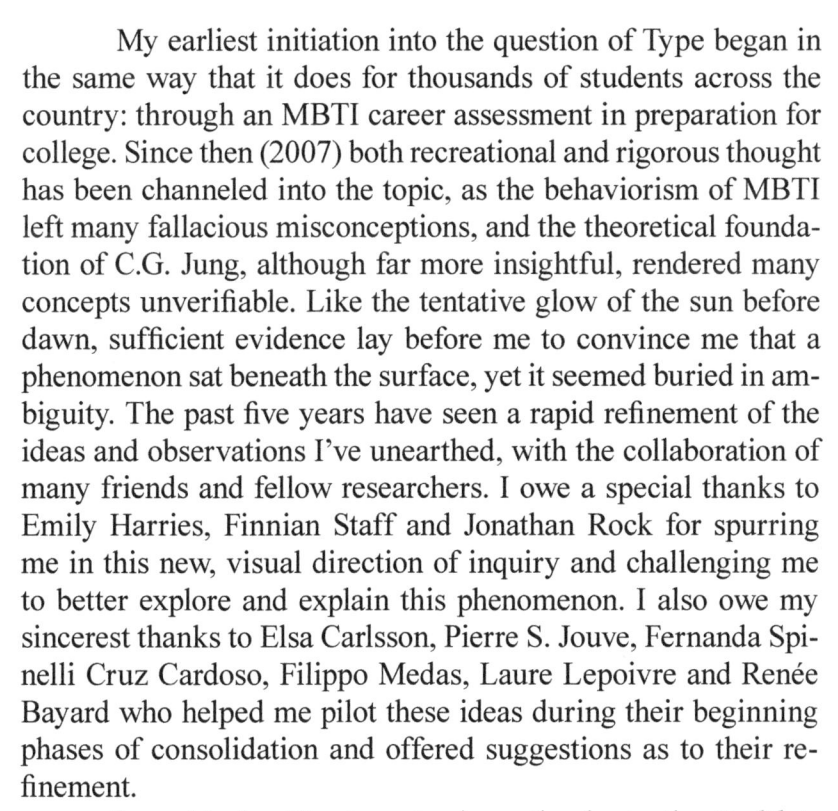

My earliest initiation into the question of Type began in the same way that it does for thousands of students across the country: through an MBTI career assessment in preparation for college. Since then (2007) both recreational and rigorous thought has been channeled into the topic, as the behaviorism of MBTI left many fallacious misconceptions, and the theoretical foundation of C.G. Jung, although far more insightful, rendered many concepts unverifiable. Like the tentative glow of the sun before dawn, sufficient evidence lay before me to convince me that a phenomenon sat beneath the surface, yet it seemed buried in ambiguity. The past five years have seen a rapid refinement of the ideas and observations I've unearthed, with the collaboration of many friends and fellow researchers. I owe a special thanks to Emily Harries, Finnian Staff and Jonathan Rock for spurring me in this new, visual direction of inquiry and challenging me to better explore and explain this phenomenon. I also owe my sincerest thanks to Elsa Carlsson, Pierre S. Jouve, Fernanda Spinelli Cruz Cardoso, Filippo Medas, Laure Lepoivre and Renée Bayard who helped me pilot these ideas during their beginning phases of consolidation and offered suggestions as to their refinement.

I would also like to extend my thanks to the *Pod'lair* research group. Having an alternative perspective on the topic of visual reading, they have acted at times as a helpful contrast point for my own direction of inquiry. And despite the many theoretical differences we face, as well as challenges in communication that have all but rendered collaboration impossible, I am grateful for their pursuit for understanding regarding the topic of vultology, as I've now come to call it.

PART V

APPENDIX

LISTING OF PEOPLE'S TYPES

NAME	TYPE	DEVELOPMENT	ALT.
Edward Witten	*FiNe*	*Scientist/Seelie Fairy*	
Brian Cox	*FiNe*	*Scientist/Seelie/Balanced*	
Neils Bohr	*FiNe*	*Seelie/Scientist*	
Linus Torvalds	*FiNe*	*Scientist*	
Liza Minnelli	*FiNe*	*Seelie Fairy*	
Evanna Lynch	*FiNe*	*Seelie Fairy*	
Joan Baez	*FiNe*	*Standard*	
Meredith Godreau	*FiNe*	*Standard*	
Regina Spektor	*FiNe*	*Standard*	
Aurora Aksnes	*FiNe*	*Standard*	
Drew Endy	*FiNe*	*Scientist*	
Eva Silverstein	*FiNe*	*Scientist/Polarized*	
Randall Munroe	*FiNe*	*Scientist/Polarized*	*TiNe*
Michael Cera	*FiNe*	*Unsocial Sensitivist*	
Joanne Rowling	*FiNe*	*Te-Heavy*	
Marilyn Manson	*FiNe*	*Unseelie*	
Jacqueline Kennedy	*FiSe*	*Seelie*	
Marilyn Monroe	*FiSe*	*Seelie*	
Audrey Hepburn	*FiSe*	*Seelie*	
Janet Jackson	*FiSe*	*Indie Artist*	
Michael Jackson	*FiSe*	*Indie Artist*	
Neri Oxman	*FiSe*	*Vegetarian*	
Bjork	*FiSe*	*Seelie/Indie Artist*	
Kanye West	*FiSe*	*Unseelie*	
Princess Diana Frances	*FiSe*	*Unseelie*	*FiNe*
Zdzisław Beksiński	*FiSe*	*Unseelie*	
Sonny Moore	*FiSe*	*Indie Artist*	
Enya Brennan	*FiSe*	*Indie Artist*	
50 Cent	*FiSe*	*Standard*	
Sarah Brightman	*FiSe*	*Harmonious Seelie*	
Liv Tyler	*FiSe*	*Harmonious Seelie*	
Bill Clinton	*FiSe*	*Balanced*	
Elijah Wood	*FiSe*	*Se-Heavy*	

COGNITIVE TYPE

Annie Laurie Gaylor	*FiSe*	*Balanced*	
Kate Bush	*FiSe*	*Ni Heavy*	*NiTe*
Elvis Presley	*FiSe*	*Ni Heavy*	*NiTe*
Marissa Mayer	*FiSe*	*Balanced/Executive*	
Angela Braly	*FiSe*	*Polarized*	
James Cameron	*TeSi*	*Entrepreneur*	
Ted Cruz	*TeSi*	*Politician/Historian*	
Stephen Colbert	*TeSi*	*Eccentric Nerd*	
John Carmack	*TeSi*	*Eccentric Nerd*	
J.R.R. Tolkien	*TeSi*	*Entrepreneur/Historian*	
Ayn Rand	*TeSi*	*Logistical Ethicist*	
Fran Lebowitz	*TeSi*	*Logistical Ethicist*	
Miley Cyrus	*TeSi*	*Individualist*	
Adele Adkins	*TeSi*	*Individualist*	
Rebecca Watson	*TeSi*	*Logistical Ethicist*	
Hugh Grant	*TeSi*	*Standard*	
Colin Firth	*TeSi*	*Standard*	
Tina Fey	*TeSi*	*Jester*	
Sarah Palin	*TeSi*	*Politician*	
Brenda Fricker	*TeSi*	*Historian*	
Germaine Greer	*TeSi*	*Individualist/Historian*	
Lady Gaga	*TeSi*	*Individualist*	
Simon Cowell	*TeSi*	*Unseelie/Dismissive*	
Erin Brockovich	*TeSi*	*Historian/Nerd*	
Kelly Eckerman	*TeSi*	*Executive*	
Chris Wallace	*TeSi*	*Politician*	
Megyn Kelly	*TeSi*	*Politician*	
Richard Dawkins	*TeSi*	*Polarized*	
Bachir Boumaaza	*TeSi*	*Individualist*	*FeSi*
Drew Barrymore	*TeSi*	*Executive*	
Savannah Guthrie	*TeSi*	*Executive*	
Joy Behar	*TeSi*	*Logistical Ethicist*	
Charlie Sheen	*TeNi*	*Fervent Eccentric*	
Tom Hanks	*TeNi*	*Fervent Eccentric*	*TeSi*
Bill O'Reily	*TeNi*	*Fervent Eccentric*	
Richard Feynman	*TeNi*	*Physicist/Seelie*	
Patricia Routledge	*TeNi*	*Fervent Eccentric*	
Maureen O'Hara	*TeNi*	*Haughty*	
Claire Pires	*TeNi*	*Executive*	
Bill Maher	*TeNi*	*Unseelie/Dismissive*	
Hugh Laurie	*TeNi*	*Balanced*	*TeSi*
Richard D Wolff	*TeNi*	*Fervent Eccentric*	*FeNi*
Mike Huckabee	*TeNi*	*Politician*	
Selena Gomez	*TeNi*	*Balanced*	

36. LISTING OF PEOPLE'S TYPES

John J. Legere	TeNi	Executive	
Kristen Hadeed	TeNi	Executive	
Tim Russert	TeNi	Balanced/Executive	
Mary Helen Bowers	TeNi	Sassy	
Mila Kunis	TeNi	Balanced	
Adolf Hitler	TeNi	Fervent Eccentric	
Rosie O'Donnell	TeNi	Fervent Eccentric	
Isaac Newton	TeNi	Fervent Eccentric	
Sarah Polley	TeNi	Standard	
Amy Poehler	TeNi	Standard	
Helena Bonham Carter	TeNi	Standard	
Carly Fiorina	TeNi	Politician/Executive	
Reese Hartwig	TeNi	Standard	
Maria Shriver	TeNi	Executive	
Ryan MacDonald	TeSi	Eccentric Nerd	TeNi
Adam Sandler	SiFe	Traditionalist	
Tom Hiddleton	SiFe	Silly-Serious	
James Franco	SiFe	Parent/Silly-Serious	
Joss Whedon	SiFe	Standard	
Vin Diesel	SiFe	Eternal Parent	
Usher Raymond	SiFe	Standard	
Joseph Gordon Levitt	SiFe	Standard	
Jeff Dunham	SiFe	Silly-Serious	
Orlando Bloom	SiFe	Silly-Serious	
Bret McKenzie	SiFe	Silly-Serious	NeTi
Heather Nova	SiFe	Ti-heavy	
Brad Pitt	SiFe	Traditionalist	
Kevin Costner	SiFe	Traditionalist	
Paul Ekman	SiFe	Traditionalist	
Ralph Fiennes	SiFe	Standard	
Hugh Whittall	SiFe	Ti Heavy	TiNe
Antero Alli	NiFe	Guru	
Ray Kurzweil	NiFe	Guru	
Garrison Keillor	NiFe	Grandfather	
Leonard Nimoy	NiFe	Grandfather	
Leonardo DiCaprio	NiFe	Balanced	
James Dean	NiFe	Delinquent	
Justin Bieber	NiFe	Delinquent	
Kendji Girac	NiFe	Persona-Sensitive	FeNi
Morgan Freeman	NiFe	Grandfather	
Larry King	NiFe	Grandfather	
Nicholas Hoult	NiFe	Balanced	
David Sinclair	NiFe	Balanced	
Jason Reitman	NiFe	Balanced	TiSe

COGNITIVE TYPE

Carl Jung	*NiFe*	*Guru*	
Elaine Aron	*NiFe*	*Guru*	*NiTe*
Fred Rogers	*NiFe*	*Grandfather*	
Matthew Gray Gubler	*NeTi*	*Comedian/Dabbler*	
Lawrence Krauss	*NeTi*	*Theorist*	
Jim Carrey	*NeTi*	*Comedian*	
Tessa Violet	*NeTi*	*Comedian*	
Tim Minchin	*NeTi*	*Introverted/Theorist*	
Adam Savage	*NeTi*	*Dabbling Theorist*	
Dave Chappelle	*NeTi*	*Comedian*	*SeTi*
Christina Perri	*NeTi*	*Standard*	
Anne Hathaway	*NeTi*	*Balanced*	
Jung Eun-ji	*NeTi*	*Introverted*	
Elizabeth Olsen	*NeTi*	*Standard*	
Chuck Thomas	*NeTi*	*Comedian*	
Michael DiMartino	*NeTi*	*Standard*	
Chris Tucker	*SeTi*	*Sensationalist*	
George Lopez	*SeTi*	*Analytical Sensationalist*	
Tyrese Gibson	*SeTi*	*Sensationalist*	
Marshall Mathers	*SeTi*	*Anti-Sage*	
Jack Black	*SeTi*	*Sensationalist*	
Auburn Williams	*SeTi*	*Standard*	
Gabby Douglas	*SeTi*	*Standard*	
Ryan Sheckler	*SeTi*	*Standard*	
Paul Rodriguez	*SeTi*	*Standard*	
Shawn Phan	*SeTi*	*Analytical Sensationalist*	
Jay McKee	*SeTi*	*Analytical/Anti-Sage*	
Fran Kranz	*SeTi*	*Analytical Sensationalist*	*TiSe*
Adriana Grande	*SeTi*	*Se-heavy*	
Rihanna	*SeTi*	*Sensationalist*	
Noam Chomsky	*TiNe*	*Scholar/Psychoanalyst*	
Lynn Hoag	*TiNe*	*Scholar*	
Hayao Miyazaki	*TiNe*	*Psychoanalyst*	
Arin Cumley	*TiNe*	*Standard*	
Mark Kessell	*TiNe*	*Armchair/Artist*	
Alanis Morissette	*TiNe*	*Psychoanalyst*	
Damon Waynes Jr.	*TiNe*	*Standard*	
Ashley Olsen	*TiNe*	*Psychoanalyst*	
Takeshi Kaneshiro	*TiNe*	*Standard*	
Amy Cuddy	*TiNe*	*Psychoanalyst*	
Andrew Bird	*TiNe*	*Armchair Philosopher*	
Richard Melville Hall	*TiNe*	*Armchair/Artist*	
Christian Hudson	*TiSe*	*Poised Actor*	
Marques Brownlee	*TiSe*	*Technical Specialist*	

36. LISTING OF PEOPLE'S TYPES

Norman Chan	*TiSe*	*Technical Specialist*	
Elon Musk	*TiSe*	*Technical Specialist*	
Yan S. Huang	*TiSe*	*Technical Specialist*	
Tony Hawk	*TiSe*	*Ace Athlete*	
Choi Min-ho	*TiSe*	*Poised Actor*	
Kim Jong-hyun	*TiSe*	*Poised Actor*	
Jamie Chung	*TiSe*	*Poised Actor*	*FiSe*
Topher Grace	*TiSe*	*Standard*	
Carl Sagan	*TiSe*	*Balanced*	*FeNi*
Kristen Stewart	*TiSe*	*Standard*	
Bryan Konietzko	*TiSe*	*Se-Heavy*	*SeTi*
Harry Lennix	*FeSi*	*Patriarch*	
Laurie Santos	*FeSi*	*Philosophical Moralist*	
Barack Obama	*FeSi*	*Philosophical Moralist*	*TiNe*
Eddie Murphy	*FeSi*	*Charismatic Charmer*	*FeNi*
Shemar Moore	*FeSi*	*Charismatic Charmer*	*FeNi*
Jill Biden	*FeSi*	*Patriarch/Martyr*	
Terry Crews	*FeSi*	*Charismatic Charmer*	
Dwayne Johnson	*FeSi*	*Charismatic Charmer*	
Tom Cruise	*FeSi*	*Patriarch*	
Rachel McAdams	*FeSi*	*Balanced*	
Emma Watson	*FeSi*	*Balanced/Martyr*	
Michael Strahan	*FeSi*	*Charismatic Charmer*	
Eddie Murphy	*FeSi*	*Comedian*	
Jackie Chan	*FeSi*	*Comedian*	
Sam Jones	*FeSi*	*Philosophical/Ti-heavy*	
Cesar Millan	*FeNi*	*Oracle*	*FeSi*
Martin Luther King Jr.	*FeNi*	*Alpha Visionary*	
Kazimierz Dąbrowski	*FeNi*	*Mystic/Oracle/Academic*	
Zbigniew Preisner	*FeNi*	*Academic*	
Mandy Patinkin	*FeNi*	*Mystic/Academic*	
Denzel Washington	*FeNi*	*Alpha Visionary*	
Neil DeGrasse Tyson	*FeNi*	*Academic*	
Oprah Winfrey	*FeNi*	*Oracle*	
Matt Damon	*FeNi*	*Standard*	*NiFe*
Patrick Stewart	*FeNi*	*Academic*	
Drew Canole	*FeNi*	*Oracle*	
Cenk Uygur	*FeNi*	*Acaemic*	
Derek Muller	*FeNi*	*Academic*	
Iyanla Vanzant	*FeNi*	*Oracle*	
Abraham Lincon	*FeNi*	*Alpha Visionary*	
Paul Michael Levesque	*FeNi*	*Alpha/Sensationalist*	
Kobe Bryant	*FeNi*	*Alpha/Athlete*	
Charlie Rose	*FeNi*	*Balanced*	

COGNITIVE TYPE

Craig Kilborn	SiTe	Jester
Ken Jennings	SiTe	Encyclopedia
Scott Adams	SiTe	Practical Dabbler
Mitt Romney	SiTe	Lawyer/Politician
George W. Bush	SiTe	Lawyer/Politician
Scott Walker	SiTe	Lawyer/Politician
Jamie Hyneman	SiTe	Practical Dabbler
Giff Nielsen	SiTe	Lawyer/Politician
Edward Norton	SiTe	Standard
Rainn Wilson	SiTe	Jester
Matthew Lewis	SiTe	Standard
Steve Carell	SiTe	Jester
Kurt Schneider	SiTe	Jester
Mira Nagayama	SiTe	Encyclopedia
Mary Landrieu	SiTe	Lawyer/Politician
Bret Baier	SiTe	Lawyer/Politician
Sean Hannity	SiTe	Lawyer/Politician	SiFe
Brian Williams	SiTe	Lawyer/Politician
Stanley Maloy	SiTe	Practical Dabbler
Tori Amos	NiTe	Critic/Mystic	FiSe
Vivien Leigh	NiTe	Haughty
Clark Duke	NiTe	Standard
Juan Manuel Rivero	NiTe	Political Critic
Joseph Marquez	NiTe	Sarcasic Jester
Stella Duffy	NiTe	Developed Te
Zinnia Jones	NiTe	Political Critic
Wolfgang Pauli	NiTe	Practical Mystic
Kat Dennings	NiTe	Deadpan
Barbara Walters	NiTe	Critic/Executive
Aubrey Plaza	NiTe	Deadpan/Jester
Brian Clough	NiTe	Standard
Asa Butterfield	NiTe	Balanced
Hillary Clinton	NiTe	Political Critic/Executive
Luke Russert	NiTe	Balanced
Jonathan Ross	NeFi	Faux-Fe
Craig Ferguson	NeFi	Faux-Fe
Kristen Schaal	NeFi	Seelie/Faux-Fe
Kate Miccuci	NeFi	Seelie
Emily Wapnick	NeFi	Seelie/Scattered
Ellen DeGeneres	NeFi	Faux-Fe
Paul Graham	NeFi	Si-Heavy	SiTe
Britney Spears	NeFi	Scattered
Chloe Agnew	NeFi	Scattered
Wally De Backer	NeFi	Aspie/Seelie

36. LISTING OF PEOPLE'S TYPES

Josh Groban	*NeFi*	*Faux-Fe*	
Robin Williams	*NeFi*	*Comedian*	
Lindsey Stirling	*NeFi*	*Seelie/Scattered*	
Amy Lee	*NeFi*	*Standard*	
Carey Mulligan	*NeFi*	*Seelie*	
Vanessa Woods	*NeFi*	*Te Heavy*	
Chrissy Costanza	*NeFi*	*Faux-Fe*	*NeTi*
Florence Welch	*NeFi*	*Introverted Extrovert*	
Jason Zimmerman	*NeFi*	*Aspie/Introverted*	
Albert Einstein	*NeFi*	*Aspie/Seelie*	
Terrence Tao	*NeFi*	*Aspie/Faux-Fe*	*SeFi*
Palmer Luckey	*NeFi*	*Eccentric Nerd*	
Jennifer Paine	*NeFi*	*Te Heavy*	
Richard Lenski	*NeFi*	*Scientist/Entrepreneur*	
Elle Fanning	*SeFi*	*Seelie Socialite*	
Sia Furler	*SeFi*	*Gypsy*	
Cillian Murphy	*SeFi*	*Standard*	
Robert Pattinson	*SeFi*	*Standard*	
Natalie Portman	*SeFi*	*Manager*	
Dakota Fanning	*SeFi*	*Seelie Socialite*	
Chris Martin	*SeFi*	*Artist/Performer*	
Bam Margera	*SeFi*	*Sensationalist*	
Keira Knightley	*SeFi*	*Artist/Performer*	
Rebecca Black	*SeFi*	*Artist/Performer*	
Kaley Cuoco	*SeFi*	*Artist/Performer*	
Cameron Diaz	*SeFi*	*Seelie Socialite*	
James Dean Bradfield	*SeFi*	*Te Heavy*	
Emma Stone	*SeFi*	*Te Heavy*	
Miranda Kerr	*SeFi*	*Seelie*	*FiSe*
Joslyn Davis	*SeFi*	*Manager*	

LEXICON OF VISUAL SIGNALS

J-1	Rigid Posture
J-2	Face Centric
J-3	Angular Motions
J-4	Exacting Hands
J-5	Subordinate Perception
P-1	Fluid Posture
P-2	Eye Centric
P-3	Ongoing Movements
P-4	Casual Hands
P-5	Subordinate Judgment
Je-1	Head Nods
Je-2	Head Shakes
Je-3	Shoulder Shrugs
Je-4	Pointed Emphasis
Je-5	Projecting Hands
Pi-1	Inertial Energy
Pi-2	Fixed Gaze
Pi-3	Diagonal Eye-drifts
Pi-4	Worldview Rambling
Pi-5	Searching Scowling
Ji-1	Receding Energy
Ji-2	Disengaging Eyes
Ji-3	Exerted Push
Ji-4	Momentum Halting
Ji-5	Meticulous Hands
Pe-1	Alert/Wide Eyes
Pe-2	Darting Eyes
Pe-3	Perk Ups
Pe-4	Bubbling Momentum
Pe-5	Body Swaying
Fi-1	Resting Tension
Fi-2	Snarling Smile
Fi-3	Asymmetrical Mouth
Fi-4	Unbridled Emotional Energy
Fi-5	Giddy Giggle

37. LEXICON OF VISUAL SIGNALS

Fi-6	Sprite-like Voice
Fi-7	Excessive Contempt
Fi-8	Wounded Expression
Fi-9	Seelie Energy
Fi-10	Unseelie Energy
Ti-1	Absent Tension
Ti-2	Flat Cheeks
Ti-3	Full Emotional Neutralization
Ti-4	Stop-Start Articulation
Ti-5	Fatigued Demeanor
Ti-6	Puppeteer Hands
Ti-7	Technical Glitching
Ti-8	Pe-Momentum Clamping
Ti-9	Passive Fe-Articulation
Ti-10	Placid Smile
Fe-1	On-Beat Emphasis
Fe-2	Emotional Shepherding
Fe-3	Warm Swelling
Fe-4	Exerting Effort
Fe-5	Semantic Disclaimers
Fe-6	Warm Head-shakes
Fe-7	Warm Head-nods
Fe-8	Upset Tension
Fe-9	Adaptive Emulation
Fe-10	Directive Pushing
Te-1	Off-Beat Expression
Te-2	Taut Square Cheeks
Te-3	Horizontally Split Cheeks
Te-4	Nasal Monotone Voice
Te-5	Snippy Head-shakes
Te-6	Snippy Head-nods
Te-7	Snippy Shoulder Shrugs
Te-8	Overbearing Yang
Te-9	Blunt Humor
Te-10	Avalanching Unbroken Articulation
Si-1	Dulled Eyes
Si-2	Confused Stare
Si-3	Slanting Edges
Si-4	Concerned Concentration
Si-5	Dancing Brow
Si-6	Anecdotal Rambles
Si-7	Indented Sockets
Si-8	Concerned Eye-Drifting
Si-9	Lightweight Inertia

COGNITIVE TYPE

Si-10   Silly Serious
Ni-1   Hypnotic Eyes
Ni-2   Unblinking Eyes
Ni-3   Permanent Stare
Ni-4   Lowered Eyelids
Ni-5   Intense Scowl
Ni-6   Abstract Rambling
Ni-7   Cryptic Speech
Ni-8   Faraway Drifting Zone-outs
Ni-9   Grounded Inertia
Ni-10   Esoteric Se Channeling
Ne-1   Naïve Eyes
Ne-2   Relaxed Eye-area
Ne-3   Diverting Gaze
Ne-4   Scattered Tangent Hopping
Ne-5   Parodies
Ne-6   Indiscriminate Correlating
Ne-7   Spritely Swaying
Ne-8   Buoyant Undercurrent
Ne-9   Amused Perk-up
Ne-10   Strong Eye-Toggling
Se-1   Amped Eyes
Se-2   Taut Eye-area
Se-3   Locked-on Eyes
Se-4   Eye-Head Parallel Motion
Se-5   Tunnel Focus
Se-6   High Stimulation
Se-7   High Sensitivity
Se-8   Bodily Presence
Se-9   Hyped Perk-up
Se-10   Moderate Eye-Toggling

TERMINOLOGY

Type, as we come to understand more intimately and empirically than through previous abstractions and arbitrary classifications, begins to signify far more within humanity. If indeed we witness, through the continual testing of cognitive type by quantifiable means, that our collective psyche is innately divided into sixteen psychologies of which we each belong to one, the legitimacy of such a discovery would have profound implications over our culture, our means of relating to one another, and our future. And while I seek to offer an objective window into this phenomenon's reality, I cannot ignore the profoundly soulful significance of such a discovery and how it touches our most intimate identity. One's cognitive type is, after all, the very seat of their consciousness. It is the essence of their psychology and the branch of the human family they belong to.

From this sacred recognition I felt an overwhelming calling to give these sixteen psychologies a new naming which moves away from the misconceptions attached to previous classification models, and which could capture the fullness of their inner symmetries and their dynamic operations. A level of artistic creativity was necessary for me to accomplish this and to give both visual and verbal metaphors to the functions. What follows is my own personal venture to birth symbolic terminologies for these sixteen sub-species of humanity, which carry for me a spiritual significance rather than any strictly academic purpose.

Symbolism

The judgment processes are denoted by a triangle, alluding to the pyramid structure of convergence they undergo as described on page 28. As a shape and visual symbol, a triangle has three sharp angles and this represents the *rigid* and exact-

COGNITIVE TYPE

Judgment **Perception**

Figure 81

ing nature of judgment. Inversely, the perception processes are denoted by a circle, alluding to the panoramic and unified operation they hold in the psyche. It represents the wholeness and expansiveness which is inherent to perception. As a shape and visual symbol it has no edges, representing the lack of differentiation between all elements within that sphere.

The Ti-Fe pairing is a triangle formed by the overlapping of three circles. This represents the diplomatic nature of Fe, which takes into consideration the perspectives (circles) of others, and strives to create a harmonious alignment between them.

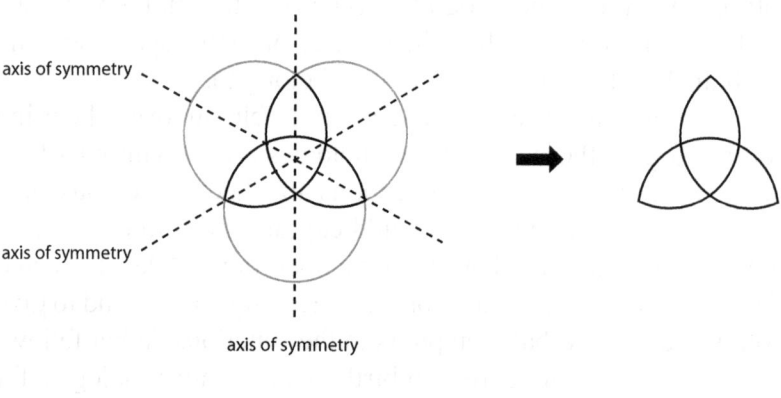

Figure 82

38. TERMINOLOGY

A few more symbols are embedded in this shape, for example, the shape also has three-fold symmetry, representing repeatability. No matter which of the three angles you approach it from, you get the same result. This alludes to the peer review process wherein Ti will use its talent for dispassion for Fe's cause; building a collective consensus. Do note that collective consensus is something different from empiricism, as Ti-Fe will be motivated more toward consensus that to a strict empiricism.

The Fi-Te pair is a more curved triangle with only one axis of symmetry running down the very middle. This represents the more independent and personal deduction-process of Fi, which strives for harmony/symmetry primarily within itself. It depicts the way in which an Fi-Te user's values can take many shapes with their own elegant symmetry, despite not being a symmetry easily or objectively traceable, nor dependent on consensual alignment.

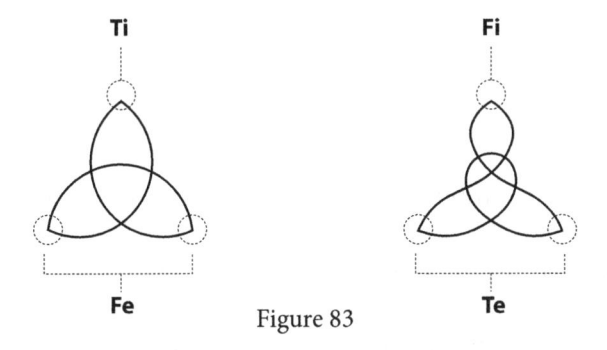

Figure 83

Furthermore, these two triangles have a central point (top) with two other points that form the base. The central point represents the compass process, while the two other points represent the articulation process. This alludes to the way the compass process compares each variable individually to itself (one point), while the articulator process compares one point to another (two points), as explained in page 31.

Below we see a solid, unbroken circle which represents the Ni-Se pairing. A pure circle is used both to represent the all-encompassing perspective of this duality, and the manner in which it views reality as one fully interconnected tapestry.

COGNITIVE TYPE

    A circle broken in three parts represents the Ne-Si duality. This is in contrast to the solid circle of Ni-Se which is more unified in its operation. The brokenness of the Ne-Si sphere symbolizes the compartmentalized nature of its operation. It alludes to the way this duality absorbs reality as individual, unrelated instances which it then connects in its own unique way.

Unified   **Compartmentalized**

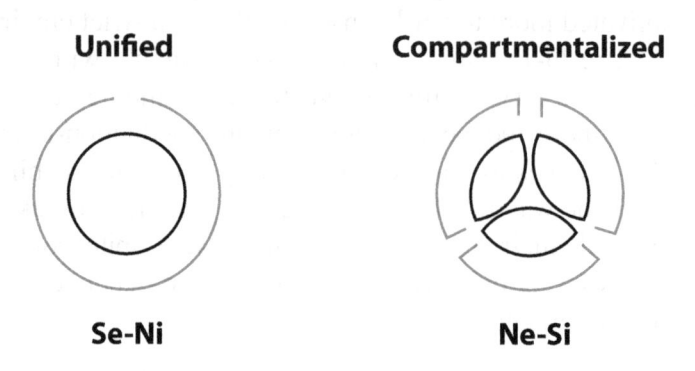

Se-Ni   **Ne-Si**

Figure 84

Heirarchy

    When combined into a cognitive hierarchy, there are two ways in which the triangle-circle symbolism is arranged. In the case that the primary oscillation is perception, then the circle will be the larger of the two and engulf the judgment triangle within it. Inversely, if the primary oscillation is judgment, the triangle will be the larger shape with the circle almost entirely embedded within it.

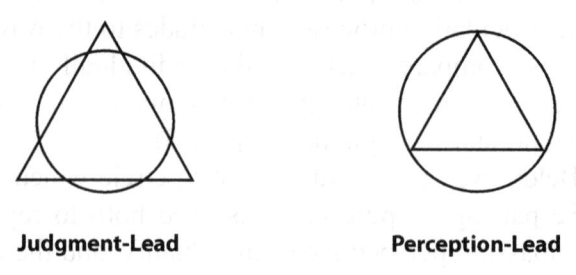

Judgment-Lead   **Perception-Lead**

Figure 85

38. TERMINOLOGY

As a result, we create the eight symbols below. Here we see the eight types which have the compass process above the articulator process, but to give us the full sixteen cognitive types, these eight are turned upside down in Figure 86.b.

a.

b.

Figure 86

Now we see the eight hierarchies where the articulator process comes before the compass process. To give us these eight types the shape of the braids was unchanged, only inverted, representing the way that each of these polar pairs has identical functionality but reversed in their energetic direction.

Through this visual symbolism we get sixteen emblems which each independently capture all of the essential qualities of the type. One could deduce all the fundamental components of that type's operation via reverse analysis of its visual structure.

Linguistics

In defining names for these processes, I took a similar approach to the formation of symbols, finding syntax metaphors which could capture the relationship between all of these elements of the psyche. The result was the formation of these terms:

EDA **ALE** **M** **V**
Fi-Te   Ti-Fe   Ne-Si   Se-Ni

Figure 87

The two judgment oscillations are three letter words with two vowels, while the two perception oscillations are single, consonant letters. The difference of three letters versus one letter alludes to the triangular and circular symbolism. The presence of vowels in the judgment processes and their absence in the perception processes alludes to the definitive nature of judgment. Vowels carry the exacting quality of judgment, as they are the points of accentuation and assertion within language, while consonants inform and compliment the execution of those vowels.

You'll also notice that the judgment oscillations hold two vowels, one on either side, with a consonant in the middle. These two vowels represent the two points of the articulation process, while the singular consonant in the middle represents the speechless, reactive, compass process.

In both judgment oscillations the vowels are E and A. However, in one they are **E_A** and in the other they are **A_E**. This represents the inversion of proactive-reactive energy flow between Te-Fi and Ti-Fe. Due to the limited number of vowels available, the selection of the vowels themselves has no particular meaning.

The consonant in the center is an allusion to the individualist vs diplomatic difference between the two judgment oscillation pairings. In linguistics, **D** and **L** differ in that the former is an obstruent consonant while the latter is a liquid consonant.

38. TERMINOLOGY

The obstruent nature of D gives it a more contrasted and defined sound as it affects other vowels, while L is fluid and flows more collaboratively. Thus the phrase "EDA" carries within it a small stop in the middle of its pronunciation, while "ALE" flows without that stop as one cohesive phrase. This is an allusion to the uniform, harmonious and collaborative nature of ALE versus the independent, often off-beat nature of EDA.

The two perception oscillations, represented as the consonants M and V have a similar differentiation. The consonant **M** is *bilabial*, requiring a break in air flow by the contact between the two lips. The consonant **V** sustains unbroken air flow, swishing its sound out of the lips as an uninterrupted stream. This alludes to the compartmentalized nature of Ne-Si and the cohesive, unified operation of Se-Ni.

We place the first oscillation at the beginning of the word, with the second right after it, giving us the following arrangements:

NAME	1st Oscillation	2nd Oscillation	Types
EDAM	Fi-Te	Si-Ne	FiNe | TeSi
EDAV	Fi-Te	Ni-Se	FiSe | TeNi
ALEM	Ti-Fe	Si-Ne	TiNe | FeSi
ALEV	Ti-Fe	Ni-Se	TiSe | FeNi
MEDA	Si-Ne	Fi-Te	SiTe | NeFi
MALE	Si-Ne	Ti-Fe	SiFe | NeTi
VEDA	Ni-Se	Fi-Te	NiTe | SeFi
VALE	Ni-Se	Ti-Fe	NiFe | SeTi

Figure 88

COGNITIVE TYPE

Type	1st Pair	2nd Pair	Direction	Name
FiNe	Fi-Te (EDA)	Si-Ne (M)	IN	Edamin
TeSi	Fi-Te (EDA)	Si-Ne (M)	ER	Edamer
FiSe	Fi-Te (EDA)	Ni-Se (V)	IN	Edavin
TeNi	Fi-Te (EDA)	Ni-Se (V)	ER	Edaver
TiNe	Ti-Fe (ALE)	Si-Ne (M)	IN	Alemin
FeSi	Ti-Fe (ALE)	Si-Ne (M)	ER	Alemer
TiSe	Ti-Fe (ALE)	Ni-Se (V)	IN	Alevin
FeNi	Ti-Fe (ALE)	Ni-Se (V)	ER	Alever
SiTe	Si-Ne (M)	Fi-Te (EDA)	IN	Medain
NeFi	Si-Ne (M)	Fi-Te (EDA)	ER	Medaer
SiFe	Si-Ne (M)	Ti-Fe (ALE)	IN	Malein
NeTi	Si-Ne (M)	Ti-Fe (ALE)	ER	Maleer
NiTe	Ni-Se (V)	Fi-Te (EDA)	IN	Vedain
SeFi	Ni-Se (V)	Fi-Te (EDA)	ER	Vedaer
NiFe	Ni-Se (V)	Ti-Fe (ALE)	IN	Valein
SeTi	Ni-Se (V)	Ti-Fe (ALE)	ER	Valeer

Figure 89

And lastly, to differentiate the proactive versus reactive versions of the two, we add the endings "ER" (extroversion) or "IN" (introversion), giving us all sixteen types.

38. TERMINOLOGY

Two-Letter Shorthand

As the reader has no doubt noticed, these ornamental names have not been explicitly utilized in the writing of this book. There are many reasons for this decision, but perhaps the strongest is that while I believe many better terminologies could be utilized, of which this is my presentation of an aesthetic alternative, it is first and foremost my desire to communicate these discoveries in a way that is comprehensible. And while the terms *intuition, sensation, feeling* and *thinking* have been omitted due to their ambiguity, the shorthand used for the eight cognitive functions (such as "Ni" and "Fe") have not suffered such profound misunderstandings in the decades after Jung's original publishing of Psychological Types. Because of this I decided to retain the use of the shorthand terminology in the creation of this book, for the sake of not wholly confusing readers who may have come to this book with a Jungian understanding of this phenomenon but also to demonstrate how these new visual signals are inescapably tied to the concepts first coined under those term. However, the necessity to update the underlying terminology still persists, and as our understanding of this reality evolves it is my hope that new terminology will develop that is capable of capturing these discoveries in their entirety. What I present here is but one suggestion for such a need.

BIBLIOGRAPHY

Adams, Scott (2013) How to Fail at Almost Everything and Still Win Big
APA (2013) Diagnostics and Statistics Manual of Mental Disorders V
Bhikkhu, Thanissaro (1997) Suñña Sutta: Empty
Bhikkhu, Thanissaro (2004) On Awareness-release
Bhikkhu, Thanissaro (2004) On the Cessation of Perception & Feeling
Boulogne, Duchenne de (1977) The mechanism of human facial expression
Briggs, Katherine (1978) An Encyclopedia of Fairies
C.G. Jung (1921) Psychological Types
C.G. Jung (1969) Archetypes and the Collective Unconscious
C.G. Jung (2009) The Red Book: Liber Novus
Chomsky, Noam (1967) The Responsibilities of Intellectuals
Chomsky, Noam (1968) Language and Mind
Chomsky, Noam (1971) Problems of Knowledge and Freedom
Chomsky, Noam (2012) The Science of Language
Clarke, Susanna (2004) Jonathan Strange & Mr.Norrell
DiTerLizzi, Tony (2009) The Spiderwick Chronicles
Ekman, Paul (1975) Telling Lies
Faigin, Gary (1990) The artist's complete guide to facial expressions
Filatova, Ekaterina Sergeevna (2010) Understanding the People around You
Hillman, James (1962) A Note on Multiple Analysis and Emotional Climate at Training Institutes
Honos-Webb, Lara (2013) The Gift of ADHD
Jennings, Ken (2011) Maphead: Charting the Wide, Weird World of Geography Wonks
Martinez-Conde, Susana (2004) The role of fixational eye movements in visual perception

39. BIBLIOGRAPHY

Meyer, Pamela (2010) Liespotting
Miller, Arthur I. (2009) Deciphering the Cosmic Number
Moore, Thomas (1994) Care of the Soul
Navarro, Joe (2008) What Every Body Is Saying
PBS (1991) How I see the World
Pianka, E.R (1970) On r and K selection
Rand, Ayn (1943) The Fountainhead
Rand, Ayn (1957) Atlas Shrugged
Rankin Jr., Arthur (1982) The Last Unicorn
Rayner, Keith (1975) The perceptual span and peripheral cues in reading
Rogen, Seth (2013) This is the End
Shaw, Philip (2007)
Singleton, John (2003) 2 Fast 2 Furious
Sorkin, Aaron (2012) The Newsroom
Taylor, Graeme J. (1997) Disorders of Affect Regulation: Alexithymia in Medical and Psychiatric Illness
Tennant, Andy (2005) Hitch
Tieger, Paul D. (1999) The Art of Speed Reading People
Tolkien, Christopher (1981) The Letters of J.R.R. Tolkien
Vala, Francis H. (2012) The Third Vision
http://www.accesstoinsight.org/
http://www.keirsey.com/
http://www.myersbriggs.org/